# PAINLESS
# Poetry

## Second Edition

## Mary Elizabeth, M.Ed.

BARRON'S

To Tanya

*All inquiries should be addressed to:*
Barron's Educational Series, Inc.
250 Wireless Boulevard
Hauppauge, New York 11788
**http://www.barronseduc.com**

*Library of Congress Catalog Card No.: 2010940870*

International Standard Book No.: 978-0-7641-4591-9

PRINTED IN CANADA
9 8 7 6 5 4 3 2 1

# BONUS MATERIAL

To access bonus materials, links to poetry you can see and hear online, and other resources, visit the author's *Painless Poetry* web page at:

http://www.edreinvented.com/products/painless-poetry/

# ACKNOWLEDGMENTS

Thank you to my editor, Anna Damaskos, the Barron's production staff, and Aodhagán O'Broin for his generous assistance.

All "original" poems are those of the author, Mary Elizabeth, and used with her permission.

Discussion of voicing text, how to scan, and the rhyming charts and accompanying explanation (pages 187–203, 205–211, 218–224, and 232–234) used by permission of the author. Also, some of the discussion of rhetorical devices is taken from the author's book, *Scintillating Syntax* and used by permission of the author.

The author gratefully acknowledges the following copyright holders for permission to reprint their poetry.

Pages 50 and 229: "On the Death of my Child," translated by A. O'Broin from "Auf meines Kindes Tod" by Joseph von Eichendorff, © 2000.

Page 69: "Samarkand: for Seamus Daly" by A. O'Broin, © 1995.

Page 108: From "Sonnet" translated by Alix Ingber from "Soneto" by Sor Juana Inés de la Cruz ("Feliciano me adora y le aborrezco"), © 1995.

Pages 142–143: "Eve Among the Perennials," copyright © 2000 by John Engels with permission of his estate.

Page 145: "Then and Now." Xin Qi-Ji (1140–1207), born in modern China's Shandong province, wrote more than 600 poems and is one of the greatest poets of the Song Dynasty. The original poem is entitled "To the Tune of *Chou Nu er*" and written in the form of "*Ci.*" This was a very popular form of poetry writing in the Song Dynasty and literally means "lyrics" or "song words." The rhythm and rhyme schemes are directly derived from existing tunes. Translation done by Ye Runxia on June 10, 1998, © 1998.

Pages 148–149: "Hen and Egg" is a poem originally written in Bulgarian by Vladimir Levchev (b. 1957), translated into English by the author with Pulitzer Prize-winning poet Henry Taylor, and published in: Levchev, Vladimir. *Black Book of the Endangered Species*. Washington, D.C.: Word Works, 1999.

Page 149: "A Mirror" is a poem originally written in Bulgarian by the famous Bulgarian poet Atanas Dalchev (1905–1978), published in his collected works: Dalchev, Atanas. *Poems, Fragments, Thoughts and Impressions*. Sofia, Bulgaria: Bulgarski Pisatel, 1978, and translated into English by Vladimir Levchev.

page 167: "Window Washing," by India Renee Douglas.

Page 224: "Ice" by Garry Smith, January, 2009.

Page 225: "Twilight" by Garry Smith, June, 2009.

Page 226: "Repose" by Garry Smith, October, 2009.

Page 229: "A Chant of Mystics" is a poem originally written in English by Ameen F. Rihani, Lebanese-American poet, writer, and philosopher. These extracts are copied, with permission, from Rihani's book *A Chant of Mystics and Other Poems* and are found on The Ameen Rihani Home Page at http://www.ameenrihani.org

Page 272: "Instant Sonnet" translated by Alix Ingber from "Soneto de repente" by Lope de Vega, © 1995.

Page 272: "Improvised Sonnet" translated by A. O'Broin from "Soneto de repente" by Lope de Vega, © 1999.

Page 280: From "More Than a Moment Ago" by John-Crow Bigler, © 1998.

Page 281: The author wishes to thank Mitsuko Yamamoto for her assistance in rendering the haiku by Basho and Issa.

Page 282: "Debate" by Geof Hewitt is reprinted with the author's permission from *Just Worlds*, published by Ithaca House Books, © Copyright 1989 by Geof Hewitt.

Page 286: "Water" and "Books" by Ivan Drago Krizanac from Essex Middle School, copyright © 2011.

Page 288: "Grow up now," copyright © 2010, and "Love the urban life," copyright © 2010, are used by permission of the author, Mike Podhaizer, a recent graduate of the University of Chicago, whose favorite poem is "Kubla Khan" by Samuel Coleridge.

**ACKNOWLEDGMENTS**

Pages 295–296: "Beneath clouds, contrails," "The old maple," "An old maple tree," "Leaving the reef," and "Fresh from saltwater sojourns," are used by permission of Wendy Zuckerman.

Pages 300–301: Section of "On Living" by Nazim Hikmet from *Poems of Nazim Hikmet*, translated by Randy Blasing and Mutlu Konuk. Translation copyright © 1994, 2002 by Randy Blasing and Mutlu Konuk. Reprinted by permission of Persea Books, Inc., New York.

Pages 302–303: "The Mad Fisherman" by Patrick Hodgkin, reprinted from *Voices from the Old Testament & Annus Domine: A Christmas Ennead,* © 1998. Used with permission from the family of Patrick H. Hodgkin.

Pages 303–304: "Arachne" from *Patterns of Descent* by Richard Foerster (Alexandria, VA: Orchises Press, 1993). Copyright © 1993 by Richard Foerster. Reprinted by permission of the author.

Page 324: "The Sandman," by Geof Hewitt is reprinted with the author's permission from *Only What's Imagined*, published by The Kumquat Press © Copyright 2000 by Geof Hewitt.

Page 325–326: "What In the Name" and "White and Wong" by Thaddeus Rutkowski.

The following three poems are used courtesy of the Young Writers Project http://youngwritersproject.org and their respective authors.

Page 327: "Remember Me" by Bridger Iverson, 2008.

Page 328: "Write. Writer. Writing" by Anna Rutenbeck—Middle of Vermont.

Page 329: "We are" by Sossina Gutema, 16.

Pages 339: "Remember" by Katie Turner © 2000, used by permission of the author.

Page 338: "The Predator and the Prey" by Mike Podhaizer, © 2000, is used by permission of the author.

Every effort has been made to contact the copyright holders. Barron's Educational Series and the author apologize for any unintentional omissions. We would be pleased to insert the appropriate acknowledgment in future editions of this book.

# CONTENTS

# Chapter Five: A Goodge Selection of Poetic Forms  **259**

# INTRODUCTION

A few years ago I taught a middle school literature course. We began with the *Odyssey*, that great epic story of the adventures and struggles of a hero returning home from war. We followed that with the *Song of Roland*, the moving tale of a battle that hangs in the balance because of treachery. I mentioned the word *poetry* one day in class, and my student Joe said disgustedly, "I hate poetry." He didn't realize that he'd read nothing BUT poetry so far in the year . . . and loved every minute of it! I'm not sure what Joe thought poetry was, but his working definition apparently didn't include exciting and well-told stories that grip the imagination.

Joe didn't realize that poems are as different as the imaginations of the poets who write them. There are book-length poems and poems that are so short we measure them in syllables. Some poems have intricate patterns of sound that the poet must conform to, and some take on the sound, and even the shape, that the poet chooses. Some poems tell a story, some express a feeling, some have no other purpose than to make you laugh.

Because the world of poetry is so broad and rich, it is helpful to have some skills, strategies, and techniques to enable you to read, write, and evaluate poetry with greater ease and authority. That's what this book will give you. Here are five pointers to help you.

- The bonus materials on the *Painless Poetry* page of my website, as well as the links and other resources, can help you in reading and writing poetry, finding more poetry by the poets in this book, and more. Check it out!
- The earliest English poem in this book was written in 1580. The most recent English poems and translations date from 2011. In these 431 years, spelling and style have changed greatly. Even today, British and American spellings differ (see p. 100).
- In the brief and compressed style of poetry, it can sometimes be hard to make out the meaning. Don't let the words get in the way! If you get stuck, grab a dictionary, look ahead to the answers, or ask someone for help.

- Not every aspect of every poem is discussed when a poem is introduced. As you learn new skills and strategies, it is worth going back and applying them to poems you met earlier in the book. Also, if a chapter is focusing on rhyme, that doesn't mean you can't take a careful look at rhythm. Each poem works as a whole: Bring everything you can to your understanding of it. Memorizing poetry that you enjoy allows you to incorporate special poems into your life and deepen your understanding.
- Part of the approach in this book includes modeling. There are model answers for the Brain Ticklers, most of which I wrote, but some of which are the work of other poets, when appropriate, and modeling of processes, such as scanning a poem, in addition to steps to follow.

## Poetry Online

There is some incredibly cool poetry available online, but remember that Web addresses are constantly changing. Although the addresses provided were current when this book was written, sooner or later, some of the addresses may no longer work. If you should come across a web address (URL) that no longer appears to be valid, either because the site no longer exists or because the address has changed, either **shorten the URL** or do a **keyword search** on the subject matter or topic. Here's how:

- To shorten the URL, **delete the end of the URL up to the first slash** that appears after a three-character extension (typically .com/ .net/ .org/ .edu/ .gov/. . .). This will usually get you to the home page of the website. From there, you may find a site map to help you, use a site search, or contact the webmaster to find out about the page you're looking for.
- To do a keyword search, type the phrase you're looking for with quotes around it, into your favorite search engine. Many search engines list the top-rated sites first, so check the blurb about the top site, and if it seems good, try it out.

**WARNING**: Not every response to your search will match your criteria, and some sites may contain adult material. If you are ever in doubt, check with someone who can help you.

# CHAPTER ONE

# The Journey Begins

# WHAT IS A POEM?

If someone were to ask you what a unicorn is, you might say it's "a shy, imaginary horselike creature with a horn in the middle of its forehead." And if you weren't sure, you could find a clear definition in a dictionary.

But if someone were to ask you what a poem is, it might be a lot harder to answer. Even though poetry is not imaginary, like a unicorn, it is still difficult to describe. This is partly because many different kinds of writing fit into the category "poetry." As we noted in the Introduction, poems can be only a few lines long or the length of a book. They may have a standard form like a sonnet, or a form made by the poet for one specific occasion. Poems may make you laugh or weep or smirk; they may teach you something or deepen your experience of life.

Dictionary definitions can make poetry sound simple. For example, one dictionary says "A poem is a composition in verse." But if you look up *verse*, you find that verse is defined as "poetry." If you read other definitions of poetry, you may conclude that poetry is even more elusive than the fabled unicorn. Eighteenth-century British statesman and writer Edmund Burke said, "Poetry is the art of substantiating shadows, and of lending existence to nothing." So what is a poem?

Let's look at what some poets say poetry is.

- "Poetry is not the thing said but a way of saying it."
  —A. E. Housman
- "Poetry is a language which tells us, through a more or less emotional reaction, something that cannot be said."
  —Edward Arlington Robinson
- Poetry is "a game of knowledge, a bringing to consciousness, by naming them, of emotions and their hidden relationships."
  —W. H. Auden

These definitions are not very easy to understand, but they seem to be saying that poetry is a specialized use of language, different than prose. They also suggest that poetry is able to capture and convey things that prose cannot, and that poetry works through emotions, not just through thoughts. Let's look at an actual poem and see if we can discover what they mean.

Read aloud this poem, written when the poet was thirty-seven.

### Loveliest of Trees (1896)
by A. E. Housman

1  Loveliest of trees, the cherry now
2  Is hung with bloom along the bough,
3  And stands about the woodland ride
4  Wearing white for Eastertide.

5  Now, of my threescore years and ten,
6  Twenty will not come again,
7  And take from seventy springs a score,
8  It only leaves me fifty more.*

9  And since to look at things in bloom
10  Fifty springs are little room,
11  About the woodlands I will go
12  To see the cherry hung with snow.

In prose, the speaker, who is not necessarily the poet (notice that he's seventeen years younger), might have said,

I see that the cherry tree is blooming and lovely. When I look at it, the lifespan of humans seems short—not enough time to properly enjoy the beauty of nature. So, I'm heading for the woods.

---

*Lines 5–8 can be difficult to understand. Here's how it works: The speaker assumes that he will have a normal lifespan—about seventy years at the time the poem was written (A score is twenty years. "Threescore years and ten" is 60 + 10 = 70). He's used up twenty years of his life span ("twenty will not come again"), which means he's twenty years old. And if he subtracts what he's "used up" from his allotment, he has "only" fifty more years in which to live and enjoy lovely things.

# BRAIN TICKLERS
*Set # 1*

1. Are there any words in "Loveliest of Trees" for which you don't know the precise pronunciation or meaning? In the prose version? What have you done about it? Look up any words that you can't define exactly or pronounce with certainty. What does the information you find add to your understanding and experience of the poem?

2. Compare and contrast the structure of the poem and the prose versions of "Loveliest of Trees."

3. Read the prose aloud. Does reading aloud add to your experience or understanding? Now read the poetry aloud. What do you notice? If the word *prettiest* were substituted for *loveliest* in the poem or *pretty* for *lovely* in the prose, how would it change your understanding and experience?

4. Can you picture the cherry tree as you read the poem? Is there really snow on the cherry, or is the speaker comparing the appearance of the white blossoms to snow? Use the details given to create a cherry tree in your imagination. What words in the poem help you? Now try with the prose. What happens? If you had to read either the poem or the prose ten times in the next week, which would you choose? Why?

5. How is the subject approached in the poem? In the prose?

6. *Evoke* means "to bring out." Besides leading to new thoughts, poems often evoke feelings. What feelings did you experience as you read the poem?

(Answers are on page 15.)

Now let's compare some key elements of prose and poetry, keeping these examples in mind.

- **use of line structure** Prose runs across the page until the paragraph is over or it reaches the right-hand margin, whichever comes first. But poetry's line lengths are decided by the poet, and this is what shapes a poem's margins.

- **special use of language** In prose fiction or nonfiction, you can start slowly, perhaps drawing your audience in with an anecdote before you get down to your topic. In poetry, there are no introductions as such, no extra words. Everything is compressed—every word counts, and every aspect of a word (its history, pronunciation, meanings, spelling, relationship to the words around it, etc.) may come into play. Poets may use ordinary words, but they do so in an extraordinary way.

- **use of sound** In some nonfiction prose, using rhyming words or other devices that call attention to the sound of the passage, rather than the meaning, can be a distraction. In reading these types of nonfiction prose, we often don't give much attention to how the passage sounds. In poetry, however, paying attention to sound is a necessity. Since most literature—all poetry and some fiction—and even some nonfiction is designed, as novelist Joseph Conrad said, "to make you hear [and] to make you feel," it's a good idea to read aloud to bring out elements that are opaque to the eye but transparent to the ear.

  Suppose you read an encyclopedia article about music. It might call melody "an agreeable succession of sounds." This is food for the mind, and our understanding of the words is purely mental. Now suppose you had a melody written on music paper. You might be able to name the key signature, the meter, the notes, and the style. But your knowledge would still be incomplete. Only the performance of a melody brings out the sound effects that the composer devised. Melody is meant to be experienced. Likewise, only the speaking aloud and hearing of a poem brings out its unique musicality—the sound effects that the poet embedded in it. Speaking the poem aloud, the poem takes shape in your body: You become the poem.

- **appeals to the reader** You can skim some nonfiction prose and still make sense of it, and sometimes skimming is the most sensible approach. But poetry is not just trying to reach your mind: the poem works through the images created in your mind, and the feelings evoked in your heart. Savor the words of a poem. Read it again and again. Maybe even memorize it. Let it work its magic on you.

- **poetic subject** In nonfiction prose, you usually state your subject fairly clearly, sometimes more than once. It may be concrete, abstract, or imaginary, but it's generally defined. In fiction, the author's theme may or may not be stated clearly in the text. In poetry, however, the subject may be the feeling that you get after reading the poet's words—a feeling that is never named in the poem but that the poem was designed to bring out.

  Poets generally choose subjects that are enhanced in some way by the special treatment that poetic language can give them. If you can say it in prose, why write a poem?

- **complete comprehension** Someone listening to or reading prose can often skip over some unknown words and still get the gist of the meaning through context clues and inference. In poetry, nothing is expendable: Every word is necessary to understanding the whole.

Some poems use more of these six aspects of poetry than others do. For example, some poems may look like prose on the page. Also, some use poetic language more successfully than others. If you find a piece of writing structured as a poem, give it the benefit of the doubt—read it as a poem, with as much care as you can, and see what happens.

# BRAIN TICKLERS
### Set # 2

1. Which of the six aspects of a poem does the following mnemonic device use? Which does it not include? Give a detailed answer.
   - use of line structure
   - special use of language
   - use of sound
   - appeals to the reader
   - poetic subject
   - complete comprehension

> *i* before *e*,
> except after *c*,
> and when sounding like *a*,
> as in *neighbor* and *weigh*.

2. Go wallow in some poetry for a while. Look through some poetry books, or go to my *Painless Poetry* web page to find links and select two poems that you like. This is a good time to buy or make a poetry notebook or journal in which to record your favorite poems.

3. Read this excerpt from a folk song lyric. Consider the six aspects of a poem. Tell why you would or would not consider this lyric to be a poem. (*Boatswain* is pronounced BO-sun.)

### Old Boatswain (folk song)

Old Boatswain was dead and laid in his grave.
Mmmm-mmmm, laid in his grave.
Old Boatswain was dead and laid in his grave.
Mmmm-mmmm-mmmm-mmmm-mmmm-mmmm.

They planted an apple tree over his head.
Mmmm-mmmm, over his head.
They planted an apple tree over his head.
Mmmm-mmmm-mmmm-mmmm-mmmm-mmmm.

Etc.

4. Choose one of the following word groups. Develop it into a poem with one or more of the six aspects of poetry. Feel free to add material, facts, ideas, details, etc.
   a. three geese flying south
   b. lightning just shattered that tree
   c. leaves of red and gold
   d. brightly twinkling stars

(Answers are on page 17.)

# JUMPSTART YOUR POETRY EXPERIENCE

No!!! You do not have to read this whole book before you can begin enjoying poetry as a reader and writer! This brief introduction will give you four key approaches that will help you get more out of poetry right away!

## Reading and writing poetry

### 1. Appearance: Notice what a poem looks like.

As we take a first look at a poem, the most obvious thing is the overall shape of the poem on the page. It often does not look like prose, even at a glance, because the lines of text do not fill the page as they do in prose. Next, you can look for space divisions between groups of lines. Poems are often displayed in one or more of these sections, called **stanzas**, as in "Old Boatswain." Each stanza is composed of a set of long, short, or varying lines. Most lines have at least several words. The shape of the words, lines, and stanzas gives each poem a unique appearance. Whether you're reading or writing poetry, think about how the poem appears on the page. More about the shape of poems will he discussed in Chapters Four and Five.

## 2. Meaning: Precise meaning is always important—every word counts.

### Dictionary

As you read poetry, keep your eyes and ears open, and don't gloss over things that don't make sense to you—check them out! Chapters Two and Three will give you more help in understanding how poems make meaning.

Reference books can help you with meaning in a variety of ways as both a reader of poetry and a poet. Dictionaries define English words and tell you how to pronounce them. Bilingual dictionaries and translation web sites do the same for words from other languages. As you write poetry, you may want to consult a thesaurus to find a precise shade of meaning. Go to my *Painless Poetry* web page to find suggestions for both print and online references.

## 3. Sound: Read poems aloud to hear the sound.

Sound is one of the keys to understanding poetry. If you can't speak out loud because others are present, say the words in your head, or mouth them quietly to yourself.

Whether you're reading or writing poetry, listen for patterns. Repetition of words, phrases, and sounds is important. Repeated word order is another pattern to which you should pay attention. Listen for the pattern of accents in each line and in each stanza.

Also, notice rhyming words—words that seem to echo each other's sound—and other sound effects. A rhyming dictionary can help, and you can find suggestions for both print and online sources on my *Painless Poetry* web page.

## 4. The whole: Sound and sense are related.

A poem that includes the line "higgledy piggledy wiggly kids" is not likely to be serious. If you find the line "Wandering far, I wondered pensively," however, you're in for a more thoughtful experience. The relationship between sound and sense is not always obvious, so practice paying attention and you'll soon begin developing an understanding of the possible relationships.

Also, think about images or memories triggered by the poem. Decide if they are relevant or helpful to your understanding.

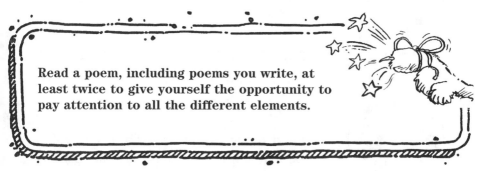

Read a poem, including poems you write, at least twice to give yourself the opportunity to pay attention to all the different elements.

## Being a good poet/audience

In the beginning of Volume II, Chapter 11 of Laurence Sterne's novel *Tristram Shandy* (1759), the narrator discusses the relationship between reader and writer:

> Writing, when properly managed . . . is but a different name for conversation: As no one, who knows what he is about in good company, would venture to talk all;—so no author, who understands the just boundaries of decorum and good breeding, would presume to think all: the truest respect which you can pay to the reader's understanding, is to halve this matter amicably, and leave him something to imagine, in his turn, as well as yourself.

The narrator is comparing reading a book to participating in a conversation. What is the reader's part in the conversation? The reader fills in what are sometimes called the "gaps" in the story (or poem). This happens in different ways with different poems, but in every poem the reader's use of imagination converts the words of the poem into experience.

### Caution—Major Mistake Territory!

The words of a poem do not hold a static meaning the way a mine holds gold or diamonds. By drawing on your prior experience to interpret the words and patterns on the page, you make meaning. The poem comes alive in and through you.

# BRAIN TICKLERS
## Set # 3

Read each poem or excerpt. For each, write an observation based on each of the four approaches:

- appearance
- meaning
- sound
- the whole.

Don't hesitate to guess about things when you don't feel sure. Feel free to use a dictionary.

1 There once was a lady from Delhi
2 Who ate nothing else besides jelly.
3 When I asked her why
4 This was her reply:
5 "Cause it feels so good in my belly."

[original]

## "The Despot" (before 1883)
### by Edith Nesbit (excerpt)

25 So he uprooted, one by one
26 The free things that had loved the sun,
27 The happy, eager, fruitful seeds
28 That had not known that they were weeds.

## "The Raven" (1844)
### by Edgar Allan Poe (excerpt)

7 Ah, distinctly I remember it was in the bleak December;
8 And each separate dying ember wrought its ghost upon the floor.
9 Eagerly I wished the morrow;—vainly I had sought to borrow
10 From my books surcease of sorrow—sorrow for the lost Lenore—
11 For the rare and radiant maiden whom the angels name Lenore—
12        Nameless *here* for evermore.

(Answers are on page 18.)

# Writing poetry

Different people use the writing process differently, but in general, the writing process that works best for poetry differs a bit from the writing process that you may use for prose. Let's take a look.

| | |
|---|---|
| **Prewriting** | the preparations you make before you begin |
| **Drafting** | the act of setting your ideas/ information down on paper |
| **Revising** | reconsidering your work in the light of your own and others' insights |
| **Proofreading** | checking for correct grammar, spelling, usage, and mechanics |
| **Publishing** | presenting your work in a way you have chosen |

## Poetic prewriting

Just as with prose, you will consider your subject, your audience, your attitude toward your subject, and the form you are going to use. But you should also consider those elements that are particular to poetry. You may want to brainstorm some feelings and images you want your reader to experience. For a rhyming poem, you can also choose rhyme words, using a rhyming dictionary as needed. As you begin to flesh out your poem, think about words that work well together and expressions that will effectively convey your ideas.

## Poetic drafting

Drafting poetry can include much more revision than drafting prose. Sometimes with prose, you can block the whole thing out and then go back and consider it section by section in revision. But words are so closely interlocked in poetry that as you write, you are not just putting down ideas in an appropriate order but also watching the interrelations of all the elements.

As a result, the introduction of a new idea can lead to changing the whole structure of your poem or all of your rhyming words.

Sound is always important. You will need to keep trying out the sound by speaking your draft aloud, something you may not be accustomed to doing with prose. In fact, you should think about those four key approaches—appearance, meaning, sound, and the whole—as you write, as well as while you are reading.

Never be shy about asking for help—you don't have to wait for a specially designated revision time if there's something you need to know right away. Also, using somebody else's insight or idea doesn't change the fact that it's your poem. Professional poets read their poetry to others all the time. It's part of the process.

## Poetic revising

Because of the way poetry evokes a response, it's important to have at least one other person to help you revise. Choosing someone who understands how poetry works is important, so choose carefully.

Here's a method you can try. Have your readers read through the poem once (aloud). Then have them do a think-aloud, going through the poem line by line or stanza by stanza and telling you how they constructed meaning from the poem and how it made them feel. This technique allows you to see how your communication is received. It may point up spots in which you need to clarify meaning, but it may also show you wonderful ideas or insights that you didn't notice.

## Poetic proofreading

The main difference between proofreading poetry and proofreading prose is that it is more often true with poetry that the official rule for something should *not* be followed. The term **poetic license** reflects our understanding that in the special uses of language that we collectively call poetry, we allow the writer liberty *if* it adds to the depth of meaning of the poem. If you can explain how ignoring a grammar or usage rule contributes to the meaning of your piece, then you probably have good and sufficient reason to do as you wish.

## Poetic publishing

Presenting poetry may mean reading it aloud, sending it away to a contest, or writing it in a journal. Currently popular are poetry slams—contests between poets performing their own verse—which were begun in Chicago in 1987 by Marc Smith.

For more on poetry slams and other types of performance poetry, see Poetry as Performance page 310.

# BRAIN TICKLERS
### Set # 4

Try out the poetic writing process on a poem about some aspect of family. Use this opportunity to find a reader or two whose responses are helpful to you.

(Answers are on page 19.)

# BRAIN TICKLERS—THE ANSWERS
## Set # 1, page 5

**Possible responses:**

1. *ride* = a path made for riding horses, especially through woodlands. *Eastertide* = the period from Easter Sunday to a feast that follows, either Ascension Thursday (forty days later), Pentecost (fifty days later), or Trinity Sunday (the Sunday after Pentecost). Before I looked up *Eastertide*, I just thought of it as a synonym for spring. But when I saw that its beginning and end are marked by feasts, that it's a period designated by people, it seemed to me that the cherry is dressed to celebrate the holiday with us, and the speaker is pointing to a connection between people and nature.

2. They are each composed of three present-tense sentences. In the poem, each sentence is a stanza of four lines in which the first two lines rhyme with each other, and the last two lines rhyme with each other (quatrains composed of two rhyming couplets).

3. Reading aloud made more of a difference with the poem because there was more in the poem that was designed to be heard. I noticed the repetition of words from stanza to stanza: *now* in the first and second stanzas, *fifty* and *springs* picked up from the second and joined together in the third, and *woodlands*, *cherry*, and *hung* in the first and third, taking me back to the beginning. I noticed the rhymes and four stresses in each line. *Pretty* seems to me to be less deep and important a quality than *lovely*, not significant enough to spend fifty years on. I think it would ruin the poem.

4. Yes, I can picture the tree. The words that help are *hung with bloom along the bough, white*, and *woodlands*. I think the tree is covered with white blossoms and "hung with snow" is a metaphor. The prose didn't seem calculated to help me form an image. I'd rather reread the poem because there's more to it, and it's a more enjoyable experience.

5. The first stanza of the poem helped me imagine the scene the speaker saw—the cherry blooming briefly in spring. The second stanza presents the speaker's context. At first it's surprising for him to say *only* when we find out that he's pretty young—just twenty. The last stanza of the poem connects the first and second stanzas. Since I could imagine how lovely the cherry tree was from the first stanza, instead of arguing with the speaker that he has plenty of time left to do whatever he wants in his life, I could see what he was saying. I think that the subject of the poem is an attitude toward life that the speaker shows in response to the cherry trees. In the prose, everything is flatter and more matter of fact. I don't share the writer's experience of loveliness; I just know it as a piece of information, and the information is the subject.

6. **Possible response:** I felt happy as I imagined the beautiful cherry tree, sad about the shortness of life when I read stanza 2, and energized to live life to the fullest by stanza 3.

## Set # 2, page 8

1. **Possible response:** It uses line structure, and every word does count. The sound—rhyme and bouncy rhythm—is what makes it easy to remember. It doesn't affect me emotionally, try to give me an experience, or work to create an image in my mind, but it does help me remember a useful bit of information.

2. The poems chosen will depend on the tastes of the reader.

3. **Possible response:** I don't consider it a poem for these reasons: The stanzas are largely composed of *mmmm's*, which might be interesting in the song but don't accomplish much as poetry; the repetition doesn't add to the sense or the feeling when read aloud—it's boring; the sound is not especially appealing; it doesn't evoke an emotional response; I can imagine something, but there's a whole lot of words for a little bit of image; I can't tell what the subject is with this excerpt.

4. **Possible response:**

Lightning just shattered that tree.
I'm lucky it didn't hit me.
It was quite a squall
That made the oak fall.
And now we've got toothpicks for free.

[original]

## Set # 3, page 12

**Possible responses:**

- **"There once was a lady from Delhi"**
  **Appearance:** I can see the rhyme words, *jelly* and *belly*, immediately. **Meaning:** I had to look up *Delhi* because I had never seen it written down before, so I didn't recognize it. **Sound:** When I read the poem aloud, I realized that it's a limerick and that *Delhi* rhymes with *jelly* and *belly*. **The whole:** *Belly* is a silly word, and this is a silly rhyme.

- **"The Despot"**
  **Appearance:** Most of the words are short, one-syllable words. **Meaning:** The meaning of the word *weeds* is important here because the poem is saying that something is not a weed by its nature but is only a weed because a gardener considers it to be one. *Merriam-Webster's Collegiate Dictionary* defines *weed* as "a plant that is not valued where it is growing." **Sound:** This poem has rhyme within the first line—*one by one*—as well as at the ends of the lines. **The whole:** For me, expecting the rhyme at the end of the last line and expecting the reason for why the plants were being uprooted went together and both were fulfilled at the same time.

- **"The Raven"**
  **Appearance:** I notice the repeated words, *Lenore, sorrow*. **Meaning:** Ha! When I looked up *surcease*, the dictionary actually quoted this line of Poe as an example! It means "a temporary respite or end." **Sound:** There are several rhyme patterns:
  - midline with line end (lines 7 and 9—*remember/December; morrow/borrow*)
  - line end with middle of following line (lines 7–8; 9–10—*December/ember; borrow/sorrow*)
  - line ends (lines 10–12—*Lenore/Lenore/evermore*)
  - midline repetition (line 9—*Sorrow*)
  
  As a result of these interlinked rhymes, the lines are more closely connected than they would be if they just had the end rhymes. **The whole:** The speaker seems all wrapped up in himself and his thoughts and feelings. The tangle of rhymes among and between lines seems like a parallel interlinking.

## Set # 4, page 15

**Possible response:**

### Dad's Gift

My dad's been in a crabby mood,
'cause things at work have not been good.
The doctor told him to relax,
enjoy his weekends to the max.
So I got a pet for Father's Day.
He really loves to run and play.
He's great at races, catches sticks,
and does all kinds of neat-o tricks.
My dad will like that kind of fun;
my dad will think it's really won-
derful to have a pet like Sam,
(that's what I've called him). And the tram
in the backyard he'll pull alone,
and sit contented with his bone.
He eats a bit much—well, that's true.
But he's got such a precious "mew."
The folks at work will be impressed;
They've thought that Dad's uptight and stressed.
But Dad's boss will be the first one vyin'
To have a chance to pet Dad's lion.

[original]

CHAPTER TWO

# Literary Elements at Your Service

The easiest way to begin our adventure in the strange and beautiful land of poetry is with the familiar elements that you've met in prose stories, also called *fiction*. In this chapter we will review the basic concepts of character, setting, plot, mood, tone, and theme. Then we'll explore them anew, looking at how they are used in the context of poetry. Finally, we'll examine situations in which readers need to know something outside of the poem in order to understand it fully.

To help us along, we'll begin with a Canadian poem that tells a story. Look up any words you don't know.

## "The Cremation of Sam McGee" (1907)
### by Robert W. Service

1  *There are strange things done in the midnight sun*
2      *By the men who moil for gold;*
3  *The Arctic trails have their secret tales*
4      *That would make your blood run cold;*
5  *The Northern Lights have seen queer sights,*
6      *But the queerest they ever did see*
7  *Was that night on the marge of Lake Lebarge*
8      *I cremated Sam McGee.*

9   Now Sam McGee was from Tennessee, where the cotton blooms and blows.
10  Why he left his home in the South to roam 'round the Pole, God only knows.
11  He was always cold, but the land of gold seemed to hold him like a spell;
12  Though he'd often say in his homely way that "he'd sooner live in hell."

13  On a Christmas Day we were mushing our way over the Dawson trail.
14  Talk of your cold! Through the parka's fold it stabbed like a driven nail.
15  If our eyes we'd close, then the lashes froze till sometimes we couldn't see;
16  It wasn't much fun, but the only one to whimper was Sam McGee.

17  And that very night, as we lay packed tight in our robes beneath the snow,
18  And the dogs were fed, and the stars o'erhead were dancing heel and toe,
19  He turned to me, and "Cap," says he, "I'll cash in this trip, I guess;
20  And if I do, I'm asking that you won't refuse my last request."

21  Well, he seemed so low that I couldn't say no; then he says with a sort of
     moan:

22  "It's the cursèd* cold, and it's got right hold till I'm chilled clean through
     to the bone.

23  Yet 'tain't being dead—it's my awful dread of the icy grave that pains;

24  So I want you to swear that, foul or fair, you'll cremate my last remains."

25  A pal's last need is a thing to heed, so I swore I would not fail;

26  And we started on at the streak of dawn; but God! he looked ghastly pale.

27  He crouched on the sleigh, and he raved all day of his home in Tennessee;

28  And before nightfall a corpse was all that was left of Sam McGee.

29  There wasn't a breath in that land of death, and I hurried, horror-driven,

30  With a corpse half hid that I couldn't get rid, because of a promise given;

31  It was lashed to the sleigh, and it seemed to say: "You may tax your
     brawn and brains,

32  But you promised true, and it's up to you to cremate those last remains."

33  Now a promise made is a debt unpaid, and the trail has its own stern code.

34  In the days to come, though my lips were dumb, in my heart how I cursed
     that load.

35  In the long, long night, by the lone firelight, while the huskies, round in a
     ring,

36  Howled out their woes to the homeless snows—O God! how I loathed the
     thing.

37  And every day that quiet clay seemed to heavy and heavier grow;

38  And on I went, though the dogs were spent and the grub was getting low;

39  The trail was bad, and I felt half mad, but I swore I would not give in;

40  And I'd often sing to the hateful thing, and it hearkened with a grin.

---

* The accent in line 22 on the word *cursèd* is called a **grave accent.** It indicates that,
for the sake of the poem's rhythm, the *-ed* ending—which is usually combined with the
previous syllable—is pronounced as a separate syllable. Say the word like this (KUR-
sid). In line 34, where it appears without an accent, it is pronounced in the usual way:
(kurst). Another example occurs in "A Poison Tree" on page 45.

41  Till I came to the marge of Lake Lebarge, and a derelict there lay;
42  It was jammed in the ice, but I saw in a trice it was called the "Alice May."
43  And I looked at it, and I thought a bit, and I looked at my frozen chum;
44  Then "Here," said I, with a sudden cry, "is my cre-ma-tor-e-um."

45  Some planks I tore from the cabin floor, and I lit the boiler fire;
46  Some coal I found that was lying around, and I heaped the fuel higher;
47  The flames just soared, and the furnace roared—such a blaze you seldom
     see;
48  And I burrowed a hole in the glowing coal, and I stuffed in Sam McGee.

49  Then I made a hike, for I didn't like to hear him sizzle so;
50  And the heavens scowled, and the huskies howled, and the wind began to
     blow.
51  It was icy cold, but the hot sweat rolled down my cheeks, and I don't
     know why;
52  And the greasy smoke in an inky cloak went streaking down the sky.

53  I do not know how long in the snow I wrestled with grisly fear;
54  But the stars came out and they danced about ere again I ventured near;
55  I was sick with dread, but I bravely said: "I'll just take a peep inside.
56  I guess he's cooked, and it's time I looked": . . . then the door I opened
     wide.

57  And there sat Sam, looking cool and calm, in the heart of the furnace
     roar;
58  And he wore a smile you could see a mile, and he said: "Please close that
     door.
59  It's fine in here, but I greatly fear you'll let in the cold and storm—
60  Since I left Plumtree, down in Tennessee, it's the first time I've been
     warm."

61  *There are strange things done in the midnight sun*
62      *By the men who moil for gold;*
63  *The Arctic trails have their secret tales*
64      *That would make your blood run cold;*
65  *The Northern Lights have seen queer sights,*
66      *But the queerest they ever did see*
67  *Was that night on the marge of Lake Lebarge*
68      *I cremated Sam McGee.*

## BRAIN TICKLERS
### Set # 5

1. Write your reaction to "The Cremation of Sam McGee." Use the words *character*, *setting*, *plot*, *mood*, *tone*, and *theme* in your reaction. Make sure that you know the meaning and pronunciation of all the words.

2. In what ways is this poem like a prose story? How does the fact that it is poetry make it different?

(Answers are on page 70.)

# WHO'S TALKING?—CHARACTER

A character is someone who acts, chooses, reflects, feels, or is addressed or referred to in a poem. One important character in every poem is the **speaker**—the person, real or imaginary, through whose mind and heart we experience reality as we read the poem. This may or may not be the poet. To be safe, assume that it is not.

The speaker may address the reader in the **first person**, speaking of personal experiences, thoughts, and insights and saying *I*, or in the **third person**, telling of things pertaining to others (*him, her, them*). Occasionally a speaker will address the reader in the **second person**, saying *you*. The second person is used more often in poetry than in prose. Here is an example.

# Barter (1920)
### by Sara Teasdale

1   Life has loveliness to sell,
2     All beautiful and splendid things,
3   Blue waves whitened on a cliff,
4     Soaring fire that sways and sings,
5   And children's faces looking up,
6   Holding wonder like a cup.

7   Life has loveliness to sell,
8     Music like a curve of gold,
9   Scent of pine trees in the rain,
10    Eyes that love you, arms that hold,
11   And for your spirit's still delight,
12   Holy thoughts that star the night.

13   Spend all you have for loveliness,
14     Buy it and never count the cost;
15   For one white singing hour of peace
16     Count many a year of strife well lost,
17   And for a breath of ecstasy
18   Give all you have been, or could be.

Notice that the first stanza seems to be in third person. Only in line 10 is the word *you*, signaling the second person, introduced. In the third stanza, the speaker directly addresses the reader.

If there is an experience or story reported, as in fiction, the speaker may relate the events in a number of different ways. In the first-person point of view, the speaker may be an important participant or have minor involvement. If the speaker is reporting something not experienced firsthand, the third-person point of view may be:

- all-knowing or *omniscient* (that is, able to see into the minds and hearts of everyone involved
- *limited* to insights into a single character, able to enter only that character's thoughts and feelings;
- *objective*, not able to see beyond the externals that everyone can see/hear/touch, etc.

"*The Cremation of Sam McGee*" (page 23) is written from the first-person point of view. The speaker, Cap—whose name is revealed in line 19—tells the tale of an experience he shared with the other important character in the poem, Sam. It is their *actions* with which we are mainly concerned. In "Loveliest of Trees" (page 4), another poem written in first person, we are not so much concerned with the speaker's actions as with his *reaction* to the scene he witnessed.

Poets, like prose writers, have a variety of techniques for revealing character.

- **Words** the character says and that others say about him or her
- **Description** of the character's appearance
- **Actions** taken by the character
- **Interactions** with others
- **Choices** the character makes
- **Growth or Development** that the character undergoes

Sometimes even a character's name is chosen to reveal characteristics to the reader. Think of names like *Superman* or *The Incredibles*, the cartoon family in which each member has super powers.

Read this poem, paying careful attention to characterization. Can you figure out enough about Mulga Bill's character at line 16 to predict the end of the poem?

### Mulga Bill's Bicycle (1895)

by A. B. ("Banjo") Patterson, national poet of Australia

1 'Twas Mulga Bill, from Eaglehawk, that caught the cycling craze;
2 He turned away the good old horse that served him many days;
3 He dressed himself in cycling clothes, resplendent to be seen;
4 He hurried off to town and bought a shining new machine;
5 And as he wheeled it through the door, with air of lordly pride,
6 The grinning shop assistant said, "Excuse me, can you ride?"
7 "See here, young man," said Mulga Bill, "from Walgett to the sea,
8 From Conroy's Gap to Castlereagh, there's none can ride like me.
9 I'm good all round at everything, as everybody knows,
10 Although I'm not the one to talk—I hate a man that blows.

11 "But riding is my special gift, my chiefest, sole delight;
12 Just ask a wild duck can it swim, a wild cat can it fight.
13 There's nothing clothed in hair or hide, or built of flesh or steel,
14 There's nothing walks or jumps, or runs, on axle, hoof or wheel,
15 But what I'll sit, while hide will hold and girths and straps are tight;
16 I'll ride this here two-wheeled concern right straight away at sight."

17 'Twas Mulga Bill, from Eaglehawk, that sought his own abode,
18 That perched above the Dead Man's Creek, beside the mountain road.
19 He turned the cycle down the hill and mounted for the fray,
20 But ere he'd gone a dozen yards it bolted clean away.
21 It left the track, and through the trees, just like a silver streak,
22 It whistled down the awful slope towards the Dead Man's Creek.

23 It shaved a stump by half an inch, it dodged a big white-box:
24 The very wallaroos in fright went scrambling up the rocks,
25 The wombats hiding in their caves dug deeper underground,
26 But Mulga Bill, as white as chalk, clung tight to every bound.
27 It struck a stone and gave a spring that cleared a fallen tree,
28 It raced beside a precipice as close as close could be;
29 And then, as Mulga Bill let out one last despairing shriek,
30 It made a leap of twenty feet into the Dead Man's Creek.

31 'Twas Mulga Bill, from Eaglehawk, that slowly swam ashore:
32 He said, "I've had some narrer shaves and lively rides before;
33 I've rode a wild bull round a yard to win a five-pound bet,
34 But that was sure the derndest ride that I've encountered yet.
35 I'll give that two-wheeled outlaw best; it's shaken all my nerve
36 To feel it whistle through the air and plunge and buck and swerve.
37 It's safe at rest in Dead Man's Creek—we'll leave it lying still;
38 A horse's back is good enough henceforth for Mulga Bill."

As you read a poem, try to find out as much
as you can about the character of the speaker.
Ask yourself whether there are other characters.
Decide whether to direct your attention to
characters' personalities, actions, choices, thoughts,
or something else.

There may be yet another kind of character in a poem—one whose presence and characterization is only hinted at—a person the speaker is addressing, but who never speaks. We can tell that someone is being addressed by the speaker's words, such as saying *you* or calling someone by name or using the form of address called apostrophe—for example, *O Muse!* (see page 118 for more on the rhetorical device apostrophe). How do we gain an impression of a character who isn't there? In such a case, we build up our idea of character from what the speaker says to him or her. Here is another Teasdale poem in second person, but in this case it is not the reader but the speaker's beloved who is addressed, and the word *you* is never used because the sentences do not require it. (*You* is always understood in imperative sentences.)

### Moods (1915)
by Sara Teasdale

1  I am the still rain falling,
2     Too tired for singing mirth—
3  Oh, be the green fields calling,
4     Oh, be for me the earth!

5  I am the brown bird pining
6     To leave the nest and fly—
7  Oh, be the fresh cloud shining,
8     Oh, be for me the sky!

# BRAIN TICKLERS
## Set # 6

1. Identify the point of view in each of these poems:
   a. "Mulga Bill's Bicycle," page 28
   b. "The Raven," page 12
   c. "The Despot," page 12
   d. "Dad's Gift," page 19
2. Read each poem, using a dictionary to check words you don't recognize or can't pronounce. Then answer the questions.

# The Death of the Hired Man (1914)
## by Robert Frost

1  Mary sat musing on the lamp-flame at the table
2  Waiting for Warren. When she heard his step,
3  She ran on tip-toe down the darkened passage
4  To meet him in the doorway with the news
5  And put him on his guard. "Silas is back."
6  She pushed him outward with her through the door
7  And shut it after her. "Be kind," she said.
8  She took the market things from Warren's arms
9  And set them on the porch, then drew him down
10  To sit beside her on the wooden steps.

11  "When was I ever anything but kind to him?
12  But I'll not have the fellow back," he said.
13  "I told him so last haying, didn't I?
14  If he left then, I said, that ended it.
15  What good is he? Who else will harbor him
16  At his age for the little he can do?
17  What help he is there's no depending on.
18  Off he goes always when I need him most.
19  He thinks he ought to earn a little pay,
20  Enough at least to buy tobacco with,
21  So he won't have to beg and be beholden.
22  'All right,' I say, 'I can't afford to pay
23  Any fixed wages, though I wish I could.'
24  'Someone else can.' 'Then someone else will have to.'
25  I shouldn't mind his bettering himself
26  If that was what it was. You can be certain,
27  When he begins like that, there's someone at him
28  Trying to coax him off with pocket-money—
29  In haying time, when any help is scarce.
30  In winter he comes back to us. I'm done."

31  "Sh! not so loud: he'll hear you," Mary said.

32  "I want him to: he'll have to soon or late."

33  "He's worn out. He's asleep beside the stove.
34  When I came up from Rowe's I found him here,
35  Huddled against the barn-door fast asleep,
36  A miserable sight, and frightening, too—
37  You needn't smile—I didn't recognize him—
38  I wasn't looking for him—and he's changed.
39  Wait till you see."

 "Where did you say he'd been?"

40  "He didn't say. I dragged him to the house,

41  And gave him tea and tried to make him smoke.

42  I tried to make him talk about his travels.

43  Nothing would do: he just kept nodding off."

44  "What did he say? Did he say anything?"

45  "But little."

                "Anything? Mary, confess

46  He said he'd come to ditch the meadow for me."

47  "Warren!"

                "But did he? I just want to know."

48  "Of course he did. What would you have him say?

49  Surely you wouldn't grudge the poor old man

50  Some humble way to save his self-respect.

51  He added, if you really care to know,

52  He meant to clear the upper pasture, too.

53  That sounds like something you have heard before?

54  Warren, I wish you could have heard the way

55  He jumbled everything. I stopped to look

56  Two or three times—he made me feel so queer—

57  To see if he was talking in his sleep.

58  He ran on Harold Wilson—you remember—

59  The boy you had in haying four years since.

60  He's finished school, and teaching in his college.

61  Silas declares you'll have to get him back.

62  He says they two will make a team for work:

63  Between them they will lay this farm as smooth!

64  The way he mixed that in with other things.

65  He thinks young Wilson a likely lad, though daft

66  On education—you know how they fought

67  All through July under the blazing sun,

68  Silas up on the cart to build the load,

69  Harold along beside to pitch it on."

70  "Yes, I took care to keep well out of earshot."

71  "Well, those days trouble Silas like a dream.

72  You wouldn't think they would. How some things linger!

73  Harold's young college-boy's assurance piqued him.

74  After so many years he still keeps finding

75  Good arguments he sees he might have used.

76  I sympathize. I know just how it feels

77  To think of the right thing to say too late.

78  Harold's associated in his mind with Latin.

79  He asked me what I thought of Harold's saying

80  He studied Latin, like the violin,

81 Because he liked it—that an argument!
82 He said he couldn't make the boy believe
83 He could find water with a hazel prong—
84 Which showed how much good school had ever done him.
85 He wanted to go over that. But most of all
86 He thinks if he could have another chance
87 To teach him how to build a load of hay—"

88 "I know, that's Silas' one accomplishment.
89 He bundles every forkful in its place,
90 And tags and numbers it for future reference,
91 So he can find and easily dislodge it
92 In the unloading. Silas does that well.
93 He takes it out in bunches like big birds' nests.
94 You never see him standing on the hay
95 He's trying to lift, straining to lift himself."

96 "He thinks if he could teach him that, he'd be
97 Some good perhaps to someone in the world.
98 He hates to see a boy the fool of books.
99 Poor Silas, so concerned for other folk,
100 And nothing to look backward to with pride,
101 And nothing to look forward to with hope,
102 So now and never any different."

103 Part of a moon was falling down the west,
104 Dragging the whole sky with it to the hills.
105 Its light poured softly in her lap. She saw it
106 And spread her apron to it. She put out her hand
107 Among the harplike morning-glory strings,
108 Taut with the dew from garden bed to eaves,
109 As if she played unheard some tenderness
110 That wrought on him beside her in the night.
111 "Warren," she said, "he has come home to die:
112 You needn't be afraid he'll leave you this time."

113 "Home," he mocked gently.

                                "Yes, what else but home?
114 It all depends on what you mean by home.
115 Of course he's nothing to us, any more
116 Than was the hound that came a stranger to us
117 Out of the woods, worn out upon the trail."

118 "Home is the place where, when you have to go there,
119 They have to take you in."

                                "I should have called it
120 Something you somehow haven't to deserve."

121 Warren leaned out and took a step or two,
122 Picked up a little stick, and brought it back
123 And broke it in his hand and tossed it by.
124 "Silas has better claim on us you think
125 Than on his brother? Thirteen little miles
126 As the road winds would bring him to his door.
127 Silas has walked that far no doubt today.
128 Why didn't he go there? His brother's rich,
129 A somebody—director in the bank."

130 "He never told us that."

                              "We know it though."

131 "I think his brother ought to help, of course.
132 I'll see to that if there is need. He ought of right
133 To take him in, and might be willing to—
134 He may be better than appearances.
135 But have some pity on Silas. Do you think
136 If he'd had any pride in claiming kin
137 Or anything he looked for from his brother,
138 He'd keep so still about him all this time?"

139 "I wonder what's between them."

                              "I can tell you.

140 Silas is what he is—we wouldn't mind him—
141 But just the kind that kinsfolk can't abide.
142 He never did a thing so very bad.
143 He don't know why he isn't quite as good
144 As anybody. Worthless though he is,
145 He won't be made ashamed to please his brother."

146 "*I* can't think Si ever hurt anyone."

147 "No, but he hurt my heart the way he lay
148 And rolled his old head on that sharp-edged chair-back.
149 He wouldn't let me put him on the lounge.
150 You must go in and see what you can do.
151 I made the bed up for him there tonight.
152 You'll be surprised at him—how much he's broken.
153 His working days are done; I'm sure of it."

154 "I'd not be in a hurry to say that."

155 "I haven't been. Go, look, see for yourself.
156 But, Warren, please remember how it is:
157 He's come to help you ditch the meadow.
158 He has a plan. You mustn't laugh at him.

159 He may not speak of it, and then he may.
160 I'll sit and see if that small sailing cloud
161 Will hit or miss the moon."

It hit the moon.
162 Then there were three there, making a dim row,
163 The moon, the little silver cloud, and she.

164 Warren returned—too soon, it seemed to her—
165 Slipped to her side, caught up her hand and waited.

166 "Warren?" she questioned.
"Dead," was all he answered.

- What point of view does this poem have?
- Look back at the list showing techniques of characterization (page 28). Through which techniques did you learn about each of the following: Mary, Warren, Silas (the Hired Man), young Harold Wilson, Silas' brother?
- Is this poem concerned with the characters' actions, reflections, choices, thoughts, personalities, change and growth, or something else? Explain your ideas.
- How is this poem like a story in prose? How is it different?

### Ozymandias (1818)
by Percy Bysshe Shelley

1 I met a traveller from an antique land
2 Who said: Two vast and trunkless legs of stone
3 Stand in the desert. Near them, on the sand,
4 Half sunk, a shattered visage lies, whose frown,
5 And wrinkled lip, and sneer of cold command,
6 Tell that its sculptor well those passions read
7 Which yet survive, stamped on these lifeless things,
8 The hand that mocked them, and the heart that fed;
9 And on the pedestal these words appear:
10 "My name is Ozymandias, king of kings:
11 Look on my works, ye Mighty, and despair!"
12 Nothing beside remains. Round the decay
13 Of that colossal wreck, boundless and bare
14 The lone and level sands stretch far away.

- Identify the four characters.
- By inserting a quotation from a character who is not the speaker, the poet can, in effect, temporarily change the point of view of a poem. How does Shelley use this technique to play with the point of view in this poem?
- Retell the information that is conveyed in "Ozymandias" in prose and in chronological (time) order from the first event to the last.

3. Write a poem in the second person. Make sure you reveal information about the speaker's character and about the character your speaker is addressing. Also think about your audience, the person or people for whom you're writing the poem.

(Answers are on page 71.)

# WHERE ARE WE?—SETTING

Everything happens somewhere, in some place at some time. The environment in which a poem takes place is its setting.

Look around you now. Perhaps you are in a room: How is it furnished? Where is it in the building? Perhaps you are outdoors: What is the weather like? What season is it? Are there buildings or mountains nearby? What country, region, city, or town is it? What year? All of these are part of your setting.

It may be helpful to you to think of setting as having three elements: physical, historical, and social/cultural.

## Physical setting

Physical setting includes the location, the weather, the natural features, the architecture, and the furnishings. This excerpt from a poem by an Australian poet focuses on physical setting.

### My Country (1908)
by Dorothea Mackellar (excerpt)

9   I love a sunburnt country,
10  A land of sweeping plains,
11  Of ragged mountain ranges,
12  Of droughts and flooding rains.
13  I love her far horizons,
14  I love her jewel-sea,
15  Her beauty and her terror—
16  The wide brown land for me!

## Historical setting

Historical setting includes the time and date in history and the events of historical significance that are occurring or have just occurred. In the following poem, an American lawyer and poet wrote about an historical event that had recently taken place.

### The Death of Lincoln (April 1865)
by William Cullen Bryant

1   Oh, slow to smite and swift to spare,
2     Gentle and merciful and just!
3   Who, in the fear of God, didst bear
4     The sword of power, a nation's trust!

5   In sorrow by thy bier we stand,
6     Amid the awe that hushes all,
7   And speak the anguish of a land
8     That shook with horror at thy fall.

9   Thy task is done; the bound are free;
10    We bear thee to an honored grave,
11  Whose proudest monument shall be
12    The broken fetters of the slave.

13  Pure was thy life; its bloody close
14    Hath placed thee with the sons of light,
15  Among the noble host of those
16    Who perished in the cause of Right.

## Social/cultural setting

The social/cultural setting includes the cultural and ethnic backgrounds of people, their socioeconomic situations, their religious or philosophical beliefs, etc. The poet's concern in this poem is to suggest a philosophy of life that will guide an individual through all kinds of social situations. By describing the circumstances in which this philosophy will be helpful, Kipling lets us see the social/cultural setting of the speaker and the person the speaker is addressing (his son).

### If (1910)
by Rudyard Kipling

1   If you can keep your head when all about you
2       Are losing theirs and blaming it on you;
3   If you can trust yourself when all men doubt you,
4       But make allowance for their doubting too;
5   If you can wait and not be tired by waiting,
6       Or, being lied about, don't deal in lies,
7   Or being hated don't give way to hating,
8       And yet don't look too good, nor talk too wise;

9   If you can dream—and not make dreams your master;
10      If you can think—and not make thoughts your aim,
11  If you can meet with Triumph and Disaster
12      And treat those two impostors just the same;
13  If you can bear to hear the truth you've spoken
14      Twisted by knaves to make a trap for fools,
15  Or watch the things you gave your life to, broken,
16      And stoop and build 'em up with worn-out tools;

17  If you can make one heap of all your winnings
18      And risk it on one turn of pitch-and-toss,
19  And lose, and start again at your beginnings,
20      And never breathe a word about your loss;
21  If you can force your heart and nerve and sinew
22      To serve your turn long after they are gone,
23  And so hold on when there is nothing in you
24      Except the Will which says to them: "Hold on!"

25  If you can talk with crowds and keep your virtue,
26      Or walk with Kings—nor lose the common touch,
27  If neither foes nor loving friends can hurt you,
28      If all men count with you, but none too much;
29  If you can fill the unforgiving minute
30      With sixty seconds' worth of distance run,
31  Yours is the Earth and everything that's in it,
32      And—which is more—you'll be a Man, my son!

## Clues that reveal setting

Because poetry is so compact, indicators of setting in a poem might perform other functions as well. Think back to "The Cremation of Sam McGee." The physical setting was also a cause of conflict, both for Sam, who couldn't stand the cold, and for Cap, who had to search long and hard for a place to carry out his promise. Without the Arctic setting, there's no story. In "Ozymandias," it is the changes in the physical setting (what was once a splendid monument is now broken and buried in the sand) *and* the historical setting (what was mighty at one moment in history is insignificant and forgotten later) that draw our interest. In "The Death of the Hired Man," the social/cultural setting was the cause of Silas's situation, including his poverty, his quest for independence and respect, and his lack of family and a social network.

### BRAIN TICKLERS
*Set # 7*

1. Read the following poems and excerpts. Use a dictionary to check words you don't recognize or can't pronounce. Then answer the questions.

   **Fog** (1916)
   by Carl Sandburg

   1  The fog comes
   2  on little cat feet.

   3  It sits looking
   4  over harbor and city
   5  on silent haunches
   6  and then moves on.

   - Describe the setting.
   - How is setting important in the poem?

# Night (1935)

by Lucy Maud Montgomery

1 A pale enchanted moon is sinking low
2    Behind the dunes that fringe the shadowy lea,
3 And there is haunted starlight on the flow
4    Of immemorial sea.

5 I am alone and need no more pretend
6    Laughter or smile to hide a hungry heart;
7 I walk with solitude as with a friend
8    Enfolded and apart.

9 We tread an eerie road across the moor
10    Where shadows weave upon their ghostly looms,
11 And winds sing an old lyric that might lure
12    Sad queens from ancient tombs.

13 I am a sister to the loveliness
14    Of cool far hill and long-remembered shore,
15 Finding in it a sweet forgetfulness
16    Of all that hurt before.

17 The world of day, its bitterness and cark,
18    No longer have the power to make me weep;
19 I welcome this communion of the dark
20    As toilers welcome sleep.

- Describe the setting.
- What setting does the speaker contrast to the one she is in as she speaks?

## Autumn's Orchestra:
## Inscribed to One Beyond Seas (1912)

by Tekahionwake (excerpts)

### The Vine

21 The wild grape mantling the trail and tree,
22 Festoons in graceful veils its drapery,
23 Its tendrils cling, as clings the memory stirred
24 By some evasive haunting tune, twice heard.

**Hare-Bell**

29 Elfin bell in azure dress,
30 Chiming all day long,
31 Ringing through the wilderness
32 Dulcet notes of song.
33 Daintiest of forest flowers
34 Weaving like a spell—
35 Music through the Autumn hours,
36 Little Elfin bell.

- How are the two excerpts similar?
- How do they differ?

2. Choose an historical event and make it the setting of a poem. Think about your chosen audience as you write.

(Answers are on page 72.)

# WHAT'S HAPPENING?—PLOT

A poem can record an unchanging scene. It may record a single thought, feeling, setting, image, or experience. But a poem can also record events that take place over time. Sometimes, as in "Fog" (page 39), this is simply movement: the fog comes, sits, and moves on. The poet may also present two contrasting states, scenes, ideas, people, or other things, and directly or indirectly encourage the reader to draw conclusions. But sometimes there is **plot**: purposeful action by one or more characters who attempt to gain a desired goal or outcome. A character who is at the center of a plot is often referred to as the **protagonist**.

A plot nearly always involves conflict. Conflict is a struggle that makes us wonder if the character will reach the goal or not. Sometimes it is something **internal**, the character's own personality or short-comings that could prevent achieving the goal. A character can also experience internal conflict about pursuing the goal if he or she desires a goal but also has reservations about it. The struggle to attain the cherished goal may lead a character to grow and change or to face the reality of his or her weaknesses or deficits.

Here is an excerpt from a poem in which the speaker faces up to his own shortcomings as a poet. He does manage to follow all the many rules for the poetic form of a French Ballade (pronounced buh-LODD), despite all the difficulties he encounters. The result, as he points out, isn't great poetry—but it is funny.

### The Ballade of the Incompetent Ballade-Monger (1891)
by J. K. Stephen (excerpt)

1  I am not ambitious at all:
2    I am not a poet, I know
3  (Though I do love to see a mere scrawl
4    To order and symmetry grow).
5    My muse is uncertain and slow,
6  I am not expert with my tools.
7    I lack the poetic argot:
8  But I hope I have kept to the rules.

9  When your brain is undoubtedly small,
10    'Tis hard, sir, to write in a row,
11  Some five or six rhymes to "Nepal,"
12    And more than a dozen to "Joe":
13    And meter is easier though,
14  Three rhymes are sufficient for "ghouls,"
15    My lines are deficient in go,
16  But I hope I have kept to the rules.

There can also be **external conflicts**, struggles with someone or something from outside the protagonist that slows or prevents progress toward the goal. A foe, called the **antagonist**, can provide conflict, but so can the environment, natural forces, or society. In "The Cremation of Sam McGee," (pages 23–25), the conflict is both internal and external. Does Cap, we may wonder, have the loyalty to honor his commitment when the environment seems to make it impossible and the continuing presence of the "corpse" is so unpleasant?

In the following poem, the speaker is the protagonist, and the antagonists are natural forces: time and death.

### The Two Highwaymen (before 1919)
by Wilfrid Scawen Blunt

1   I long have had a quarrel set with Time
2   Because he robb'd me. Every day of life
3   Was wrested from me after bitter strife:
4   I never yet could see the sun go down
5   But I was angry in my heart, nor hear
6   The leaves fall in the wind without a tear
7   Over the dying summer. I have known
8   No truce with Time nor Time's accomplice, Death.
9   The fair world is the witness of a crime
10   Repeated every hour. For life and breath
11   Are sweet to all who live; and bitterly
12   The voices of these robbers of the heath
13   Sound in each ear and chill the passer-by.
14   —What have we done to thee, thou monstrous Time?
15   What have we done to Death that we must die?

In analyzing plots, we can also see a **beginning**, when the goal is set; a **middle**, during which the character struggles to achieve the goal; and an **end**, when we find out the conclusion of the character's quest—successful, unsuccessful, or undetermined. For examples, through Mary's and Warren's conversation in "The Death of the Hired Man," we can imagine Silas's struggle for dignity throughout his life and reconstruct in our imagination the conflicts with family, coworkers, and those who hired him, until his value, sadly, is proclaimed by Mary only at his death.

# BRAIN TICKLERS
### Set # 8

1. Read this excerpt from a seventeenth-century poem about Odysseus/Ulysses.* Check words you don't know in a dictionary.

### Ulysses and the Siren (1605)
by Samuel Daniel (excerpt)

SIREN:
1    Come worthy Greek, Ulysses, come,
2  Possess these shores with me;
3  The winds and seas are troublesome,
4  And here we may be free.
5    Here may we sit and view their toil
6  That travail in the deep,
7  And joy the day in mirth the while,
8  And spend the night in sleep.

ULYSSES:
9    Fair nymph, if fame or honour were
10  To be attain'd with ease,
11  Then would I come and rest me there,
12  And leave such toils as these.
13    But here it dwells, and here must I
14  With danger seek it forth;
15  To spend the time luxuriously
16  Becomes not men of worth.

SIREN:
17    Ulysses, O be not deceiv'd
18  With that unreal name;
19  This honour is a thing conceiv'd
20  And rests on others' fame.
21    Begotten only to molest
22  Our peace, and to beguile
23  The best thing of our life, our rest,
24  And give us up to toil.

---

* *Ulysses* is the Latin form of the name *Odysseus*. Odysseus was one of the Greek heroes of the Trójan War, whose adventures Homer recounted in the *Iliad* and the *Odyssey*. As Odysseus traveled home after the war, he and his shipmates passed the island of the Sirens, mythological creatures who tried to lure the men to their destruction.

- Plot often begins with someone who wants something. What does the Siren want?
- What argument does Ulysses use against her? How does she respond?
- Predict how the conflict will end.

2. Read this poem from the eighteenth century using a dictionary to check words you don't know. Then answer the questions. Note that in this poem, in the words *waterd*, *veild*, and *outstretchd*, the poet has left out an *e*, signaling us to not make—*ed* a separate syllable. This is called **elision**. (For more on syllables see pages 24, 189, and 279.)

### A Poison Tree (1794)
by William Blake

1  I was angry with my friend:
2  I told my wrath, my wrath did end.
3  I was angry with my foe:
4  I told it not, my wrath did grow.

5  And I waterd it in fears,
6  Night & morning with my tears;
7  And I sunnéd it with smiles,
8  And with soft deceitful wiles.

9  And it grew both day and night,
10  Till it bore an apple bright.
11  And my foe beheld it shine,
12  And he knew that it was mine,

13  And into my garden stole,
14  When the night had veild the pole;
15  In the morning glad I see
16  My foe outstrechd beneath the tree.

- Recount the plot of this story in your own words.
- Why do you think Blake introduced the character of the friend rather than just of the speaker and the speaker's foe?
- How is setting important in this poem?

3. Read this nineteenth-century poem and use a dictionary to check any words you don't know. Then answer the questions. It may help to know that the first line of this poem was originally "O what can ail thee, knight-at-arms." Knowing this will help you imagine the character that Keats had in mind. The title is in French. It means "the beautiful woman without pity."

## La Belle Dame Sans Merci (1819)

### by John Keats

1 Ah, what can ail thee, wretched wight,
2    Alone and palely loitering;
3 The sedge is wither'd from the lake,
4    And no birds sing.

5 Ah, what can ail thee, wretched wight,
6    So haggard and so woe-begone?
7 The squirrel's granary is full,
8    And the harvest's done.

9 I see a lily on thy brow,
10    With anguish moist and fever dew;
11 And on thy cheek a fading rose
12    Fast withereth too.

13 I met a lady in the meads
14    Full beautiful, a faery's child;
15 Her hair was long, her foot was light,
16    And her eyes were wild.

17 I set her on my pacing steed,
18    And nothing else saw all day long;
19 For sideways would she lean, and sing
20    A faery's song.

21 I made a garland for her head,
22    And bracelets too, and fragrant zone;
23 She look'd at me as she did love,
24    And made sweet moan.

25 She found me roots of relish sweet,
26    And honey wild, and manna dew;
27 And sure in language strange she said,
28    I love thee true.

29 She took me to her elfin grot,
30    And there she gaz'd and sighed deep,
31 And there I shut her wild sad eyes—
32    So kiss'd to sleep.

33 And there we slumber'd on the moss,
34    And there I dream'd, ah woe betide,
35 The latest dream I ever dream'd
36    On the cold hill side.

37 I saw pale kings, and princes too,
38    Pale warriors, death-pale were they all;
39 Who cry'd—"La belle dame sans merci
40    Hath thee in thrall!"

41 I saw their starv'd lips in the gloam
42    With horrid warning gaped wide,
43 And I awoke, and found me here
44    On the cold hill side.

45 And this is why I sojourn here
46    Alone and palely loitering,
47 Though the sedge is wither'd from the lake,
48    And no birds sing.

- Identify the characters in the poem.
- Explain the change that takes place between lines 12 and 13.
- Tell the plot of the poem in chronological order.
- How is setting important in this poem?

4. Write a poem of any kind in which setting is important to the plot. If you're stumped for ideas, it may help to choose an extreme setting—very cold, very hot, very wet, very remote (Pluto?), very high, very low. Or close your eyes, spin a globe, and put down your finger somewhere.

(Answers are on page 73.)

# HOW DOES IT FEEL?—MOOD

You can probably tell when those close to you are in a bad mood or a really good mood, when they are hyper, relaxed, tense, or scared. Like people, poems have moods. Often the mood of a poem is closely related to the way the setting is described, to what is happening in the plot, and/or to the rhythm of the poem.

Read these three brief excerpts that describe a forest setting in a poem.

### Stopping By Woods on a Snowy Evening (1923)
by Robert Frost (see page 129)

. . . the woods are lovely, dark and deep . . .

### *Autumn's Orchestra* (1912)
by Tekahionwake (see page 40)

#### The Vine

The wild grape mantling the trail and tree,
Festoons in graceful veils its drapery,
Its tendrils cling, as clings the memory stirred
By some evasive haunting tune, twice heard.

## Alone in the Dark

I dare to broach the deepening dark.
The darkness deepens more and more.
The owls screech, the goblins jape,
As I scrape along the forest floor.

—original

Notice that the setting itself does not set the mood. For example, a furnace seems to be a deadly place, but Sam McGee was happy there. We might have some preconceived ideas about a forest setting, but the three excerpts show us that the feeling is in the description, not in the place.

In the first instance, the darkness of the forest and its mystery are inviting. In the second, the setting evokes a mood of longing—*haunting* here does not refer to ghosts, but to a lingering presence that is pleasurable yet not able to be captured and contained. In the third case, there is a sense of foreboding and suspense. This forest is a place where evil lurks. Read the excerpts aloud. Try to express the mood with your voice.

Now let's think about how plot interacts with mood. Think back to "The Death of the Hired Man" (pages 31–35). Think of Mary's urgent attempts to communicate to Warren what she sees in Silas and how she elaborates her plan to help him feel welcomed. Think of her sitting and contemplating the cloud and the moon as she waits for Warren to help put her plan into action. Now recall the abrupt ending:

'Dead,' was all he answered.

Does the sharp cutting off of the plot convey to you the frustration of both Silas' life and Mary's plans? Does it create a sudden mood change for you, from hopeful expectation (even though you know the title, and so know that Silas will die) to sudden emptiness? If this was not your experience, take some time to consider it as a possible interpretation.

Now let's consider mood and meter. Look back at "Hare-Bell" from *Autumn's Orchestra* (page 41) and read it aloud. Notice how the lines move quickly and lightly. Now read the excerpt from "The Raven" (page 12), noticing how it drags along, tumbling over itself. In each case, the rhythm contributes to the mood.

The mood of a poem can change, usually as circumstances in the plot change. Think back to the first two lines of "A Poison Tree" (page 45). The speaker quickly deals with the friction between himself and his friend: Two brief lines and the matter is done. But by the end of line 4, the festering, brooding hatred that accompanies the injury of the foe has taken root and changed the mood.

Remember that just as a variety of elements can contribute to the mood of a person, so a poem's mood can be shaped by several factors.

## BRAIN TICKLERS
### Set # 9

1. Read the following poems. Use a dictionary to check words you don't recognize. Then answer the questions.

### Bird Language (1875)
by Christopher Pearse Cranch

1 One day in the bluest of summer weather,
2     Sketching under a whispering oak,
3 I heard five bobolinks laughing together
4     Over some ornithological joke.

5 What the fun was I couldn't discover.
6     Language of birds is a riddle on earth.
7 What could they find in whiteweed and clover
8     To split their sides with such musical mirth?

9 Was it some prank of the prodigal summer,
10     Face in the cloud or voice in the breeze,
11 Querulous catbird, woodpecker drummer,
12     Cawing of crows high over the trees?

13 Was it some chipmunk's chatter, or weasel
14     Under the stone-wall stealthy and sly?
15 Or was the joke about me at my easel,
16     Trying to catch the tints of the sky?

17 Still they flew tipsily, shaking all over,
18    Bubbling with jollity, brimful of glee,
19 While I sat listening deep in the clover,
20    Wondering what their jargon could be.

21 'Twas but the voice of a morning the brightest
22    That ever dawned over yon shadowy hills;
23 'Twas but the song of all joy that is lightest,—
24    Sunshine breaking in laughter and trills.

25 Vain to conjecture the words they are singing;
26    Only by tones can we follow the tune
27 In the full heart of the summer fields ringing,
28    Ringing the rhythmical gladness of June!

- How would you describe the mood of the poem?

### On the Death of My Child (1832)
by Joseph von Eichendorff,
translated by Aodhagán O'Broin (2000)

1 The distant clocks are striking,
2 It is already late,
3 The lamp is burning dimly,
4 Your little bed is made.

5 The winds are blowing still,
6 They wail around the house,
7 Inside we sit here lonely
8 And often listen out.

9 It is as if that must be
10 You tapping on the door,
11 You lost your way a little,
12 But now you've made it home.

13 What silly foolish folk we are!
14 It's we who are misled—
15 While we're still lost in darkness
16 You've long since found your bed.

- Who are the characters in this poem?
- At which line does the mood change? What realization does the speaker have that changes the mood? Describe the mood before and after the change.

2. Write a poem in which you create a mood in a forest, different from those in the three examples (pages 47–48).

(Answers are on page 75.)

# SOMEONE WITH AN ATTITUDE—TONE

"Don't use that tone of voice to me!" we may hear person A say to person B. This can happen if person A feels that person B has been rude, condescending, disrespectful, etc. It's important to realize that person A is *not necessarily* objecting to the content of what person B said but to the *way* person B said what he or she said. Tone of voice is expressed through the pitch, volume, and inflection of the voice. Tone in writing is similar: It consists of the cues, not vocal but written, that tell us what attitude toward the subject the poet chose to convey.

## Caution—Major Mistake Territory!

What the poet has chosen to express in a particular piece of writing, and how the poet feels may be two quite different things.

A love poem can convey admiration simply by the fact that the poet took the time to write and perfect it. A poet from the American colonies wrote the following love poem for her husband, and we know that she herself is the speaker. Notice the devices she uses within the poem to convey her attitude toward her husband.

## To My Dear and Loving Husband (1678)

### by Anne Bradstreet

1  If ever two were one, then surely we.
2  If ever man were lov'd by wife, then thee.
3  If ever wife was happy in a man,
4  Compare with me, ye women, if you can.
5  I prize thy love more than whole Mines of gold
6  Or all the riches that the East doth hold.
7  My love is such that Rivers cannot quench,
8  Nor ought but love from thee give recompense.
9  Thy love is such I can no way repay.
10  The heavens reward thee manifold, I pray.
11  Then while we live, in love let's so persever
12  That when we live no more, we may live ever.

Bradstreet uses terms of endearment in the title, never mentioning her husband's name. *If ever* conveys her belief that in the history of married love they have reached the peak. She favorably compares her love for him to love of gold, and deems it unquenchable. Even so, she says, this great depth of her love is insufficient to repay *his* love. She prays that the depth and loyalty of their mutual love will win them the reward of heaven. Over and over in various ways, she tells of her love for him and her delight in his love for her. The repetition and the invention join to convey how much she cherishes him.

Love poetry often uses these devices: language that is emotionally charged, comparison, invention, and repetition. Poems that express other strong feelings may use some of the same devices. This poet uses invention, comparison, and repetition to create a playful tone in celebrating the happiness of spring. Notice that he also uses enumeration, listing the things that characterize spring.

### Spring (1600)

#### by Thomas Nashe

1  Spring, the sweet Spring, is the year's pleasant king;
2  Then blooms each thing, then maids dance in a ring,
3  Cold doth not sting, the pretty birds do sing—
4     Cuckoo, jug-jug, pu-we, to-witta-woo!

5  The palm and may make country houses gay,
6  Lambs frisk and play, the shepherds pipe all day,
7  And we hear aye birds tune this merry lay—
8  Cuckoo, jug-jug, pu-we, to-witta-woo!

9  The fields breathe sweet, the daisies kiss our feet,
10  Young lovers meet, old wives a-sunning sit,
11  In every street these tunes our ears do greet—
12    Cuckoo, jug-jug, pu-we, to-witta-woo!
13    Spring, the sweet Spring!

This poet uses emotional language and invention to celebrate dedicated effort and perseverance in this poem, in which the tone moves between disdain and admiration.

### Success (before 1887)
#### by Emma Lazarus

1  Oft have I brooded on defeat and pain,
2  The pathos of the stupid, stumbling throng.
3  These I ignore to-day and only long
4  To pour my soul forth in one trumpet strain,
5  One clear, grief-shattering, triumphant song,
6  For all the victories of man's high endeavor,
7  Palm-bearing, laurel deeds that live forever,
8  The splendor clothing him whose will is strong.
9  Hast thou beheld the deep, glad eyes of one
10  Who has persisted and achieved? Rejoice!
11  On naught diviner shines the all-seeing sun.
12  Salute him with free heart and choral voice,
13  'Midst flippant, feeble crowds of spectres wan,
14  The bold, significant, successful man.

## BRAIN TICKLERS
### Set # 10

1. Read the poems on pages 54–55. Use a dictionary to check words you don't recognize. For each poem, answer questions a and b.
   a. Do you think that the speaker is the poet? Why or why not?
   b. What is the tone of the poem? What devices work to achieve that tone?

# Psalm 100 (1611)

King James translation

1 Make a joyful noise unto the Lord, all ye lands.

2 Serve the Lord with gladness: come before his presence with singing.

3 Know ye that the lord he is God: it is he that hath made us, and not we ourselves; we are his people, and the sheep of his pasture.

4 Enter into his gates with thanksgiving, and into his courts with praise: be thankful unto him, and bless his name.

5 For the Lord is good; his mercy is everlasting; and his truth endureth to all generations.

# The Curse (1907)

by J. M. Synge*

1 Lord, confound this surly sister,

2 Blight her brow with blotch and blister,

3 Cramp her larynx, lung, and liver,

4 In her guts a galling give her.

5 Let her live to earn her dinners

6 In Mountjoy with seedy sinners:

7 Lord, this judgment quickly bring,

8 And I'm your servant, J. M. Synge.

# Charge of the Light Brigade (1854)

by Alfred, Lord Tennyson

### I

1 Half a league, half a league,

2     Half a league onward,

3 All in the valley of Death

4     Rode the six hundred.

5 'Forward, the Light Brigade!

6 Charge for the guns!' he said:

7 Into the valley of Death

8     Rode the six hundred.

### II

9 'Forward, the Light Brigade!'

10 Was there a man dismay'd?

11 Not tho' the soldier knew

12     Some one had blunder'd:

13 Theirs not to make reply,

14 Theirs not to reason why,

15 Theirs but to do and die:

16 Into the valley of Death

17     Rode the six hundred.

### III

18 Cannon to right of them,

19 Cannon to left of them,

20 Cannon in front of them

21     Volley'd and thunder'd;

22 Storm'd at with shot and shell,

23 Boldly they rode and well,

24 Into the jaws of Death,

25 Into the mouth of Hell

26     Rode the six hundred.

---

* The playwright Synge wrote this poem about a woman who criticized one of his plays; she was the sister of a man Synge considered to be his enemy. *Mountjoy* is the name of a prison in Dublin.

#### IV

27 Flash'd all their sabres bare,
28 Flash'd as they turn'd in air
29 Sabring the gunners there,
30 Charging an army, while
31    All the world wonder'd:
32 Plunged in the battery-smoke
33 Right thro' the line they broke;
34 Cossack and Russian
35 Reel'd from the sabre-stroke
36    Shatter'd and sunder'd.
37 Then they rode back, but not
38    Not the six hundred.

#### V

39 Cannon to right of them,
40 Cannon to left of them,

41 Cannon behind them
42    Volley'd and thunder'd;
43 Storm'd at with shot and shell,
44 While horse and hero fell,
45 They that had fought so well
46 Came thro' the jaws of Death,
47 Back from the mouth of Hell,
48 All that was left of them,
49    Left of six hundred.

#### VI

50 When can their glory fade?
51 O the wild charge they made!
52    All the world wonder'd.
53 Honour the charge they made!
54 Honour the Light Brigade,
55    Noble six hundred!

2. Recall that in "Ozymandias" (page 35) there are four characters—the speaker, the traveler, the sculptor, and Ozymandias himself. The speaker merely gives a factual report of what he heard. The traveler shares his opinion about what manner of man the statue showed and the sculptor's skill. Ozymandias had recorded his own impressions of his place in the world on the statue.

   a. What is the tone of Ozymandias, the king, in his statement?

   b. Whose tone in the poem is most like the poet's? Why do you think so? Define that tone.

   c. Of what use is the speaker in the poem? What would be different if the poem had begun:

1  I am a traveller from an antique land
2  Who saw: Two vast and trunkless legs of stone . . . ?

(Answers are on page 76.)

**Irony** is a tone in which someone means the opposite of what is said. You may need to pay very close attention to recognize irony because, unlike the speaking voice, which adds clues to the words with pitch and inflection, the clues to irony in written language are very subtle. **Sarcasm** is a particular kind of irony in which what one says is intended to hurt or severely criticize someone else.

Let's read through a poem together, pausing after each line to reflect on how one author develops tone. We'll use the poem "Comment" (1925) by Dorothy Parker. We know that a comment is a response to something, but as yet we don't know what is being commented on or whether Parker herself is the speaker.

1   Oh, life is a glorious cycle of song,

This seems to be a poem of celebration. Although the first line is rather overstated (we know that not all of life is so wonderful as all that), we might accept it for the moment as a rather uncritical, sentimental view, and wait to see what happens.

2   A medley of extemporanea;

A medley is an assortment of dissimilar items; extemporanea are things that happen spontaneously, without planning. Is it true that life is unplanned and always pleasantly surprising? Well, no, but we still might take this as joyous exaggeration resulting from a delightful and surprising experience.

3   And love is a thing that can never go wrong;

Now the subject is narrowing. One explanation of the poem so far would be the joyous response of someone in love, whose vision is temporarily filled with only the good things of life. And so we read on.

4   And I am Marie of Roumania.

Well, it is absolutely certain that Dorothy Parker was *not* the queen of Roumania. Would it make sense that she would write a poem in which the speaker was Marie? It's not immediately apparent why she would.

How do we know what to do next? The word *and* that begins the last line puts the four lines on an equal footing:

It gives us a cue that we must assign the same truth-value to all of them. It is obvious that the last line is not only untrue but ludicrous. So we must go back and reassess the others in the same way.

Is life "a glorious cycle of song" really? No. There is suffering, sickness, death, loneliness, despair. Is life a "medley of extemporanea"? Consider how much planning is required to run a government, build a submarine, put out a forest fire, get the laundry done for a family of six. Is love "a thing that can never go wrong"? Hardly. This poem is completely ironic.

And what of the title? Well, it's clearly a comment on life itself, and maybe also a comment on sentimental, fuzzy-headed poetry that paints life with falsely bright colors . . . and on the foolish readers who, let's face it, got tricked.

If you were familiar with Dorothy Parker's poetry before you began reading this poem, you would know that many of her poems are ironic or sarcastic. In this situation, you could use your **prior knowledge** as another tool to inform your reading. For more on irony, see page 150.

## BRAIN TICKLERS
### Set # 11

Rewrite "Charge of the Light Brigade" with a different tone. (You can try sarcasm, if you wish.) Feel free to change the poem as necessary to achieve your end. Think about your audience as you work.

(Answers are on page 78.)

# WHAT'S IT ALL ABOUT?—THEME

The theme is the central thought of a poem. It's not the same as the poem's subject, although the subject and the poet's tone are good clues to the theme. Sometimes the theme is directly stated by the poet, as in this excerpted poem. An explicitly stated theme is often a **moral**, a lesson the poet draws for the reader.

### The Retired Cat (1803)
by William Cowper (excerpts)

1  A poet's cat, sedate and grave
2  As poet well could wish to have,
3  Was much addicted to inquire
4  For nooks to which she might retire,
5  And where, secure as mouse in chink,
6  She might repose, or sit and think.

. . .

35  A drawer, it chanc'd, at bottom lin'd
36  With linen of the softest kind,
37  With such as merchants introduce
38  From India, for the ladies' use—
39  A drawer impending o'er the rest,
40  Half-open in the topmost chest,
41  Of depth enough, and none to spare,
42  Invited her to slumber there;
43  Puss with delight beyond expression
44  Survey'd the scene, and took possession.
45  Recumbent at her ease ere long,
46  And lull'd by her own humdrum song,
47  She left the cares of life behind,
48  And slept as she would sleep her last,
49  When in came, housewifely inclin'd
50  The chambermaid, and shut it fast;
51  By no malignity impell'd,
52  But all unconscious whom it held.

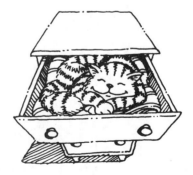

53    Awaken'd by the shock, cried Puss,
54  "Was ever cat attended thus!
55  The open drawer was left, I see,
56  Merely to prove a nest for me.
57  For soon as I was well compos'd,
58  Then came the maid, and it was clos'd.
59  How smooth these kerchiefs, and how sweet!
60    Oh, what a delicate retreat!
61  I will resign myself to rest
62  Till Sol, declining in the west,
63  Shall call to supper, when, no doubt,
64  Susan will come and let me out."

65    The evening came, the sun descended,
66  And puss remain'd still unattended.
67  The night roll'd tardily away
68  (With her indeed 'twas never day),
69  The sprightly morn her course renew'd,
70    The evening gray again ensued,
71  And puss came into mind no more
72  Than if entomb'd the day before.
73  With hunger pinch'd, and pinch'd for room,
74  She now presag'd approaching doom,
75  Nor slept a single wink, or purr'd,
76  Conscious of jeopardy incurr'd.

77    That night, by chance, the poet watching
78  Heard an inexplicable scratching;
79  His noble heart went pit-a-pat
80  And to himself he said, "What's that?"
81  He drew the curtain at his side,
82  And forth he peep'd, but nothing spied;
83  Yet, by his ear directed, guess'd
84  Something imprison'd in the chest,
85  And, doubtful what, with prudent care
86  Resolv'd it should continue there.
87  At length a voice which well he knew,
88  A long and melancholy mew,
89  Saluting his poetic ears,
90  Consol'd him, and dispell'd his fears:
91  He left his bed, he trod the floor,

92   He 'gan in haste the drawers explore,
93   The lowest first, and without stop
94   The rest in order to the top;
95   For 'tis a truth well known to most,
96   That whatsoever thing is lost,
97   We seek it, ere it come to light,
98   In ev'ry cranny but the right.
99   Forth skipp'd the cat, not now replete
100   As erst with airy self-conceit,
101   Nor in her own fond apprehension
102   A theme for all the world's attention,
103   But modest, sober, cured of all
104   Her notions hyperbolical,
105   And wishing for a place of rest
106   Anything rather than a chest.
107   Then stepp'd the poet into bed,
108   With this reflection in his head:

   MORAL

109   Beware of too sublime a sense
110   Of your own worth and consequence.
111   The man who dreams himself so great,
112   And his importance of such weight,
113   That all around in all that's done
114   Must move and act for him alone,
115   Will learn in school of tribulation
116   The folly of his expectation.

Cowper tells us plainly that we may learn from his cat not to think too much of ourselves.

When the theme is not explicitly stated, often it is wise to begin with the title. The title may state the subject, or at least cast light on it, and theme is closely related to subject. The subject of "Ozymandias" is the wreckage of a statue of a monarch of that name; the theme could be said to be the workings of time: What is mighty in one age is of no account and nearly forgotten in another. The subject of "The Death of the Hired Man" is the hired man, Silas. The theme might be stated as the inherent dignity of every individual.

Remember that we looked at excerpts of three poems set in the forest and discovered that they had different moods. Similarly, poems with the same subject may have different themes. "A Poison Tree" and "Charge of the Light Brigade" are both about a fight with an enemy. The theme of "A Poison Tree" is the evil brought about by unresolved anger and hatred, whereas the theme of Tennyson's poem is the heroism of those who give their lives for their country.

Not every poem has a clearly defined theme—some poems seem capable of more than one interpretation, or are so rich that they teem with possibility. Humorous poems, on the other hand, may be intended primarily for entertainment rather than to convey a message. The search for a theme in "The Cremation of Sam McGee" might bring you to something like "keep your promises, no matter what," or "necessity is the mother of invention," or "one man's meat is another man's poison." But none of them seem to be a satisfactory way to convey the gist of that poem. Although I am not saying that humorous poems have no theme, I will let their themes stand unnamed.

# BRAIN TICKLERS
## Set # 12

1. Read the following poems and excerpts. Use a dictionary to check words you don't recognize. Then answer the questions.

### "Hope" is the thing with feathers—
(c. 1861)
by Emily Dickinson

1  "Hope" is the thing with feathers—
2  That perches on the soul—
3  And sings the tune without the words—
4  And never stops—at all—

5  And sweetest—in the Gale—is heard—
6  And sore must be the storm—
7  That could abash the little Bird
8  That kept so many warm—

9  I've heard it in the chillest land—
10  And on the strangest Sea—
11  Yet, never, in Extremity,
12  It asked a crumb—of Me.

- What is the subject of this poem?
- What is its theme?

### Sonnets from the Portuguese XIV (1845–1846)
#### by Elizabeth Barrett Browning

1   If thou must love me, let it be for nought
2   Except for love's sake only. Do not say
3   'I love her for her smile . . . her look . . . her way
4   Of speaking gently, . . . for a trick of thought
5   That falls in well with mine, and certes brought
6   A sense of pleasant ease on such a day'—
7   For these things in themselves, Belovèd, may
8   Be changed, or change for thee,—and love, so wrought,
9   May be unwrought so. Neither love me for
10  Thine own dear pity's wiping my cheeks dry,—
11  A creature might forget to weep, who bore
12  Thy comfort long, and lose thy love thereby!
13  But love me for love's sake, that evermore
14  Thou may'st love on, through love's eternity.

- What is the subject of this poem?
- How is this poem similar to and different from Anne Bradstreet's poem, "To My Dear and Loving Husband" (page 52)?
- What is Browning's theme?

2. Choose an animal, anything from a slug to a unicorn, a diplodocus to a Pekingese, a fruit fly to a dromedary, or a cat, if you like. Write two poems with the animal as the subject. Construct the poems to have two different themes, or write one poem with a clear theme and one humorous poem. Keep your intended audience in mind.

(Answers are on page 78.)

# HAVEN'T I HEARD THAT BEFORE?—ALLUSIONS AND REFERENCES

Everybody brings prior knowledge, experience, and understanding with them to their reading of poetry. But sometimes in reading poetry and other literature, we encounter mentions of things with which we are not familiar. When this happens, it is important to find out what the poet's reference is.

Some references are so well known to us, we take them for granted. But if we were trying to figure out the plot of "The Cremation of Sam McGuee" and we had never heard of the *Land of the Midnight Sun* (line 1), *the Arctic* (line 3), *the Northern Lights* (line 5), or *Tennessee* (line 9), we would have had a difficult time.

In the past, when the readership of any particular poet's work was local and education was more standardized, poets writing in English could count on readers knowing the Bible, classical allusions, geography, and their shared history. Today— when the available information is so vast and we may use the Internet to read poems from virtually any culture in any age—it is unlikely that we know all these fields so well that we will recognize every reference we come across. So it is important to learn techniques for uncovering their meaning. Poets count on readers' willingness to go beyond what they happen to already know.

First, let's clarify our terminology. In this book we will use the word **allusion** to refer to all kinds of references, both explicit and indirect references—the ones for which your first task is to figure out that there is a reference, even before you go about figuring out what is being referenced and why.

Poets use allusions for a variety of purposes. Comparing a character in a poem to a real person or another character quickly brings his or her attributes and situation to mind. So, a character compared to Samson (from the Hebrew Scriptures/ Old Testament) or Hercules (from Greek mythology) will be strong. A character compared to Mata Hari (a Dutch woman who lived from 1876 to 1917, apparently engaging in espionage for the Germans) is likely a spy.

Poets also create allusions in the following ways: by retelling historical or mythical stories, by using historical or mythological figures as characters in their poems, by setting their characters in situations that are similar to historical or mythical situations, and by using historical or mythical settings. The poem "Ulysses and the Siren" (page 44) is an example of a poem that uses mythical characters and story.

How do you identify an allusion? Let's look at some of the clues that may indicate an allusion.

- Quotation marks can indicate use of material from an earlier source.
- A capitalized word or phrase may be the name of a significant person or place.
- An italicized word or phrase may be from a foreign language.
- *O* or *Oh* before a name indicates someone or something being called or called upon, likely a deity or someone beloved.

Some allusions are more subtle, like the reuse of a few unmarked words from another literary work or historically important document or speech. If you come across words in an English-language poem that look like they might be from another language, it may signal an allusion.

Remember that in poetry every word counts. This especially includes allusions. Allusions can bring with them an entire background, story, culture, and setting. It's better to look up too much than too little. Do keep in mind that some material that looks like allusion may actually be from the poet's imagination.

Don't think that just because someone is a poet, he or she is unapproachable. If you have a question about a poem written by a living poet and after careful thought and searching can't come up with a satisfactory answer, write and ask your question. It is standard, and always correct, to contact a poet in care of his or her publisher. Format your request as a standard business letter.

## Sources

Sometimes, tracking down an allusion can require pretty canny detective work. Sources that poetry readers and poets find useful from time to time include the Bible and other sacred works, dictionaries of mythology, dictionaries of biography and geography, dictionaries of quotations, and concordances. Check the reference section of your library for text versions. If you can't find what you need, try your librarian. Links to useful sources for allusion research can be found on my *Painless Poetry* web page.

## Steps in your search

First, try a print or online dictionary. It may give you a hint to get you started. It's better to use a dictionary that wasn't especially prepared for children: Children's and student dictionaries may not have the entries you need.

A citation is a short reference to direct you to a particular line or verse in a poem, play, or Scripture. Knowing how to read citations will help you. There are three common source citations. Poetry references or citations are given by line number. If you discover that the moral of "The Retired Cat" is in l. 109–116, you read that as "lines 109 to 116." Scripture passages (both Hebrew Scriptures/Old Testament and New Testament) are listed *chapter number colon verse number.* Semicolons separate distinct references. If you discover that the story of Moses receiving the Ten Commandments is in Exodus 24:12–18; 31:18–34:35, you read that as "chapter 24, verses 12 to 18 and chapter 31, verse 18 to chapter 34, verse 35."

Play citations are listed *act number, scene number, line number*, with the act being a large Roman numeral, the scene being a small Roman numeral, and the line number an Arabic numeral. If you discover that the clause "Full fathom five thy father lies" comes from *The Tempest* I, ii, 400 (a play by English poet William Shakespeare), you read that as "act one, scene two, line 400." If books, software, and Internet references aren't helping with citation questions, try real people: Even if they don't know the answer, they may be able to point you on your way.

When you find a useful source, make a note of it. Bookmark useful websites using *Favorites* on your browser. Note the names and call numbers of library references you find helpful. It's easier to reuse a source than to start all over again looking for one.

## BRAIN TICKLERS
### Set # 13

1. Read the following poems and excerpts. Use a dictionary to check words you don't recognize. (This is the last time I'll remind you to do that.) For the first five poems or excerpts, choose and use appropriate references to check each underlined allusion. Record its meaning.

### First Epigram: Upon being Contented with a Little (1686)
by Anne Killigrew (excerpt)

6   If both the *Indies* unto some should fall,
7   Such Wealth would yet *Enough* but only be,
8   And what they'd term not Want, or Luxury.
9     Among the Suits, O *Jove*, my humbler take;
10   *A little give, I that Enough will make.*

### The Discontent (1686)
by Anne Killigrew (excerpt)

30   For few do run with so Resolv'd a Pace,
31   That for the Golden Apple will not loose [lose] the Race.

## The New Colossus (1883)
### by Emma Lazarus

1   Not like the brazen giant of Greek fame,
2   With conquering limbs astride from land to land;
3   Here at our sea-washed, sunset gates shall stand
4   A *mighty woman with a torch*, whose flame
5   Is the imprisoned lightning, and her name
6   Mother of Exiles. From her beacon-hand
7   Glows world-wide welcome; her mild eyes command
8   The air-bridged harbor, that twin cities frame.
9   "Keep, ancient lands, your storied pomp!" cries she
10   With silent lips. "Give me your tired, your poor,
11   Your huddled masses yearning to breathe free,
12   The wretched refuse of your teeming shore.
13   Send these, the homeless, tempest-tost to me,
14   I lift my lamp beside the golden door!"

## Sonnet: On the Sonnet (1848)
### by John Keats

1   If by dull rhymes our English must be chain'd,
2   And, like *Andromeda*, the Sonnet sweet
3   Fetter'd, in spite of painèd loveliness,
4   Let us find, if we must be constrain'd,
5   Sandals more interwoven and complete
6   To fit the naked foot of Poesy:
7   Let us inspect the *Lyre*, and weigh the stress
8   Of every chord, and see what may be gain'd.
9   By ear industrious, and attention meet;
10   Misers of sound and syllable, no less
11   Than *Midas* of his coinage, let us be
12   Jealous of dead leaves in the *bay wreath crown*;
13   So, if we may not let the *Muse* be free,
14   She will be bound with garlands of her own.

## Dies Irae (1826)
### by Thomas MacCauley (excerpt)

1   On that great, that awful day,
2   This vain world shall pass away.
3   Thus the *sibyl* sang of old,
4   Thus hath *Holy David* told . . .

2. For the next three poems, you need to identify the allusions, research and record their meanings, and explain how the poet used the allusion. The last poem of the three is especially challenging. For this poem, *Samarkand*, first identify and research the allusions, and then explain how they are necessary to the poem's meaning.

### Common Things (1893)
by Paul Laurence Dunbar

1  I like to hear of wealth and gold,
2      And El Doradoes in their glory;
3  I like for silks and satins bold
4      To sweep and rustle through a story.

5  The nightingale is sweet of song;
6      The rare exotic smells divinely;
7  And knightly men who stride along,
8      The role heroic carry finely.

9  But then, upon the other hand,
10      Our minds have got a way of running
11  To things that aren't quite so grand,
12      Which, maybe, we are best in shunning.

13  For some of us still like to see
14      The poor man in his dwelling narrow,
15  The hollyhock, the bumblebee,
16      The meadow lark, and chirping sparrow.
17  We like the man who soars and sings
18      With high and lofty inspiration;
19  But he who sings of common things
20      Shall always share our admiration.

## Prayer of a Soldier in France (1918)
### by Joyce Kilmer

1  My shoulders ache beneath my pack
2  (Lie easier, Cross, upon His back).

3  I march with feet that burn and smart
4  (Tread, Holy Feet, upon my heart).

5  Men shout at me who may not speak
6  (They scourged Thy back and smote Thy cheek).

7  I may not lift a hand to clear
8  My eyes of salty drops that sear.

9  (Then shall my fickle soul forget
10 Thy agony of Bloody Sweat?)

11 My rifle hand is stiff and numb
12 (From Thy pierced palm red rivers come).

13 Lord, Thou didst suffer more for me
14 Than all the hosts of land and sea.

15 So let me render back again
16 This millionth of Thy gift. Amen.

## Samarkand: for Seamus Daly* (1995)
### by Aodhagán O'Broin

1  Seek me not in the wilds of Samarkand;
2  Search not the Gobi's fastness for my trail.
3  I am not in a hot and desert land.
4  No pilgrim I, I seek no holy grail.

5  The depths of Wall Street's canyon know me not.
6  Nor in The City's most corrupted Mile,
7  Nor in Hang Seng, nor in Nikkei where rot
8  Abounds, is my faint footfall found. A while

9  In such dry places is enough for most —
10 While desert's dust on bodies takes its toll,
11 The other sites still duller dangers boast,
12 For here the thing at mortal risk is soul.

13     For me the tranquil life, the calming image:
14     The Buddha on a modem, here in Kimmage.

---

* If you need help with this poem, hints appear above the answers on page 83.

3. Write a poem in which allusion plays a central role. Idea: You could begin with a person or place from history (Annie Oakley, Warsaw, Gandhi, the Amazon River, Queen Hatshepsut, the moon on July 20, 1969) or from literature (the planet Naboo, Sherlock Holmes, Atlantis, Juliet Capulet, Hogwarts, Cassandra). Think about your audience and whether they are likely to know what you mean as you make choices about how obvious or subtle to be.

(Answers are on page 80.)

# BRAIN TICKLERS—THE ANSWERS

## Set # 5, page 26

1. **Possible response:** The speaker—a man called Cap—and Sam McGee are the two main characters. The setting is the Arctic, where the men are on an expedition. The plot is basically this: Sam, a Tennessee native suffering greatly from the Arctic cold, asks Cap to promise to cremate Sam if Sam dies on the trip. Cap promises but then has regrets when he cannot locate a place in which to fulfill the promise. Finally, Cap finds an abandoned wreck of a boat, lights a fire in it, and shoves Sam in. Unable to watch, he walks away. Returning to make sure the promise is fulfilled, he finds Sam alive and happy, warm for the first time since he left Tennessee. From the start, the mood is not typical for the story of a death. The italicized passage that begins the poem has a kind of bouncy rhythm that doesn't sound grim and serious. Also, Cap calls the occurrence "queer" rather than dire or terrifying. I enjoyed the surprise ending of this entertaining poem.

2. Like other stories, this one has a beginning, middle, end, a conflict (how to get rid of the corpse), characters, and setting. The main difference between this poem and a prose story is that the rhythm signals a humorous tone right from the beginning. You know immediately it's not a horror story, even though the word *horror* is used (line 29). The misspelling forced mispronunciation of the word *crematorium* to rhyme with *frozen chum* are other humorous poetic devices.

## Set # 6, page 30

**Possible responses:**
1. a. It is third-person omniscient.
   b. It's in first-person.
   c. It is third-person omniscient.
   d. It's in first person.

2. **The Death of the Hired Man**
   - It has a third-person point of view.
   - We learn about the character of Mary and Warren through their words, their dialogue with each other, their choices, and their actions. We learn about the characters of Silas (the Hired Man), young Harold Wilson, and Silas' brother through Mary's and Warren's reports of their actions and words, and through Mary's and Warren's opinions about each of the three.
   - The poem is concerned with differences between various characters' attitudes toward Silas and, beyond that, toward the poor. It is about Mary's concept of home— " 'something you somehow haven't to deserve' " (line 125)—becoming a reality for Silas: He comes back to her to die because he understands that she will welcome him. The poem affirms that the ultimate question about someone is not " 'What good is he?' " (line 15).
   - The poem has narration and dialogue, like a prose tale, but it also has rhythm. The text is divided into lines, most of which have ten syllables, even when both Mary and Warren speak in one line. It has many very simple words, as if that were the poet's conscious choice. Sometimes several words close together begin with the same letter and there are some rhyming words within lines: " 'he hurt my heart the way he lay' " (line 154).

**Ozymandias**
**Possible responses:**
- The four characters are the speaker, the traveler, the sculptor, and Ozymandias.
- The point of view shifts, in effect, because the speaker only speaks the first line himself; then he quotes the words of the traveler, who in turn quotes the words on the statue, which we take to be those of Ozymandias.

- Once the all-powerful ruler of a huge empire, Ozymandias had himself commemorated in a great statue. The sculptor had the insight and skill to convey Ozymandias's pride and arrogance. At some point, Ozymandias's kingdom and those of his rivals fell and were lost. In the "now" of the poem, his broken statue is the only remaining trace of the kingdom in the desert sand. One traveler was so impressed by the sight that he reported it to the speaker.

3. **Possible response:**

### You and I

You are short, and I am tall.
I play hockey, you play ball.
I paint with oils, while you play tuba.
You like to snorkle; I like scuba.
You like FM, I like AM.
You like quiet, I like mayhem.
I smile broadly, you just grin.
Say, how'd you get to be my twin?

[original]

## Set # 7, page 39

1. **Possible responses:**
   **Fog**
   - The setting is a harbor by a city to which fog comes and from which fog goes.
   - In this case, the setting, with its change in weather, is the subject of the poem.

**Night**

- The setting is night over the dunes and moor by the sea. The moon is going down, but the stars still shine. It is cool.
- She contrasts the cares and worries of "the world of day" (line 17) with the undemanding, friendly solitude of night.

***Autumn's Orchestra***

- Both excerpts are set in autumn in a forest. But the sound of the poetry is different in the two: The first has longer lines and is more somber, whereas the second is livelier and more like a dance. The sound fits the setting in each case.

2. **Possible response:**

### Out of the Depths, October 13, 2010

1 One by one through the narrow darkness,
2 Thirty-three who know too much of cramped dark
3 Rise to the wide, bright light
4 Of the world's embrace.

5 Drawing on the wisdom of all who go deep—
6 whether in space or dirt or water—
7 Deep in Earth, they kept each other whole,
8 Until a hoist could help them home.

[original]

## Set # 8, page 47

**Possible responses:**

1. **Ulysses and the Siren** by Samuel Daniel
   - The Siren wants Ulysses to stay with her and enjoy a peaceful, happy life.
   - Ulysses tells her that he is seeking fame and honor, and to acquire them he must continue with his "toils." The Siren argues that honor is not real and that seeking it interrupts the things of true value in life: peace and rest.
   - Ulysses has a strong ethic and the Siren's cheap arguments won't persuade him.

### A Poison Tree by William Blake

- The speaker was angered by a friend, confronted the friend, and cleared the matter up. But when a foe angered the speaker, he nursed the grudge until it grew completely out of proportion. The foe, too, continued the conflict, and the result of their refusal to make peace was the foe's death.
- The two lines devoted to the friend show that the difference between friend and foe was *not* that the friend never angered the speaker. The difference lay in the speaker's response to the conflict in each case: He worked to make peace after the incident and (apparently) forgave his friend, whereas he worked to increase enmity with his foe.
- The foe uses the cover of night to steal the apple.

### La Belle Dame Sans Merci by John Keats

- The characters are the speaker, the "wretched wight" (or knight-at-arms), the beautiful faery, and the pale figures in the dream.
- The knight was riding in the meadows when he met a faery. He took her up on his horse with him and was so entranced that she totally occupied his thoughts. It seems to have been the height of summer for he was able to use blossoms to make her a crown, bracelets, and a belt. He had the impression that she was in love with him. She brought him food, and he is positive that she told him that she loved him. Then she took him to her home, he kissed her, and they both fell asleep. He had a disturbing dream of kings, princes, and warriors, all pale as death, who told him that he had been enchanted by the faery, whom they called the beautiful lady without mercy. When he awoke from this nightmare, he was alone on the hillside where the speaker discovered him. And he stays there, despite the coming on of winter (he has been there for a long, long time), for love of the faery, in the hopes of finding her again, which will not happen.
- Setting along with the man's pale coloring provides the first clue to the speaker that something is wrong with the man he has met—it's no place to be out wandering in the raw weather of winter. The stark setting in which they stand speaking presents a radical contrast to the

summer flowers mentioned to describe the knight's brow and face (lines 9–12), and to the setting in which he met the faery, which was so full of so many flowers he could make her a belt, bracelets, and a crown.

2. **Possible response:**

### Forced Back to Earth

I'd struggled hard to reach this peak,
I'd planned each step I took.
I'd packed my backpack carefully,
Each cranny and each nook.

My route was charted on a map,
allowing for the clime.
I thought for sure that I would reach
the pinnacle this time.

How carefully I chose the pals
to make ascent with me!
How carefully I chose the day!
But I could not foresee

the reverberating landslide that
would end my hopes of fame.
What mind can dream and body do
are not always the same.

[original]

## Set # 9, page 49

1 **Possible responses:**
**Bird Language** by Christopher Pearse Cranch
- The poem expresses curiosity, fascination with nature, and joy in living.

**On the Death of My Child** by Joseph von Eichendorff, translated by Aodhagán O'Broin
- The characters are a little child who has died and the child's parents: The speaker is one or both parents (it says we).
- The mood changes at line 13 due to the parents' coming to terms with the reality of their child's death. They had been thinking of themselves as their child's safest haven and considered their child lost because he or she could not return to them. They suddenly are able to accept that their child has entered a better place than their home—heaven (the child finding the bed means finding eternal rest). The parents' longing turns to solace—they are consoled by the idea that their child is with God.

2. **Possible response:**

## The Forest

I was searching alone in the forest.
I was fearful, but had to go on.
For I'd heard a sharp cry from the forest,
And I had to know what had gone wrong.

My small brother had run in before me.
He had somehow got out of my sight.
I was lingering by the edge calling,
when that single shrill cry broke the night.

I had neither flashlight nor candle,
but I still hurried in towards Will's call.
I was thwarted and tripped by the tree roots,
which frequently caused me to fall.

The blackness was suddenly broken,
by a glint and a glimmer of gleams,
as the branches above burst asunder
and let in the moon's piercing beams.

"I freed her, I freed her," cried Willy,
as a falcon now fled and was gone.
He had found the poor bird ensnarled in a snare,
and was sure she'd have died before dawn.

For a hunter had entered the forest,
And Willy had gone in pursuit,
had cried for the bird all entangled,
and worked hard to undo her foot.

Now Willy and I stumbled homeward,
and in spite of the fast-fading light,
I walked with the memory of moonlight aglow
As the falcon burst free through the night.

[original]

## Set # 10, page 53

1. **Possible responses:**
   **Psalm 100**
   a. The poet seems to be the speaker. Nothing indicates another persona.

b. The tone is awe and worship blended with a certain urgency. The speaker repeatedly reminds listeners to praise the Lord and tells them in what manner ("with gladness," "with thanksgiving"), how ("with singing," "with praise," by blessing "his name"), and why ("the Lord is God," "we are his people," "the Lord is good," merciful, and truthful forever) they should do so.

## The Curse

a. The circumstances of the poem and the signature at the end clearly indicate that Synge is the speaker. He is getting playful revenge on someone who found fault with his work. This revenge is limited to the feeling of satisfaction in writing the tongue-in-cheek poem. Obviously, Synge does not believe that God would honor a request for revenge in order to obtain Synge's services.

b. At the beginning, the tone appears malicious, but the last two lines and the special uses of language make it humorous. Someone who was really angry probably wouldn't take the trouble to match the beginning letters of words and make rhymes about it. You might call it humorous frustration.

## Charge of the Light Brigade

a. The speaker does not seem to be a character. The poem seems to be an honest appraisal of an historic event, so I think it's Tennyson's own voice.

b. The tone is admiration. Repeated praise of the troops and avoidance of treating the elements that might lead one to question the wisdom of the incident make me think so.

2. a. Ozymandias is proud and condescending.

   b. The traveler's tone, like the poet's, is contemptuous. By juxtaposing Ozymandias's words, the words "colossal wreck," and the description of how and where the statue now stands, the traveler completely undercuts Ozymandias's claim to glory, without saying anything directly about it. He exposes Ozymandias's vanity, his tyrannical treatment of others, and his self-importance. The poet uses the traveler to lay out the information that will lead us to understand what he wishes us to know.

c. The speaker's words hint to us that of all the things the traveler saw, the statue of Ozymandias was what most impressed him. The sense of having chosen this, of all the things he saw, to tell the speaker would be lost with the poem rewritten as indicated.

## Set # 11, page 57

**Possible response:**

### The Easy Life

I loved to be a follower,
'Twas such an easy life.
I'd always obey orders
And save myself from strife.

I was in the Crimea,
By cannons all surrounded,
And when my leader gave the word,
Why, down that hill I bounded.

'Twere cannons to the left of me,
'Twere cannons to the right,
'Twere cannons ranged in front of me,
Thundering in the night.

I thought the order foolish—
To ride into such a plight
To go on horseback down to face
Guns front, and left, and right.

But, hey, I'm just a private:
'ts not mine to make reply;
'ts not mine to know the wherefore;
'ts just mine to do and die.

Well, therein ends my story,
'Cause sabers don't beat guns.
But I'm glad you have this jolly poem
To remind you of what I've done.

[original]

## Set # 12, page 61

**Possible responses:**
1. **"Hope" is the thing with feathers—**
   - Hope is the subject.
   - The theme is that hope is nearly impossible to drive away, and no matter how difficult the circumstances, demands nothing of the one who entertains it.

*Sonnets from the Portuguese* **XIV**
   - The subject is the love between the poet and her husband.
   - The subject of this poem is the same as the subject of "To My Dear and Loving Husband." Bradstreet focuses on how greatly she loves and on perseverance in love, but Browning attends more to what is loved and why.

- Browning's theme is that only love that dotes on what is unchanging can itself be unchanging and last into eternity.

2. **Possible response:** Two poems about cats: one on the self-sufficiency of cats and one humorous.

### Burrs

Sheba,
self-contained, solitary she-cat—
self-admiring, self-absorbed, self-assured—
stuck
in a burdock bush.
Suddenly she seeks
solicitude, solace, succor.
Burrs removed.
Sheba's herself:
sleek, shining, self-admiring,
she strolls
away.

[original]

### Maître d'

My dinner party's ready.
The only problem's Freddy—
I've been so busy all the day,
I haven't had much time to play.
I've got to feed him quickly;
he's acting queer and sickly.
I pour some cat chow in his bowl,
I go to check the welcome mat,
and there's a gift left by my cat—
a mole.

The party's underway now.
I'm serving the soufflé now,
and Freddy's mewing to come in.
"He just wants scratching on his chin,"
I tell my guests and serve
the compote and preserves.
"My cat is acting so absurd!"
I let him in and watch him strut
into the dining room, and what's
he carrying but a bird!

My mind is in a whirl.
I let Fred out again.
This time he's back in ten.
This time he has a squirrel.

The moral of this story
is very simply that
you should check your party's menu
with your cat.

[original]

## Set # 13, page 66

1. **First Epigram: Upon being Contented with a Little**
*Indies*—the East and West Indies. The East Indies in Asia
are the source of aromatic spices and wealth that Columbus
was seeking when he discovered the Caribbean Islands,
referred to as the West Indies. Together, they symbolize the
wealth and beauty of both hemispheres.
*Jove*—Roman name for Zeus, head of the pantheon of
gods and goddesses; the ruler of the universe, in that
tradition.

**The Discontent**
*Race that could be lost on account of Golden Apples*—If you
found this, congratulations! It refers to the Greek
mythological story of Atalanta, a fine athlete who agreed to
marry the man who could outrun her. Hippomenes bested
her by a trick: He dropped three golden apples (given him by
Venus in answer to a prayer), one at a time, during the race,
and Atalanta paused to pick them up, permitting Hippomenes
to win the contest.

**The New Colossus**
*Colossus*—The Colossus of Rhodes, a statue of the Greek
God Apollo that stood 120 feet high, was one of the Seven
Wonders of the Ancient World. Built in 280 B.C.E., it was set at
the entrance to the harbor at ancient Rhodes, a commercial
center until its destruction by earthquake in 155 C.E.
*Mighty woman with a torch*—the "New Colossus," the
Statue of Liberty (full name: "Liberty Enlightening the
World"), given to the United States by the people of France
on July 4, 1884, and erected in New York Harbor. The poem
*The New Colossus* was inscribed on a tablet on the statue's
pedestal in 1903.

**Sonnet: On the Sonnet**
*Andromeda*—in Greek mythology, the lovely daughter of
King Cepheus and Queen Cassiopeia. The queen had
offended Poseidon, god of the seas. Andromeda, though
completely innocent, was chained to a rock as an offering
for a sea monster sent by Poseidon in retribution. The
Greek hero Perseus, a son of Zeus, rescued Andromeda by
turning the monster to stone.

*Lyre*—the first instrument, invented by the god Hermes using a tortoise shell and traded to Apollo in exchange for Apollo's cattle. **Lyric poetry**, of which this sonnet is an example (see more on page 265), originally referred to words sung to the accompaniment of a lyre.

*Midas*—the greedy king of Phrygia in Greek mythology who was granted a wish by Dionysus in exchange for a favor, wished that everything he touched might turn to gold. But Midas had not reckoned on the consequences—for example, when his food turned to gold, becoming inedible, and when, according to some versions, he accidentally turned his daughter into a golden statue when she embraced him.

*Bay wreath crown*—another tough one! The crown was made of laurel (or bay) leaves and awarded to prizewinning athletes, heroes, and poets in ancient times. This custom is the origin of the modern term *poet laureate* for the official poet of a country or state.

*Muse*—one of the nine daughters of Zeus and Mnemosyne (Memory). The muses are goddesses of the arts and sciences:

| | |
|---|---|
| Calliope | Epic poetry |
| Clio | History |
| Erato | Love poetry |
| Euterpe | Lyric poetry |
| Melpomene | Tragedy |
| Polyhymnia | Sacred poetry |
| Terpsichore | Choral dance |
| Thalia | Comedy |
| Urania | Astronomy |

### Dies Irae

*Dies Irae*—Latin phrase meaning the "day of wrath," another name for the "Day of Judgment" at the end of the world in the Christian tradition.

*sibyl*—a Greek or Roman prophetess or oracle.

*Holy David*—the second king of Judah and Israel in about the tenth century B.C.E.; father of King Solomon the Wise and ancestor of Jesus. He is considered to be the author of the Psalms recorded in the Hebrew Scriptures/Old Testament.

2. **Common Things**

*El Dorado*—The Spanish words literally mean "the gilded" [land]; it is a mythical city of gold sought by sixteenth-century explorers in what is now Latin America. Dunbar has used it as if it were an English word and added the plural suffix–*es*. It is part of a contrast Dunbar draws, presenting (in the first two stanzas) the fine subjects that poetry might treat but then (in the third and fourth stanzas, in which there are no allusions) showing the value of treating less extraordinary subjects, and finally (in the fifth stanza) reasserting the worth of both types of poetry.

**Prayer of a Soldier in France**

This poem rests on a comparison of the sufferings of a soldier in World War I with the sufferings of Jesus Christ as he carried his cross to Calvary and was crucified. The story of the crucifixion can be found in the Gospels of the New Testament (Matthew 27–28; Mark 1.5–16; Luke 23–24; John 19–20). By identifying his own sufferings with those of Christ, the speaker not only puts his own ordeals in perspective but also presents them to Jesus as a gift in response to the great gift of salvation that Christians believe Jesus merited by his death.

# HINTS

| Allusion | What is it? | What source should I try? |
|----------|-------------|---------------------------|
| Samarkand | place | geographical dictionary |
| pilgrim | kind of person | regular dictionary; note lowercase |
| holy grail | object | regular dictionary |
| Wall Street | place | regular dictionary |
| The City/Mile | place | Look up *city* in a regular dictionary; find the specification "cap" to indicate the capitalized form of the word. *Mile* is short for *Square Mile* and refers to a particular section of a particular city. Once you know the city, look for "Square + Mile + (city name)" in an Internet search. |
| Hang Seng | thing | Internet search |
| Nikkei | thing | mentioned on business reports; if not familiar, try an Internet search |
| Buddha | person | biographical dictionary |
| Kimmage | small place | Google Maps search |

## "Samarkand" for Seamus Daly

*Samarkand*—Now a city in Uzbek, Samarkand was one of the earliest cities in the USSR, an important point on the trade route to the East (the "Silk Route"), and a center of Arab culture. The palace and tomb of the Islamic ruler Tamerlane (Timur the Lame) commemorate it as the capital of his empire (1370).

*Gobi*—a central Asian desert; the second largest desert in the world.

*pilgrim*—a person who journeys to a shrine or other holy place or embarks on a quest with a sacred end.

*holy grail* (usually capitalized)—the cup or chalice used by Jesus at the Last Supper; the legendary object of quests in medieval tales of King Arthur and the Knights of the Round

Table. Absolute personal purity and integrity were prerequisites for being allowed to approach it. As a lower case word, it might mean the object of a devoted quest.

*Wall Street*—site of the financial district and the New York Stock Exchange in New York City.

*The City's . . . Mile*—"The City" is the older part of London. The "Square Mile" refers to London's financial district.

*Hang Seng*—the Hong Kong Stock Index.

*Nikkei*—the Japanese Stock Index.

*Buddha*—name (meaning enlightened one) for Prince Siddhartha Gautama (*c.* 563–483 B.C.E.) born in a town in what is now Nepal, who, weary of the luxuries of palace life, became a wandering ascetic. He finally gave up asceticism and taught his doctrine (Buddhism) to others throughout the Ganges Valley.

*Kimmage*—a small parish in South Dublin, outside the city proper.

In the first four lines, the speaker evokes (and distances himself from) exotic adventure and quest by reference to two places and two quests, all four of which inspire the imagination with thoughts of great heroic deeds and romantic adventures. Explaining that he is neither a conqueror nor a religious seeker, the speaker does not choose to inhabit a remote and exotic country. (Note that the two places mentioned are in the East, whereas the words *pilgrim* and *Grail* are associated with the West.) In lines 5–8, the speaker disassociates himself from the greed and corruption of the modern world, both in the East and in the West, by saying that he cannot be found in financial districts or stock markets.

In the next four lines, the speaker summarizes: Most people abandon these places of high adventure and financial wizardry—whether past or present, near or far—after "a while." The harsh landscape is hard on the body, but the effects of greed and corruption are worse because they threaten the soul.

The speaker finally reveals his choice of life: a tranquility that brings together past and present, East and West, but with peace and integrity—through his own appreciation and use of art and technology (evidenced by a statue of Buddha sitting on an external modem for a computer) in a small place of no great note.

3. **Possible response:**

### The Awful Day

I tumbled down a hill like Jill,
Ran through the town like Willie.
I lost my shoe-a-doodle-doo,
And, boy, did I feel silly!

I sang for supper, just like Tommy,
But I got not any.
And when I got home, the cupboard was bare,
And for hot cross buns I had no penny.

The knave of hearts had got my tarts
On this fine summer's day.
A spider came to gloat at me,
All filled with curds and whey.

The rat had eaten all the malt,
The dish had run off with the spoon.
I went to bed and bumped my head.
I hope this day ends soon!

[original]

# CHAPTER THREE

# Getting Your Wordsworth!

Poetry does not have to rhyme. It does not have to have the same number of syllables in every line. It does not have to look a certain way. But it has to have words! There is no poetry without them.

It is impossible to talk about poetry without talking about words, and we are attentive to words in special ways when we read and write poems. When you are writing a poem, words can seem like puzzle pieces that you are trying to fit together, shifting and substituting them until you achieve the sound and the sense that satisfies you. When you are reading a poem, words can seem like a set of clues in a mystery until you can make sense of them all together and reach a coherent understanding.

What's in a poem? Words. What's in a word? We're about to explore the answer to that question. After an overview, we'll review kinds of words and parts of speech. Then we'll go on to various ways of analyzing word use, spending some time on rhetorical figures, some of which will very likely be familiar to you already. We'll look at how words provide sensory detail and conclude with a consideration of levels of meaning. All these aspects of word use are elements of a poet's **style**.

We'll begin with a poem that captures a scene that moved the poet when he first saw it and came to have an even deeper meaning with time.

### I Wandered Lonely as a Cloud (1804)
by William Wordsworth

1  I wandered lonely as a cloud
2  That floats on high o'er vales and hills,
3  When all at once I saw a crowd,
4  A host, of golden daffodils;
5  Beside the lake, beneath the trees,
6  Fluttering and dancing in the breeze.

7   Continuous as the stars that shine
8   And twinkle on the milky way,
9   They stretched in never-ending line
10  Along the margin of a bay:
11  Ten thousand saw I at a glance,
12  Tossing their heads in sprightly dance.

13  The waves beside them danced; but they
14  Out-did the sparkling waves in glee;
15  A poet could not but be gay,
16  In such a jocund company;
17  I gazed—and gazed—but little thought
18  What wealth the show to me had brought:

19  For oft, when on my couch I lie
20  In vacant or in pensive mood,
21  They flash upon that inward eye
22  Which is the bliss of solitude;
23  And then my heart with pleasure fills,
24  And dances with the daffodils.

# BRAIN TICKLERS
## Set # 14

1. Which words that Wordsworth used stand out for you or evoke an emotional response?

2. What do you notice about his word choice?

3. Can you find the simile and personification, two of the rhetorical figures Wordsworth uses in the poem?

4. Which senses does Wordsworth appeal to using sensory language?

5. Consider the possibility that this is a poem about poetry—the speaker mentions that he is a poet. In what way(s) could the experience of reading a poem be similar to the experience of seeing a lovely field of daffodils?

(Answers are on page 158.)

# WHAT'S IN A WORD?

## A short history of words

When poetry began, there was no writing. Words didn't have letters; they were simply sounds. Language was oral and aural, so poetry was oral and aural. So all the written/visual aspects of poetry are later developments. In the beginning, the *sound* of poetry as spoken by a poet or storyteller *was* poetry.

Poets couldn't jot their words down for next time. If they wanted to keep their poems, they had to memorize them. So they developed techniques like meter (the rhythm of a poem), rhyme, and other patterns, sound effects, and uses of repetition to make poetry memorable.

Many of us experienced this as children with poems we learned by repeating them out loud. We learned counting out rhymes like "Eenie, meenie, minie, mo; catch a tiger by the toe" and skipping rhymes like "Bluebells, cockleshells, evie, ivy, over," but probably never saw them written down. We remember such poems, not because of the meaning but because the meter and rhyme and other sound effects make them easy for our minds to grasp.

When poetry was first written down, writing was simply a way of recording the sounds so that they could be reproduced. But then poets saw that they could use the appearance of single words and groups of words to create additional visual effects for their readers, and poetry actually changed as a result.

When someone speaks words to us, our brains automatically separate the flow of sounds into words, figure out the grammar and syntax, and create meaning, which may be primarily mental but may also evoke an emotional response. For most people, responding to poetry in all these ways becomes almost automatic. The important thing to realize is that writing didn't just give us a means to record sounds; it changed the way we think.

- First, we have added a whole series of mental processes: We must make the connection between the symbols on the page (the written words) and the pronunciation of the words.
- Second, we do not have to memorize because we can go back to our written record. This permits us to pay attention to trivial things as well as critically important ones.
- Third, our literary connections in the world have grown broader and deeper. With a written record, we can know how a word was used, what events happened, and what people thought about and felt hundreds of years before we were born, or in contemporary times in the most distant countries, which we may never visit.

Writing changed the world.

## Words in poetry

In the Shakespeare play *Romeo and Juliet* (II, ii, 43–47), written about 1594 to 1595, Juliet asks the question, "What's in a name?" And she answers herself:

43  . . . That which we call a rose
44  By any other name would smell as sweet.
45  So Romeo would, were he not Romeo called,
46  Retain that dear perfection which he owes*
47  Without that title.

Juliet says that the name does not shape the thing named. She suggests that even while using words to name things we can look beyond words—beyond language—to recognize the deeper reality of the things themselves.

Let's extend Juliet's insight. When we read and write poetry, we are not dealing directly with the realities of things themselves. When we try as poets to evoke in a reader the ideas and experiences that make up the poem, all we have are words to work with. How do we make the leap from words to experience?

_____

* owns

Language is full of possibility. Words, which we slide our eyes over so quickly and vaguely in reading prose, are packed with meaning, and the poet may take advantage of every aspect of a word. That is why no two words are interchangeable in poetry. Imagine if Wordsworth had told us the daffodils were *yellowish* instead of *golden*, or that there were a *bunch* rather than a *host*. To change a word is to change the poem and change our experience, for better or for worse. So we need to understand how words work in our understanding to know how poems work and to apply this knowledge to reading and writing poems.

When a poet uses a word in a poem, he or she *knows* certain things about the word and *feels* certain things about the word. The poet also knows some things that the reader will know about the word, but there are things about the reader's experience that the poet cannot know.

Let us imagine a poet writing a poem in English. What can be known about the reader of an English poem? He or she may live in Nigeria, Australia, Ireland, the United States, Canada, Jamaica, or the United Kingdom—all countries in which English is the official language. Our reader may be an English-speaking person living in any country in the world or a person who has learned English as a second (or third or fourth) language. The poet cannot know whether the reader has ever seen a particular word, though if the reader is a native speaker of English who is old enough to read, there are a great many words that the poet can guess the reader will know. The poet knows for sure only that, when the reader reads the poem, the reader will share the words as the poet has written them. Readers may pronounce the word differently than the poet pronounces it and will almost certainly have at least *some* different associations with it and feelings about it. But the poet also knows that there are tools that readers hold in common, most notably the dictionary. Although dictionaries differ somewhat, the poet can count on the readers knowing certain things about the word's pronunciation, history, and meaning, *if* they use the dictionary.

If we consider poetry as communication—as a message or expression of some sort from the poet to the reader—then it makes sense to invest the effort to study and try to understand the special tools and techniques of poetry and their uses. This will enhance our experience not only as readers of poetry but also as poets. One way to increase our understanding is to develop a love of words.

## The attraction of words

What's your favorite word? Is it a name, like *Ramón*? A short word, like *nit*? A funny word, like *gargantuan*? A long word, like *Australopithecus*? A word with a special meaning, like *love*? A word you made up yourself, like *skiddelysnippet*? A word with an interesting sound, like *Tanganyika*? A word with an interesting visual pattern of letters, like *tintinabulation*?

People's favorite words aren't usually words like *to* or *when*. They're words with specific meanings, words that name important ideas or beautiful sights, words with wonderful sounds, words that trigger deep feelings, words that capture life's vividness.

Let's stop and think about words. Words are chock full of information that we take in as we read.

## 1. Something for the eyes and ears

### Pronunciation and spelling

Most words have a unique sound and a unique look. A few overlap in sound or spelling with at least one other word. This chart shows the terminology we will use to discuss such instances.

| Category | Name | Examples |
|----------|------|----------|
| alike in sound and alike in spelling | homonym | bear (noun, an animal); bear (verb, to carry) |
| alike in sound, different in spelling | homophone | pear, pair, pare |
| different in sound, alike in spelling | homograph | record (noun, RE-cord); record (verb, re-CORD) |

You need to use your eyes and ears in tandem to pick up on the use of homonyms, homophones, and homographs in poems. Looking at the poem while hearing the sound of the word is a great way to become aware of the connections between the shape and pronunciation of the words, and link those elements to meaning. Remember that "out loud" is the best way to experience poetry—both as a reader and as a writer, but you should look for visual patterns as well.

You can test your skills with homonyms and homophones using these excerpts from a humorous poem by a teenage poet. How many homonyms and homophones can you find?

### Mathematics (1869?)
by Arthur Clement Hilton (excerpts)

1  I've really done enough of sums,
2      I've done so very many,
3  That now instead of doing sum
4      I'd rather not do any.

5  I've toiled until my fingers are
6      With writing out of joint;
7  And even now of Decimals
8      I cannot see the point.

9  Subtraction to my weary mind
10     Brings nothing but distraction,
11 And vulgar and improper I
12     Consider every fraction.
              . . . .
17 Discount is counted troublesome
18     By my unlearned pate;
19 For cubic root I entertain
20     A strongly rooted hate.
              . . . .
33 "Apply yourself," my master said,
34     When I my woes confided,
35 "And, when you multiply, bestow
36     Attention undivided."

Hilton creates humor by using words in ways that reference more than one of their meanings. This type of wordplay is a form of pun. See pages 118–119 for more.

*Sum* in line 3 really should be spelled *some*: it is purposely misspelled to add to the humor. It is also a tipoff about the type of humor based on puns that Hilton uses throughout the rest of the poem. All the rest of the wordplay is based on homonyms: *point* (line 8), *improper* (line 11), *counted* (line 17), *rooted* (line 20), and *undivided* (line 36). In each case, Hilton wants the reader to understand two meanings—one ordinary and one mathematical. *Point* means both "importance" and "decimal point." *Improper* means both "not proper" and "a fraction in which the numerator is greater than or equal to the denominator." *Counted* means both "considered" and "reckoned by listing numerals in ascending order." *Rooted* means "engrained" and "a number that is multiplied by itself a given number of times to obtain a product." And *undivided* means both "entire" and "not having had the process of division applied to it."

## BRAIN TICKLERS
### Set # 15

Glance at this brief poem without reading it.

1 Fuzzy Wuzzy was a bear.
2 Fuzzy Wuzzy had no hair.
3 Fuzzy Wuzzy wasn't fuzzy, was he?
4 No, he was a bare bear.

1. What gets the attention of your eyes?
2. Now read it aloud. What gets the attention of your ears?

(Answers are on page 158.)

# 2. Something for the mind

## Meaning and imagination

Besides yielding information to our eyes and ears, words open up avenues into our mind and our mind's eye, as our imagination is sometimes called. Read the following two lists of words. Note your thoughts.

LIST 1:
that, instead, which, but, sometimes, when, him, rather, over

LIST 2:
Moon, peacock, Tibet, music, firelight, temple, danced, joy

The first list contains more words than the second, but alone they do not tell us much, and it is hard to think about them. Reading the second list may have already led you to form an image in your mind. These words can each evoke an image and also be put together to create a scene.

When you read and write poetry, let the words work on your mind. Practice using your ability to make moving pictures in your head to call up, not only visual imagery, but sounds, textures, and even smells and tastes, if it makes sense in the context.

## Prior use

Some words are famous in their own right. If you hear a phrase like "Oh, say can you see," it probably sets off a whole array of thoughts including the music and all the words you know of our country's national anthem. None of the individual words in that phrase is very picturesque, and the phrase taken out of context doesn't have a lot of meaning. But most citizens of the United States immediately recognize this important phrase.

Even single words can have a powerful effect because of prior use. Here's an example. What do you think about when you hear the word *nevermore*? For anyone who's read it, the word *nevermore* is forevermore connected with Poe's poem "The Raven." Any professional poet writing in English and using this word is likely to have Poe's poem in mind and be hoping that readers recall it. You can use connections like this to your advantage when you write, and you should keep an eye out for them as you read. The *Oxford English Dictionary* includes famous and important uses of particular words and is an excellent source for seeking information about word history.

# BRAIN TICKLERS
### Set # 16

1. In the following two poems, things that are very different become alike. Read them and tell what differences there are in how your eyes, ears, and mind apprehend the two of them.

**Love Equals Swift and Slow** (1849)
by Henry David Thoreau

1 Love equals swift and slow,
2    And high and low,
3 Racer and lame,
4    The hunter and his game.

**Death of the Day** (1858)
by Walter Savage Landor

1 My pictures blacken in their frames
2    As night comes on,
3 And youthful maids and wrinkled dames
4    Are now all one.

5 Death of the day! a sterner Death
6    Did worse before;
7 The fairest form, the sweetest breath,
8    Away he bore.

2. Read each scenario. Recalling that, as a poet, you are trying to help readers make a transition from words on the page to a meaningful experience, make a list of seven words you might use in creating a poem in each situation. Write a poem for the scenario that you find most appealing.
   a. You are trying to convince your parents to buy a pet skunk.
   b. You want to thank a relative for giving you a particularly nice gift (you can decide for yourself what the gift is).

c. The president of the United States is coming to a school assembly at which you must read a poem.

d. You are designing a menu for the school cafeteria. Each main dish is going to be the subject of a brief poem.

e. Your English teacher has asked you to write a poem to go with this illustration.

(Answers are on page 159.)

# THE NITTY GRITTY OF WORDS: RHETORIC 101

**Rhetoric** is the art of using words effectively, whether in speech or in writing. You already use many rhetorical devices, and you will recognize many more at once, even though you may not know their names.

Rhetoric helps us to communicate more sucessfully. We all want people to laugh at our jokes and be serious about our deep concerns. We want to share our sadness in a way that will call forth compassion and our joy in a way that will inspire delight. The study of rhetoric helps us to accomplish these ends, by making us aware of the ways that words work.

Rhetoric, because it involves choices, also expresses our individuality. Just as people can learn to recognize our speaking voices by their unique characteristics, so our writing (which also has a "voice") carries our personal and unique mark and will, if we take the time and trouble to develop it, become distinctive and recognizable to our readers.

Our voices have a variety of aspects: the kinds of sentences we use, our diction (word choice), our use of rhetorical figures (like similes and metaphors), and our use of sensory detail and imagery. But one element of our voice is not usually a choice, but a given—our dialect.

## Dialect—How we talk

We don't all pronounce all words in the same way. Even for those of us who speak English as our first language, our pronunciation depends on our cultural background and the region(s) in which we have lived. You've probably heard the word **dialect**. A dialect is a variety of a language distinguished from other varieties of the same language by differences in pronunciation, grammar, and vocabulary. It is usually confined to a particular region, but not always: Black American English is an example of a dialect that is *not* regionalized.

There are three main dialect areas in the United States: Northern, Southern, and Midland. But the differences are so specific, that a dialect specialist can listen to you and tell whether you are from the Northern Middle West; New England; Chicago; the Central Atlantic Seaboard; Gary, Indiana; the Southern Coast; New York City, etc. In linguistic terms, no particular dialect is better than any other dialect.

This poem shows a dialect of English. We know the poem is English by its title, but few people who don't speak the Scottish dialect of English will understand all the vocabulary, especially in the first six lines.

# TO A MOUSE, ON TURNING UP HER NEST WITH THE PLOUGH, NOVEMBER, 1785
### by Robert Burns (excerpt)

1 Wee, sleekit, cow'rin, tim'rous beastie,
2 O, what a panic's in thy breastie!
3 Thou need na start awa sae hasty
4      Wi' bickering brattle!
5 I wad be laith to rin an' chase thee,
6      Wi' murd'ring pattle!

7 I'm truly sorry man's dominion
8 Has broken Nature's social union,
9 An' justifies that ill opinion
10      Which makes thee startle
11 At me, thy poor earth-born companion,
12      An' fellow-mortal!

If we find a poem written in English dialect as different from ours as this poem is, we know to resort to a good dictionary. But the effects of pronunciation on dialect are more complicated. Here's why.

## EXAMPLE 1:
Some people pronounce the following words identically, whereas other people give them three distinct pronunciations, using a different vowel sound for each: *Mary, merry, marry.* (Try saying them aloud.)

## EXAMPLE 2:
Pronunciation of words has changed over time. Look at this excerpt from a poem by an Englishman.

### Going Down Hill on a Bicycle:
### A Boy's Song (c. 1900)
#### by Henry Charles Beeching (excerpt)

1 With lifted feet, hands still,
2 I am poised, and down the hill
3 Dart, with heedful mind;
4 The air goes by in a wind.

5 Swifter and yet more swift,
6 Till the heart with a mighty lift
7 Makes the lungs laugh, the throat cry:—
8 'O bird, see; see, bird, I fly. . . .'

Most speakers of English in the Western Hemisphere say *wind* (meaning "moving air") to rhyme with *thinned*, not to rhyme with *mind*. Yet, the *Oxford English Dictionary* explains that the word was once universally pronounced to rhyme with *mind* (and still is in some dialects).

## EXAMPLE 3:

Some words are also pronounced differently depending on their context—the words that come before and after them and whether they receive stress in the sentence. The two most striking are *a* and *The*. *A* is pronounced [AY] when stressed and [UH] when unstressed. *The* is pronounced [THUH] before words that begin with a consonant sound and [THEE] before words that begin with a vowel sound, although this may vary with the dialect of English that you speak. The pronunciation [THEE] can also be used to emphasize the uniqueness of the single thing being identified.

## EXAMPLE 4:

A syllable is a single vowel sound, whether by itself or with the preceding and/or following consonant sound(s). Sometimes dialects differ in how many syllables they give a word in their pronunciation. For example, some people say [RES-ling] for *wrestling*, giving it two syllables, but some give it three, saying [REH-suhl-ing].

For these reasons, what rhymes for me may not rhyme for you and your rhythm may not be the same as my rhythm.

Use of the phonetic pronunciations in a dictionary can be helpful both for reading and writing poems. But dictionaries have to take the various dialects of English into account. As a result:

1. Dictionaries often offer multiple pronunciations of a word, the first being the most widely accepted.
2. Dictionaries can differ about which pronunciation of a word they list first.

In the end, it will be up to you to make the best choice you can.

## BRAIN TICKLERS
### Set # 17

Use a dictionary to look up each of the following words. (It's probably best to choose one dictionary and use it consistently so that you get to know it well.) After the pronunciation key, indicate how many pronunciations are given. Compare the dictionary's first pronunciation with yours. Write "same" or "different" to indicate if your pronunciation and the dictionary's first choice match or not.

1. February
2. jewelry
3. Wednesday
4. garage
5. often

6. dog
7. coyote
8. rodeo
9. taut
10. tot

(Answers are on page 160.)

## Words about words

To discuss effective use of words, we need to share a vocabulary. This means that you will need to recall and/or learn the words writers use to discuss the uses of language, beginning with the terms for the parts of speech. These technical terms help us to understand and analyze how poets use grammar to achieve the effects they desire. This vocabulary is also a tool for planning your own writing. You will find a short grammar review among the resources on my *Painless Poetry* website.

# BRAIN TICKLERS
## Set # 18

1. Let's return to our consideration of how words appeal to our mind's eye. Look once again at these lists:

LIST 1:
that, instead, which, but, sometimes, when, him, rather, over

LIST 2:
Moon, peacock, Tibet, music, firelight, temple, danced, joy

The effectiveness of the second list in arousing images in the mind can be explained by the parts of speech that make up each list. Copy the words from each list and write their part(s) of speech, consulting the short grammar review from the *Painless Poetry* website and/or a dictionary if necessary. What conclusions can you draw?

2. Read this poem about slavery in the United States prior to the Civil War. Analyze each sentence, using the categories simple, compound, complex, declarative, imperative, interrogative, and/or exclamatory.

### The Slave Mother (1854)
by Frances Ellen Watkins

1 Heard you that shriek? It rose
2 　So wildly on the air,
3 It seemed as if a burden'd heart
4 　Was breaking in despair.

5 Saw you those hands so sadly clasped—
6 　The bowed and feeble head—
7 The shuddering of that fragile form—
8 　That look of grief and dread?

9 Saw you the sad, imploring eye?
10 　Its every glance was pain,
11 As if a storm of agony
12 　Were sweeping through the brain.

13 She is a mother, pale with fear.
14 　Her boy clings to her side,
15 And in her kirtle vainly tries
16 　His trembling form to hide.

17 He is not hers, although she bore
18 　For him a mother's pains;
19 He is not hers, although her blood
20 　Is coursing through his veins!

21 He is not hers, for cruel hands
22 　May rudely tear apart
23 The only wreath of household love
24 　That binds her breaking heart.

25 His love has been a joyous light
26    That o'er her pathway smiled,
27 A fountain gushing ever new,
28    Amid life's desert wild.

29 His lightest word has been a tone
30    Of music round her heart,
31 Their lives a streamlet blent in one—
32    Oh, Father! must they part?

33 They tear him from her circling arms,
34    Her last and fond embrace.
35 Oh! never more may her sad eyes
36    Gaze on his mournful face.

37 No marvel, then, these bitter shrieks
38    Disturb the listening air;
39 She is a mother, and her heart
40    Is breaking in despair.

3. Write a poem in which the names of the parts of speech (for example, *noun, verb, adjective, adverb, pronoun, article*) somehow play an important role.

(Answers are on page 160.)

# CHOOSE YOUR WORDS CAREFULLY: DICTION

Understanding grammatical terms helps us analyze how poets organize words, but it doesn't tell us why a poet chose the particular nouns, verbs, adjectives, etc. that he or she did. A grammatical structure (say, subject-verb-object) can be filled with any number of particular words, and the poet must apply some criteria to make useful decisions. The technical term for word choice is **diction**, our subject in this section. Sometimes people mistakenly think that writing poetry requires a certain, special "poetic" vocabulary. All that is required, in fact, is what works for the particular poem being written.

The following five sentences describe the same person in the same place doing the same thing. But you can see that they wouldn't fit interchangeably into a single poetic context.

- A guy got some food.
- The gentleman sampled a dish.
- Iggy gulped guacomole.
- Inigo ate an avocado concoction.
- Señor Jiminez enjoyed an appetizer.

Each has a different flavor, so to speak, and that's because of the diction. You can probably imagine that the substitution of different words over the course of a whole poem could lead to a very different overall impression.

As we discuss word choice, we will pay attention to the following five areas: the level of formality, the currency of expression, denotation and connotation, variety, and length and etymological origin of words.

## Formal and informal language

Formal language isn't better than informal language, or vice versa. The key is to choose language appropriate to your context and social setting. In poetry, levels of formality are linked to the subject matter, the audience, and the tone. A poem about farm chores is probably not deserving of lofty language: If the poet used language that was too formal, it would seem "inappropriate" unless the tone were obviously humorous.

Look again at the examples above. *Guy* and *Iggy* are informal. *Señor Jiminez* is formal address. *Man* and *Inigo* are somewhere in between. In formal language, we tend not to use slang, contractions, and nicknames. We are more careful about following grammatical and usage rules (*going to*, rather than *gonna*). Since we make these adaptations every day in our speech, we already have the basis for learning how to choose the level of formality of our writing in a particular instance.

There are differences in the standards for language used in most school writing, on the one hand, and poetry on the other. Run-ons and fragments may both be used, at times, in poetry. While it is important to observe rules of grammar and mechanics because these standards help smooth communication, in poetry there may be a good reason to break the rules. If you use either fragments or run-ons, make sure you can explain why.

## Currency

Samuel Daniel, one of the earliest English speakers to write sonnets, encouraged the use of contemporary (current—hence *currency*) language in one of the sonnets (XLVI) from his Delia cycle:

1   Let others sing of knights and paladines
2   In aged accents and untimely words;

In 1592, this was plain speaking, and Daniel was contrasting his own choice of simple, contemporary usage with other poets who wrote more fancifully and used antiquated language. In the twenty-first century, Daniel's language seems stilted and immediately recognizable as being from another era.

You may wish to take Daniel's advice, but in the present age in the United States, you can't do it the way he did in sixteenth-century England. Finding the expression that works for you in the context in which you live is part of the process referred to as "finding your voice."

## Denotation and connotation

Imagine a person who is speaking quite loudly. If you called that person *stentorian* (extremely loud), your choice would carry the overtones of the history of the word: Stentor was a Greek herald in the Trojan War, known to us from Homer's epic poem the *Iliad* on account of his powerful voice. If you described the person as *obstreperous* (noisy and unruly), you would be implying that the person is obnoxious and possibly self-centered and unconcerned about others; for most readers, however, the word would not carry any particular historical reference.

**Denotation** is the word we use for the literal meaning of a word. But even words that have similar or nearly identical literal meanings do not share **connotations**, the meanings associated with a word beyond the explicit, literal meaning.

The connotations of a word separate one synonym from another. *Obstreperous, stentorian, clarion, resonant, shrill,* and *squawky* are all synonyms for *loud,* but we're more likely to want to hear someone whose voice is clarion or resonant than someone whose voice is shrill or squawky. Because of the sound, shape, etymology, length, and history of its use, each word has a different feel, and even words that we refer to as synonyms are never equivalent.

## Variety

Synonyms, nevertheless, are very important in English style because we English speakers often find it distracting, or even annoying, when words or forms from the same root are repeated too often or too close together. This love of variety is one of the aspects that differentiates the diction of literary culture from that of oral culture, in which repetition is one of the key aids to understanding. But beyond the literary/oral distinction, there are stylistic preferences within cultures.

The first eight lines of this 1995 translation of a sonnet written in the seventeenth century by a Mexican nun (with her verb choices in parentheses) can help to demonstrate the two preferences in diction. You do not need to know Spanish to see that the original poem takes a different approach to words with the same roots than the English version does. Although Ingber's choices may be partially due to the demands of making a coherent translation, they also reflect taste.

### Sonnet

1　Philip worships (*adora*) me and I abhor (*aborrezco*) him;
2　Leonard hates (*aborrece*) me; and for him I yearn (*adoro*);
3　for him who would desire (*apetece*) me not, I'm weeping (*lloro*),
4　and him who weeps (*llora*) for me I always spurn (*no apetezco*).

5　To him who'd shame (*desdora*) me most, my soul I offer (*ofrezco*);
6　him who'd sacrifice (*ofrece*) for me, I shame (*desdoro*);
7　I scorn (*desprecio*) him who'd exalt (*enriquece*) my reputation,
8　of him who'd scorn (*desprecios*) it, I exalt (*enriquezco*) the name.

Since Spanish is an inflected language, the endings of the Spanish verbs differ, but you can easily see how repetitious Sor Juana's diction is as opposed to Ingber's.

In the first stanza, there are only four different verbs in Spanish but seven in English. Overall, there are twelve different

| Stanza 1 | | Stanza 2 | |
|---|---|---|---|
| **Spanish** | **English** | **Spanish** | **English** |
| adora | worships | desdora | shame |
| adoro | yearn | desdoro | shame |
| aborrezco | abhor | ofrezco | offer |
| aborrece | hates | ofrece | sacrifice |
| apetece | desire | desprecio | scorn |
| no apetezco | spurn | desprecios | scorn |
| lloro | weeping | enriquece | exalt |
| llora | weeps | enriquezco | exalt |

English verbs in the two sentences, whereas the Spanish has only eight verbs, each used twice.

The title and first line of this German poem makes the same point, packing in five forms of *wunder* (wonder) in nine words:

### Wunder über Wunder (1819)
by Josef von Eichendorff

1    Du wunderst wunderlich dich über Wunder

## Word length and word origins

Word length is related to several different aspects of language. English vocabulary, more than that of most languages, is remarkable for its inclusion of words from many other languages. Building on Germanic origins of the early tribes who controlled Britain (Angles, Saxons, and Jutes), English added many Latin words beginning with the Roman conquest and continuing with the influx of Christian missionaries, Scandinavian words stemming from the Viking incursions, French words beginning with the Norman Conquest, Greek and Latin debuting when the

Renaissance brought classical studies to renewed vigor, and some words from just about everywhere else. English has words derived from languages as distinct as Algonquian (*skunk*) and Arabic (*alcohol*), as Dutch (*cookie*) and Dharuk, an Australian aborigine language from near Port Jackson (*boomerang*). English keeps evolving as it continues to be used in international politics and economics, and it continues to add new words.

Anglo-Saxon words tend to be short. Of the top 100 most frequently used words in English, every single one is Anglo-Saxon, and most of them are short: *the, of, in, on, to, me*—you get the idea. French words are still a predominant part of the language—40 percent of our vocabulary is of French origin. Words from French tend to be longer: *boulevard, garage, salon, etiquette, reverie*. In addition, vocabulary in the United States has long been influenced by our Spanish-speaking population, giving us for example: *sombrero* (1599), *llama* (1600), *cockroach* (1623—ever heard of *la cucaracha*?), *mesa* (1759), *burro* (1800), *ranch* (1831), *rodeo* (1834), *canyon* (1837), and *fiesta* (1844), and phrases like "Hasta la vista, baby," and "Adios, amigos."

Many of the long, multisyllabic words in our language, especially those with multiple prefixes and suffixes, are from Latin: *recrimination, symbiosis, extricate, voracious, quaternary, equilibrium*. Much of our vocabulary for sophisticated ideas and concepts comes from Latin.

Sometimes poets use words from other languages in their poems. Here is an example showing how foreign words can add humor.

### The Hippopotamus (1899)
#### by Oliver Herford

1  "Oh, say, what is this fearful, wild,
2  Incorrigible cuss?"
3  "This creature (don't say 'cuss,' my child;
4  'Tis slang)—this creature fierce is styled
5  The Hippopotamus.
6  His curious name derives its source
7  From two Greek words: hippos—a horse,
8  Potamos—river. See?
9  The river's plain enough, of course;
10  But why they called that thing a horse,
11  That's what is Greek to me."

**Neologisms** (new words) are words that have no prior history because they were invented by the poet. Shakespeare was responsible for many new words that are now part of the language, even if you wouldn't use them every day: *bodement* meaning "omen", *intrenchant* meaning "not capable of being cut", *multitudinous* meaning "the great bulk of the waters", and *incarnadine* meaning "to redden" all were used for the first time in Shakespeare's 1605 play *Macbeth*. Lewis Carroll and Edward Lear invented many nonsense words, e.g., *jabberwocky*, an imaginary beast—Carroll; *runcible spoon*, an obscure piece of silverware—Lear.

Information about a word's history can be found in most dictionaries. The history of a word's meaning and passage from language to language is called its **etymology**. Finding words with similar etymologies may be important if you are working in a context in which you wish to establish consistent diction.

Even from these brief examples, you can begin to get a feel for the kinds of choices that were made by poets whose poetry you have read and that *you* can make to shape the language in your poetry.

It's important to be aware of usage and customs that differ from your own. Here's an example: Until recently, English usage accepted the noun *man* or *mankind* to stand for a person or all people, regardless of gender, and the third-person singular masculine pronoun (*he, him, his*) to stand for a single person, whether male or female. This reflects the usage of the times and is still commonly done in other languages and occasionally in English. It does not necessarily suggest bias or prejudice against women on the part of the writer.

Currently, in the United States, it is common to replace such usage with usage that is considered nondiscriminatory. However you choose to express your ideas, don't make the mistake of using a plural pronoun to replace a singular noun. "*A poet* chooses the words that *they* consider best" is not grammatically correct English.

## BRAIN TICKLERS
### Set # 19

1. Read the following three pieces of nineteenth-century poetry (one complete poem and two excerpts). Then, using the words *formal, informal, currency, denotation* and *connotation, variety, length,* and *origin,* describe the diction of each piece. If you notice any allusions, note those as well.

### The Football Match* (1892)
#### Author Unkown

1  O wild kaleidoscopic panorama of jaculatory arms and legs.
2  The twisting, twining, turning, tussling, throwing, thrusting, throttling, tugging, thumping, the tightening thews.
3  The tearing of tangled trousers, the jut of giant calves protuberant.
4  The wriggleness, the wormlike, snaky movement and life of it;
5  The insertion of strong men in the mud, the wallowing, the stamping with thick shoes;
6  The rowdyism, and *élan*, the slugging and scraping, the cowboy Homeric ferocity.
7  (Ah, well kicked, red legs! Hit her up, you muddy little hero, you!)
8  The bleeding noses, the shins, the knuckles abraded:
9  That's the way to make men! Go it, you border ruffians, I like ye.

---

* This is an excerpt from an anonymous Canadian poem. The subject is a game between McGill University in Quebec and the University of Toronto. The McGill team is called the "Redmen," and they wear red uniforms.

### The Land of Nod (1885)
by Robert Louis Stevenson

1  From breakfast on through all the day
2  At home among my friends I stay,
3  But every night I go abroad
4  Afar into the land of Nod.

5  All by myself I have to go,
6  With none to tell me what to do—
7  All alone beside the streams
8  And up the mountain-sides of dreams.

9  The strangest things are there for me,
10 Both things to eat and things to see,
11 And many frightening sights abroad
12 Till morning in the land of Nod.

13 Try as I like to find the way,
14 I never can get back by day,
15 Nor can remember plain and clear
16 The curious music that I hear.

### The Rubáiyát of Omar Khayyám (c. 1100)
translated from Persian
by Edward FitzGerald (1859) (excerpt)

XI
41 Here with a Loaf of Bread beneath the Bough,
42 A Flask of Wine, a book of Verse—and Thou
43 　　Beside me singing in the Wilderness—
44 And Wilderness is Paradise enow.

2. Choose an interesting word (maybe your favorite word) and construct a poem around it. Think carefully about your diction, and making a fitting setting for your special word. Also consider your audience.

(Answers are on page 162.)

# SPECIAL TREATMENT:
# RHETORICAL DEVICES

In the last section we discussed English language speakers' preference for variety rather than repetition in word choice. In English usage, repetition such as the following is not effective:

> My friendly friend befriended me
> When I was friendless and alone
> Our friendship grew apace and we
> are friendlier now with everyone.

Most people would find that passage very boring. And yet, other patterns of repetition are key to **rhetorical devices**, ways of using language that have been found effective for thousands of years.

Just as auto manufacturers who find that including a Global Positioning System (GPS) will be effective in selling cars make sure their cars are equipped with GPS devices, so writers and speakers, knowing how effective rhetorical devices are, use them often. But it is important for you to know that some of these devices that you see and hear in advertisements, movies, speeches, and even nursery rhymes, haven't been taught in some schools for a long time. So, while some—simile and metaphor, personification, and pun, for example—you'll probably recognize right away, others will be new to you, and their names, often being from Greek, will look unusual. To show you how easy they really are, we'll start by looking at them in nursery rhymes and folk songs. Then, when you've had a chance to get used to them, we'll work with them in poetry written for more mature readers so you can see how they work in more sophisticated contexts.

**Not only are these rhetorical devices useful for poetry, but they're also great to embed in your prose and speech (and you'll find them used often in the prose and poetry of great writers and public speakers). Once you become familiar with their uses, you'll want to employ them in essays, persuasive writing, etc. And soon, you'll start noticing them all over the place.**

# Anadiplosis

**Anadiplosis** (ann-uh-duh-PLO-suhs) is repetition of a word from the end of one clause or line at the beginning of the next clause or line for emphasis or development. Here is an example from a nursery rhyme. The rhetorical device is in red.

### Hickory, Dickory Dock

1   Hickory Dickory Dock,
2   A Mouse ran up **the Clock**.
3   **The Clock** struck One,
4   The Mouse ran down.
5   Hickory, Dickory Dock.

# Anaphora and epistrophe

**Anaphora** (uh-NAH-fuh-uh) is repetition of the same word(s) at the beginning of a series of phrases or lines, whereas **epistrophe** (ih-PIH-struh-fee) is repetition of the same word(s) at the end of a series of phrases or lines. Sometimes it creates a refrain. Either one can be used to focus attention, expand on an idea, and/or create expectation. Here is an example of anaphora from a nursery rhyme. The rhetorical device is in red, and the repetition contributes to the characterization of Taffy as a scoundrel.

### Taffy Was a Welshman

1   **Taffy** was a Welshman,
2   **Taffy** was a thief.
3   **Taffy** came to my house
4   And stole a piece of beef.

Here is an example of epistrophe from a nursery rhyme in which the repetition of *hot* emphasizes how very hot the peas (formerly spelled *pease*) are. The rhetorical device is in red.

1   Piping **hot**
2   Smoking **hot**
3   What I've got,
4   You know not,
5   Hot hot pease, hot, hot, **hot**;
6   Hot are my pease, **hot**.

Notice that the poem at the bottom of page 115 has anaphora in lines 5 and 6 with the same word that's used for epistrophe in lines 1, 2, 5, and 6. Also note the use of anadiplosis from line 5 to line 6.

# BRAIN TICKLERS
## *Set # 20*

1. Identify and explain the effect of anadiplosis in the selection.

### Samson Agonistes (1667–1671)
by John Milton (excerpt)

16  Retiring from the popular noise, I seek
17  This unfrequented place to find some ease;
18  Ease to the body some, none to the mind
19  From restless thoughts, that like a deadly swarm
20  Of hornets arm'd, no sooner found alone,
21  But rush upon me thronging, and present
22  Times past, what once I was, and what am now.

2. Identify and explain the effect of anaphora in the selection.

### I Do Not Love Thee (mid-1800s)
by Caroline Elizabeth Sarah Norton

1    I do not love thee!—no! I do not love thee!
2  And yet when thou art absent I am sad;
3    And envy even the bright blue sky above thee,
4  Whose quiet stars may see thee and be glad.

5    I do not love thee!—yet, I know not why,
6  Whate'er thou dost seems still well done, to me:
7    And often in my solitude I sigh
8  That those I do love are not more like thee!

9    I do not love thee!—yet, when thou art gone,
10  I hate the sound (though those who speak be dear)
11    Which breaks the lingering echo of the tone
12  Thy voice of music leaves upon my ear.

13    I do not love thee!—yet thy speaking eyes,
14  With their deep, bright, and most expressive blue,
15    Between me and the midnight heaven arise,
16  Oftener than any eyes I ever knew.

17    I know I do not love thee!—yet, alas!
18  Others will scarcely trust my candid heart;
19    And oft I catch them smiling as they pass,
20  Because they see me gazing where thou art.

3. Identify and explain the effect of epistrophe in the selection.

### The Death of the Hired Man (1914)
by Robert Frost (excerpt)

114  "Warren," she said, "he has come home to die:
115  You needn't be afraid he'll leave you this time."

116  "Home," he mocked gently.

117                          "Yes, what else but home?
118  It all depends on what you mean by home.
119  Of course he's nothing to us, any more
120  Than was the hound that came a stranger to us
121  Out of the woods, worn out upon the trail."

122  "Home is the place where, when you have to go there,
123  They have to take you in."

124                          "I should have called it
125  Something you somehow haven't to deserve."

(Answers are on page 163.)

## Aporia

**Aporia** (ah-puh-REE-uh) is the questioning of where to begin or end or what to do or say next. It can be used to convey true uncertainty or feigned in order to try to awaken the listener's interest or to get another person to reveal what he or she is thinking. Here is an example from a song. The rhetorical device is in red.

### The Drunken Sailor
Traditional Sea Chanty

1  What shall we do with the drunken sailor?
2  What shall we do with the drunken sailor?
3  What shall we do with the drunken sailor early in
     the morning?

In this song, the initial question gives rise to a number of verses in which various answers are proposed:

- Put him in the long boat till he's sober.
- Put him in the scuppers with the hosepipe on him.

Etc.

Other verses may be invented, but the song often ends with:

- That's what we'll do with the drunken sailor.

## Apostrophe

**Apostrophe** (uh-PAHS-truh-fee) is a direct address to someone or something. It often interrupts a speech and often (but not always) begins with *O* or *Oh*. It may be a simple exclamation to show deep feeling, or it may be used in supplication or prayer. Here is an example from a song in which it helps establish that the song is reporting a conversation between two people. The rhetorical device is in red.

### Billy Boy
Traditional Folk Song (excerpt)

1  Oh, where have you been, Billy Boy, Billy Boy?
2  Oh, where have you been, charming Billy?
3  I have been to see my wife:
4  She's the joy of my life.
5  She's a young thing and cannot leave her mother.

Notice the use of anaphora in lines 1 and 2 and lines 4 and 5. It is common for both songs and poems to have multiple rhetorical devices in them.

## Antanaclasis

**Antanaclasis** (ann-tah-nuh-KLAH-sis) is one of several types of pun or play on words. The words in the pun are either homonyms or homophones. Puns often work better said out loud, because when it's written down, the words have to be spelled, and if they're homophones, this gives away the joke or forces the poet to spell one incorrectly. Here is an example from a nursery rhyme riddle. The rhetorical device is in red.

### Twelve Pears

1 Twelve pears hanging high,
2 Twelve knights riding by;
3 Each knight took a pear
4 And yet left a dozen there.

The riddle is solved by interpreting the word *pears* as *pairs*.

## BRAIN TICKLERS
### Set # 21

1. Identify and explain the effects of aporia in the following passage.

### The Love Song of J. Alfred Prufrock
#### (1910–1911)
by T. S. Eliot (excerpt)

68 And should I then presume?
69 And how should I begin?

70 Shall I say, I have gone at dusk through narrow streets
71 And watched the smoke that rises from the pipes
72 Of lonely men in shirt-sleeves, leaning out of windows? . . .

2. Identify and explain the effects of apostrophe in this passage.

### *The Odyssey* by Homer (c. 700 B.C.E)
translated into prose by Samuel Butler (1900)
(excerpt from the beginning)

Tell me, O muse, of that ingenious hero who travelled far and wide after he had sacked the famous town of Troy.

3. The author of the lyrics for *America the Beautiful* wrote the poem on page 120. Identify and explain the effects of puns or antanaclasis in this passage.

## Don't You See? (c. 1900)
### by Katherine Lee Bates

1 The day was hotter than words can tell,
2 So hot the jelly-fish wouldn't jell.
3 The halibut went all to butter,
4 And the catfish had only force to utter
5 A faint sea-mew—aye, though some have doubted,
6 The carp he capered and the horn-pout pouted.

7 The sardonic sardine had his sly heart's wish
8 When the angelfish fought with the paradise fish.
9 'T was a sight gave the bluefish the blues to see,
10 But the seal concealed a wicked glee—

11 The day it went from bad to worse,
12 Till the pickerel picked the purse-crab's purse.

13 And the crab felt crabbier yet no doubt,
14 Because the oyster wouldn't shell out.
15 The sculpin would sculpt, but hadn't a model,
16 And the coddlefish begged for something to coddle.

17 But to both the dolphin refused its doll,
18 Till the whale was obliged to whale them all.

(Answers are on page 164.)

# Asyndeton and polysyndeton

**Asyndeton** (uh-SIHN-duh-tawn) is the purposeful omission of coordinating conjunctions from a series of items. It can be used to suggest that the list is incomplete, just a token of items too numerous to enumerate. Here is an example from a nursery rhyme in which a conjunction is not used because the series is actually referring to parts of one man's name, not a group of men. The rhetorical device is in red.

### Mr. Punchinello

1   O, Mother, I shall be married to
2   Mr. Punchinello,
3     To Mr. Punch,
4      To Mr. Joe,
5       To Mr. Nell,
6        To Mr. Lo.
7   **Mr. Punch, Mr. Joe,**
8   **Mr. Nell, Mr. Lo,**
9   To Mr. Punchinello.

Notice also the use of the rhetorical device called apostrophe in line 1 (*O, Mother*) and the use of anaphora in lines 3–6 and 9 (*To Mr.*) and lines 7–8 (*Mr.*).

    **Polysyndeton** (paw-lee-SIHN-duh-tawn) is approximately the "opposite" of asyndeton—the use of a conjunction before every (or almost every) item in the series. It can be used to draw attention to each and every element in a list, to give them added weight. Here is an example from a nursery rhyme that may have been about an uprising against King Richard II of England. It's an add-on rhyme, which starts off with one line and adds on an additional line each time. The word *and* emphasizes the long chain of events being formed. The rhetorical device is in red.

1   John Patch made the match,
2   **And** John Clint made the flint,
3   **And** John Puzzle made the muzzle,
4   **And** John Crowder made the powder,
5   **And** John Block made the stock,
6   **And** John Brammer made the rammer,
7   **And** John Wiming made the priming,
8   **And** John Scott made the shot,
9   **But** John Ball shot them all.

Did you notice that the polysyndeton is also anaphora because *And John* is repeated at the beginning of many consecutive lines?

## Epanalepsis

**Epanalepsis** (eh-puh-nuh-LEHP-sis) is the repetition of a word or phrase (sometimes at the beginning and end of the same line or sentence) after an interruption, which is sometimes an apostrophe. It can be used for emphasis or to return to a focus that was temporarily changed. Here is an example from a nursery rhyme in which it emphasizes the command for Thumbkin to kick up his heels. The rhetorical device is in red.

### Dance, Thumbkin, Dance

1 Dance, Thumbkin, Dance.
2 Dance, ye merry men, every one;
3 But Thumbkin, he can dance alone,
4 Thumbkin, he can dance alone.

There is also anaphora in lines 1–2 (*Dance*), and epistrophe in lines 3–4 (*alone*).

## BRAIN TICKLERS
### Set # 22

1. Identify and explain the effects of asyndeton in this passage.

### On the Pulse of Morning (1993)
by Maya Angelou (excerpt), transcribed in newspaper accounts from her reading

54 Each of you, descendant of some passed
55 On traveler, has been paid for.
56 You, who gave me my first name, you,
57 Pawnee, Apache, Seneca, you
58 Cherokee Nation, who rested with me, then
59 Forced on bloody feet,
60 Left me to the employment of
61 Other seekers—desperate for gain,
62 Starving for god.
63 You, the Turk, the Arab, the Swede, the German, the Eskimo, the Scot,
64 You, the Ashanti, the Yoruba, the Kru, bought
65 Sold, stolen, arriving on the nightmare
66 Praying for a dream.

2. Identify and explain the effects of polysyndeton in this passage.

### The Tragedy of Macbeth (1605)
IV, I, 12–19 by William Shakespeare (excerpt)

12   Fillet of a fenny snake,
13   In the cauldron boil and bake;
14   Eye of newt and toe of frog,
15   Wool of bat and tongue of dog,
16   Adder's fork and blind-worm's sting,
17   Lizard's leg and owlet's wing
18   For a charm of powerful trouble,
19   Like a hell-broth boil and bubble.

3. Identify and explain the effects of epanalepsis in this passage.

### Lycidas (1637)
by John Milton

165   Weep no more, woeful shepherds, weep no more,
166   For Lycidas, your sorrow, is not dead. . . .

(Answers are on page 164.)

## Epithet

An **epithet** (EH-puh-thet) is a modifier that draws attention to a key characteristic of the noun it modifies (Richard the Lionhearted; Aethelred the Unready) or a noun phrase used in place of a name ("The Father of His Country" for George Washington). The device originated in oral poetry to help poets fill their lines (the bard had a stock of epithets and added one that fit the empty space). It can provide further identification of characters, or function as a nickname. On page 124 is an example from a nursery rhyme, in which it helps to identify the subject of the poem. The rhetorical device is in red.

### Tom, Tom, the Piper's Son

1 Tom, Tom, the piper's son
2 Stole a pig and away did run;
3 The pig was eat, and Tom was beat,
4 Till he run crying down the street.

## Epizeuxis

**Epizeuxis** (eh-pih-ZOOK-suhs) creates emphasis by repeating a single word several times in a row. Here is an example from a nursery rhyme. The rhetorical device is in red.

### Twinkle, Twinkle, Little Star

1 Twinkle, twinkle, little star,
2 How I wonder what you are!
3 Up above the world so high,
4 Like a diamond in the sky.

## Hyperbole

**Hyperbole** (hi-PUR-buh-lee) is exaggeration for emphasis or humor. Here is an example from a folk song where exaggeration is meant to be funny. The rhetorical device is in red.

### Billy Boy
Traditional Folk Song (excerpts)

...

15 Can she bake a cherry pie, Billy Boy, Billy Boy
16 Can she bake a cherry pie, charming Billy?
17 **She can bake a cherry pie**
18 **Quicker than a cat can wink its eye.**
19 She's a young thing and cannot leave her mother.

20 How old is she, Billy Boy, Billy Boy?
21 How old is she, charming Billy?
22 **Three times six, four times seven,**
23 **Twenty-eight, and eleven,**
24 She's a young thing and cannot leave her mother

## BRAIN TICKLERS
### Set # 23

1. Identify and explain the effects of epithet in this passage.

### The Frog (1896)
by Hillaire Belloc

1 Be kind and tender to the Frog,
2    And do not call him names,
3 As "Slimy skin," or "Polly-wog,"
4    Or likewise "Ugly James,"
5 Or "Gap-a-grin," or "Toad-gone-wrong,"
6    Or "Bill Bandy-knees":
7 The Frog is justly sensitive
8    To epithets like these.
9 No animal will more repay
10    A treatment kind and fair;
11 At least so lonely people say
12    Who keep a frog (and, by the way,
13 They are extremely rare).

2. Identify and explain the effects of epizeuxis in this passage.

### Break, Break, Break (1842)
by Alfred Lord Tennyson

1  Break, break, break,
2      On thy cold gray stones, O Sea!
3  And I would that my tongue could utter
4      The thoughts that arise in me.

5  O, well for the fisherman's boy,
6      That he shouts with his sister at play!
7  O, well for the sailor lad,
8      That he sings in his boat on the bay!

9  And the stately ships go on
10      To their haven under the hill;
11  But O for the touch of a vanish'd hand,
12      And the sound of a voice that is still!

13  Break, break, break
14      At the foot of thy crags, O Sea!
15  But the tender grace of a day that is dead
16      Will never come back to me.

3. Identify and explain the effects of hyperbole in this passage.

### To His Coy Mistress (1681)
by Andrew Marvell (excerpt)

1  Had we but world enough, and time,
2  This coyness, lady, were no crime.
3  We would sit down and think which way
4  To walk, and pass our long love's day. . . .

13  An hundred years should go to praise
14  Thine eyes, and on thy forehead gaze. . . .

(Answers are on page 164.)

# Simile

**Simile** (SIM-uh-lee) is comparison using *like* or *as*. It is one way of adding description without using modifiers. Here is a nursery rhyme riddle in which all the clues are expressed as similes.

### As White as Milk

1 As white as milk,
2 And not milk;
3 As green as grass,
4 And not grass;
5 As red as blood,
6 And not blood;
7 As black as soot,
8 And not soot.

The riddle describes the stages of development of a blackberry.

## Metaphor, personification, and extended metaphor

**Metaphor** (MEH-tuh-for) is a comparison in which one thing is identified with another by saying that the first thing *is* the second. Metaphors can surprise us into taking a fresh look at something. They are useful in explaining qualities indirectly.

**Personification** (pur-SAW-nuh-fuh-KAY-shun) is a type of metaphor, a metaphorical figure in which an animal or an inanimate object is given one or more human attributes.

See the top of page 128 for an example from a folk song where metaphor, simile, and personification are all used to explain the different faces of romantic love. The metaphor and personification are in red. The metaphor compares love to a jewel, and the personification speaks about the timeless love as if it were a living thing that could age and be hot or cold. See if you can identify the simile.

### The Water Is Wide
Traditional Folk Song (excerpt)

9   Oh, love is gentle, and love is kind,
10  And **love's a jewel** when first 'tis new.
11  But **love grows old and waxes cold**
12  And fades away like morning dew.

The simile is in line 12.

**Extended metaphor** simply takes a metaphor and develops it in a variety of directions, giving a rich depth to a description.

# BRAIN TICKLERS
### Set # 24

1. Identify and explain the effects of simile in this passage.

### A Red, Red Rose (1794)
by Robert Burns

1   O my Luve's like a red, red rose,
2       That's newly sprung in June;
3   O my Luve's like the melodie
4       That's sweetly play'd in tune.

5   As fair art thou, my bonnie lass,
6       So deep in luve am I;
7   And I will luve thee still, my Dear,
8       Till a' the seas gang dry.

9   Till a' the seas gang dry, my Dear,
10      And the rocks melt wi' the sun;
11  I will luve thee still my Dear,
12      While the sands o' life shall run.

13  And fare thee weel, my only Luve,
14      And fare the weel, a while!
15  And I will come again, my Luve,
16      Tho' it ware ten thousand mile!

2. Identify and explain the effects of metaphor in this passage.

### The Tragedy of Macbeth (1605)
(V, v, 24–28) by William Shakespeare

24  Life's but a walking shadow, a poor player
25  That struts and frets his hour upon the stage
26  And then is heard no more: it is a tale
27  Told by an idiot, full of sound and fury,
28  Signifying nothing.

3. Identify and explain the effects of personification in this passage.

### Stopping by Woods on a Snowy Evening (1923)
by Robert Frost

1   Whose woods these are I think I know.
2   His house is in the village though;
3   He will not see me stopping here
4   To watch his woods fill up with snow.

5   My little horse must think it queer
6   To stop without a farmhouse near
7   Between the woods and frozen lake
8   The darkest evening of the year.

9   He gives his harness bells a shake
10  To ask if there is some mistake.
11  The only other sound's the sweep
12  Of easy wind and downy flake.

13  The woods are lovely, dark and deep.
14  But I have promises to keep,
15  And miles to go before I sleep,
16  And miles to go before I sleep.

Look back at the poem "On the Death of my Child" on page 50. By using the word *bed* in the last line, the translator O'Broin creates a metaphor connecting death and sleep. He's not the first one to do so—it's a tradition, so well known now (think of the fairy tale "Sleeping Beauty" for another example) that Frost uses *sleep* in his poem, expecting the reader to make the connection.

4. Identify and explain the effects of extended metaphor in this passage.

### October (1896)
by Paul Laurence Dunbar

1  October is the treasurer of the year,
2     And all the months pay bounty to her store:
3  The fields and orchards still their tribute bear,
4     And fill her brimming coffers more and more.
5  But she, with youthful lavishness,
6  Spends all her wealth in gaudy dress,
7     And decks herself in garments bold
8     Of scarlet, purple, red, and gold.

9  She heedeth not how swift the hours fly,
10     But smiles and sings her happy life along;
11  She only sees above a shining sky;
12     She only hears the breezes' voice in song.
13  Her garments trail the woodland through,
14  And gather pearls of early dew
15     That sparkle till the roguish Sun
16     Creeps up and steals them every one.

17  But what cares she that jewels should be lost,
18     When all of Nature's bounteous wealth is hers?
19  Though princely fortunes may have been their cost,
20     Not one regret her calm demeanor stirs.
21  Whole-hearted, happy, careless, free,
22  She lives her life out joyously,
23     Nor cares when Frost stalks o'er her way
24     And turns her auburn locks to gray.

(Answers are on page 165.)

## Metonymy

**Metonymy** (muh-TAH-nuh-mee) is the substitution of one concept for another to which it is closely related. This can be done for emphasis, for meter, or just to make writing either more colorful or less wordy. Here is an example from a nursery rhyme. The metonymy is in red, with *crown* being a short and colorful way of explaining that the fight was for control of the government.

## The Lion and the Unicorn

1 The Lion and the Unicorn
2     Were fighting for the Crown
3 The Lion beat the Unicorn
4     All about the Town.

5 Some gave then white bread,
6     And some gave them brown;
7 Some gave them plum cake
8     And drummed them out of town.

# Paraprosdokian

**Paraprosdokian** (pair-uh-prohs-DOH-kee-un) means a surprise ending. In this folk song, there are several surprises at the end, shown in red. Surprise endings may tend to be found in longer works because it takes awhile to build up a strong enough impression that reversing it creates a surprise.

### Frog Went A-Courtin'

1 Frog went a-courtin' and he did ride, mm-hmm, mm-hmm
2 Frog went a-courtin' and he did ride, mm-hmm, mm-hmm
3 Frog went a-courtin' and he did ride
4 Sword and a pistol by his side, mm-hmm, mm-hmm

5 He rode right up to Miss Mousie's door, mm-hmm, mm-hmm
6 He rode right up to Miss Mousie's door, mm-hmm, mm-hmm
7 He rode right up to Miss Mousie's door
8 Where he had been many times before, mm-hmm, mm-hmm

9 "Mistress Mouse, are you within?" mm-hmm, mm-hmm
10 "Mistress Mouse, are you within?" mm-hmm, mm-hmm
11 "Mistress Mouse, are you within?"
12 "Yes, kind Sir, I sit and spin," mm-hmm, mm-hmm

13 Took Miss Mousie on his knee, mm-hmm, mm-hmm
14 Took Miss Mousie on his knee, mm-hmm, mm-hmm
15 Took Miss Mousie on his knee,
16 Said, "Miss Mousie, will you marry me?" mm-hmm, mm-hmm

17 "Without my Uncle Rat's consent," mm-hmm, mm-hmm
18 "Without my Uncle Rat's consent," mm-hmm, mm-hmm
19 "Without my Uncle Rat's consent,
20 I wouldn't marry the President," mm-hmm, mm-hmm

21 Uncle Rat laughed, and he shook his fat sides . . .
24 To think his niece would be a bride.

25 Uncle Rat, he went downtown . . .
28 To buy Miss Mouse a wedding gown.

29 Where shall the wedding supper be . . .
32 Way down yonder in the hollow tree.

33  What shall the wedding supper be . . .
36  Two green beans and a black-eyed pea.

37  First to come in was a bumblebee . . .
40  Sat a mosquito on his knee.

41  Next to come in was a broken back flea . . .
44  Danced a jig with the bumblebee.

45  Next to come in was the big black snake . . .
48  Ate up all of the wedding cake.

49  Mr. Frog went a-hoppin' over the brook . . .
52  But a white duck came and swallowed him up.

53  Little piece of corn bread layin' on the shelf . . .
56  If you want anymore you can sing it yourself.

## Parataxis

**Parataxis** (pair-uh-TAK-sis) is a series of independent clauses, relating a series of actions or a series of propositions. The nursery rhymes that build up by adding new material in each stanza, called cumulative poems, are examples of this. The parataxis is in red.

### The Key of the Kingdom

1   This is the key of the kingdom.
2   In that kingdom there is a city.
3   In that city there is a town.
4   In that town there is a street.
5   In that street there is a lane.
6   In that lane there is a yard.
7   In that yard there is a house.
8   In that house there is a room.
9   In that room there is a bed.
10  On that bed there is a basket.
11  In that basket there are some flowers.

12  Flowers in the basket,
13  Basket in the bed,
14  Bed in the room,
15  Room in the house,
16  House in the yard,
17  Yard in the lane,
18  Lane in the street,
19  Street in the town,
20  Town in the city,
21  City in the kingdom—
22  And this is the key of the kingdom.

## Polyptoton

Now we're going to learn to use the technique that was so overdone in the "friendly" example (page 114). **Polyptoton** (pah-LIP-tuh-tahn) is the use of a word in its different inflectional forms (as different parts of speech, in different tenses, etc.). When used sparingly, it can add cleverness and create connections between phrases and clauses. The technique also occurs frequently in the wordplay known as tongue twisters, as in this example. The red text shows the different words containing *thatch*.

### A Thatcher of Thatchwood

1 A thatcher of Thatchwood went to Thatchet a-thatching;
2 Did a thatcher of Thatchwood go to Thatchet a-thatching?
3 If a thatcher of Thatchwood went to Thatchet a-thatching,
4 Where's the thatching the thatcher of Thatchwood hath thatch'd?

## BRAIN TICKLERS
### Set # 25

1. Identify and explain the effects of metonymy in this passage.

**Psalm 99\*** (1609/revised 1752)
Douay-Rheims version (excerpt)

2 Sing joyfully to God, all the earth; serve ye the Lord with gladness. Come in before his presence with exceeding great joy.

---

\*You saw the King James Version of this psalm earlier, but there it was referred to as Psalm 100, due to numbering differences in the different translations of the Bible.

2. Identify and explain the effects of paraprosdokian in this passage. As you read the following poem, note how you think it is going to end, and how your thoughts develop as you read.

## The Owl Critic (1800s)
### by James T. Fields

1 "Who stuffed that white owl?" No one spoke in the shop:
2 The barber was busy, and he couldn't stop;
3 The customers, waiting their turns, were all reading
4 The "Daily," the "Herald," the "Post," little heeding
5 The young man who blurted out such a blunt question;
6 Not one raised a head, or even made a suggestion;
7         And the barber kept on shaving.

8 "Don't you see, Mister Brown,"
9 Cried the youth, with a frown,
10 "How wrong the whole thing is,
11 How preposterous each wing is,
12 How flattened the head is, how jammed down the neck is—
13 In short, the whole owl, what an ignorant wreck 't is!
14 I make no apology;
15 I've learned owl-eology.
16 I've passed days and nights in a hundred collections,
17 And cannot be blinded to any deflections
18 Arising from unskilful fingers that fail
19 To stuff a bird right, from his beak to his tail.
20 Mister Brown! Mister Brown!
21 Do take that bird down,
22 Or you'll soon be the laughing-stock all over town!"
23         And the barber kept on shaving.

24 "I've studied owls,
25 And other night fowls,
26 And I tell you
27 What I know to be true:
28 An owl cannot roost
29 With his limbs so unloosed;
30 No owl in this world
31 Ever had his claws curled,
32 Ever had his legs slanted,
33 Ever had his bill canted,
34 Ever had his neck screwed
35 Into that attitude.

36 He can't do it, because
37 'T is against all bird-laws.
38 Anatomy teaches,
39 Ornithology preaches
40 An owl has a toe
41 That can't turn out so!
42 I've made the white owl my study for years,
43 And to see such a job almost moves me to tears!
44 Mister Brown, I'm amazed
45 You should be so gone crazed
46 As to put up a bird
47 In that posture absurd!
48 To look at that owl really brings on a dizziness;
49 The man who stuffed him don't half know his business!"
50              And the barber kept on shaving.

51 "Examine those eyes.
52 I'm filled with surprise
53 Taxidermists should pass
54 Off on you such poor glass;
55 So unnatural they seem
56 They'd make Audubon scream,
57 And John Burroughs laugh
58 To encounter such chaff.
59 Do take that bird down;
60 Have him stuffed again, Brown!"
61              And the barber kept on shaving.

62 "With some sawdust and bark
63 I could stuff in the dark
64 An owl better than that.
65 I could make an old hat
66 Look more like an owl
67 Than that horrid fowl,
68 Stuck up there so stiff like a side of coarse leather.
69 In fact, about him there's not one natural feather."

70 Just then, with a wink and a sly normal lurch,
71 The owl, very gravely, got down from his perch,
72 Walked round, and regarded his fault-finding critic
73 (Who thought he was stuffed) with a glance analytic,
74 And then fairly hooted, as if he should say:
75 "Your learning's at fault this time, any way;
76 Don't waste it again on a live bird, I pray.
77 I'm an owl; you're another. Sir Critic, good-day!"
78              And the barber kept on shaving.

3. Identify and explain the effects of parataxis in this passage.

### Malcolm's Katie: A Love Story (1884)
by Isabella Valency Crawford (excerpt)

399  O, Love builds on the azure sea,
400    And Love builds on the golden sand;
401  And Love builds on the rose-wing'd cloud,
402    And sometimes Love builds on the land.

403  O, if Love build on sparkling sea—
404    And if Love build on golden strand—
405  And if Love build on rosy cloud—
406    To Love these are the solid land.

407  O, Love will build his lily walls,
408    And Love his pearly roof will rear,—
409  On cloud or land, or mist or sea—
410    Love's solid land is everywhere!

4. Identify and explain the effects of polyptoton in this passage.

### Astrophel and Stella Sonnet I (1580–1582)
by Sir Philip Sidney (excerpt)

1  Loving in truth, and fain in verse my love to show,
2  That she, dear she, might take some pleasure of my pain,–
3  Pleasure might cause her read, reading might make her know,
4  Knowledge might pity win, and pity grace obtain,–
5  I sought fit words to paint the blackest face of woe;
6  Studying inventions fine her wits to entertain,
7  Oft turning others' leaves, to see if thence would flow
8  Some fresh and fruitful showers upon my sunburn'd brain.

(Answers are on page 166.)

# BRAIN TICKLERS
## Set # 26

1. Read the two poems below. Then identify each instance of the rhetorical devices you have learned in this chapter.

### Robin Hood (1818)
#### by John Keats
##### To a Friend

1 No! those days are gone away
2 And their hours are old and gray,
3 And their minutes buried all
4 Under the down-trodden pall
5 Of the leaves of many years:
6 Many times have winter's shears,
7 Frozen North, and chilling East,
8 Sounded tempests to the feast
9 Of the forest's whispering fleeces,
10 Since men knew nor rent nor leases.

11 No, the bugle sounds no more,
12 And the twanging bow no more;
13 Silent is the ivory shrill
14 Past the heath and up the hill;
15 There is no mid-forest laugh,
16 Where lone Echo gives the half
17 To some wight, amaz'd to hear
18 Jesting, deep in forest drear.

19 On the fairest time of June
20 You may go, with sun or moon,
21 Or the seven stars to light you,
22 Or the polar ray to right you;
23 But you never may behold
24 Little John, or Robin bold;
25 Never one, of all the clan,
26 Thrumming on an empty can
27 Some old hunting ditty, while
28 He doth his green way beguile
29 To fair hostess Merriment,
30 Down beside the pasture Trent;
31 For he left the merry tale
32 Messenger for spicy ale.

33 Gone, the merry morris din;
34 Gone, the song of Gamelyn;
35 Gone, the tough-belted outlaw
36 Idling in the "grenè shawe";
37 All are gone away and past!
38 And if Robin should be cast
39 Sudden from his turfed grave,
40 And if Marian should have
41 Once again her forest days,
42 She would weep, and he would craze:
43 He would swear, for all his oaks,
44 Fall'n beneath the dockyard strokes,
45 Have rotted on the briny seas;
46 She would weep that her wild bees
47 Sang not to her—strange! that honey
48 Can't be got without hard money!

49 So it is: yet let us sing,
50 Honour to the old bow-string!
51 Honour to the bugle-horn!
52 Honour to the woods unshorn!
53 Honour to the Lincoln green!
54 Honour to the archer keen!
55 Honour to tight little John,
56 And the horse he rode upon!
57 Honour to bold Robin Hood,
58 Sleeping in the underwood!
59 Honour to maid Marian,
60 And to all the Sherwood-clan!
61 Though their days have hurried by
62 Let us two a burden try.

## America the Beautiful (1893, revised in 1904 and 1911)
### by Katherine Lee Bates

1   O beautiful for spacious skies,
2       For amber waves of grain,
3   For purple mountain majesties
4       Above the fruited plain!
5   America! America!
6       God shed his grace on thee
7   And crown thy good with brotherhood
8       From sea to shining sea!

9   O beautiful for pilgrim feet,
10      Whose stern, impassioned stress
11  A thoroughfare for freedom beat
12      Across the wilderness!
13  America! America!
14      God mend thy every flaw,
15  Confirm thy soul in self-control,
16      Thy liberty in law!

17  O beautiful for heroes proved
18      In liberating strife,
19  Who more than self their country loved,
20      And mercy more than life!
21  America! America!
22      May God thy gold refine,
23  Till all success be nobleness
24      And every gain divine!

25  O beautiful for patriot dream
26      That sees beyond the years
27  Thine alabaster cities gleam
28      Undimmed by human tears!
29  America! America!
30      God shed his grace on thee
31  And crown thy good with brotherhood
32      From sea to shining sea!

2. Write a poem in which you use at least two rhetorical devices that you learned in this chapter and that you have never used before.

(Answers are on page 166.)

# BE SENSIBLE!: SENSORY DETAIL AND IMAGERY

All experience comes to us through our senses. We may later apply our minds and hearts to it, but it enters our consciousness through the senses. Details that specifically appeal to one or more senses are called **sensory details**. Extended description with attention to sensory detail is called **imagery**.

Poetry immediately engages two of our senses—seeing and hearing—when we read it, but this is only the first level at which we experience poetry. If we imagine as we read, if we allow the experiences named within the poem—the sights, sounds, tastes, smells, and textures, as well as the emotional and intellectual impact of the topic or plot—to move us, we create a deep layer of sensory experience that helps us to understand the poem's meaning. When we write, we use sensory detail and images to give the reader access to our world, allowing another person to share in our imagination and our journey.

Often, sight is the predominant sense to which the poet's imagery appeals. For example, in this excerpt from a poem, the poet tries to evoke the world as a new baby perceives it.

### Portrait of a Baby (before 1918)
by Stephen Vincent Benét (excerpt)

1 He lay within a warm, soft world
2 Of motion. Colors bloomed and fled,
3 Maroon and turquoise, saffron, red,
4 Wave upon wave that broke and whirled
5 To vanish in the grey-green gloom,
6 Perspectiveless and shadowy.
7 A bulging world that had no walls,
8 A flowing world, most like the sea,
9 Compassing all infinity
10 Within a shapeless, ebbing room,
11 An endless tide that swells and falls . . .
12 He slept and woke and slept again.

The next three poems evoke the wind and the sea, appealing to sound as well as sight.

### My Soul Is Awakened (mid 1800s)
by Anne Brontë

1 My soul is awakened, my spirit is soaring,
2 And carried aloft on the wings of the breeze;
3 For, above, and around me, the wild wind is roaring,
4 Arousing to rapture the earth and the seas.

5 The long withered grass in the sunshine is glancing,
6 The bare trees are tossing their branches on high;
7 The dead leaves beneath them are merrily dancing,
8 The white clouds are scudding across the blue sky.

9 I wish I could see how the ocean is lashing
10 The foam of its billows to whirlwinds of spray,
11 I wish I could see how its proud waves are dashing
12 And hear the wild roar of their thunder today!

### The Sun Has Set (mid 1800s)
by Emily Brontë

1  The sun has set, and the long grass now
2      Waves dreamily in the evening wind;
3  And the wild bird has flown from that old gray stone
4      In some warm nook a couch to find.

5  In all the lonely landscape round
6      I see no light and hear no sound,
7  Except the wind that far away
8      Come sighing o'er the healthy sea.

### Adventure (early 1900s)
by Adelaide Crapsey

1  Sun and wind and beat of sea,
2  Great lands stretching endlessly . . .
3  Where be bonds to bind the free?
4  All the world was made for me!

## BRAIN TICKLERS
### Set # 27

1. Read the poems and answer the questions that follow.

### A Birthday (1857)
by Christina Rossetti

1   My heart is like a singing bird
2       Whose nest is in a water'd shoot;
3   My heart is like an apple-tree
4       Whose boughs are bent with thickset fruit;
5   My heart is like a rainbow shell
6       That paddles in a halcyon sea;
7   My heart is gladder than all these
8       Because my love is come to me.

9   Raise me a dais of silk and down;
10      Hang it with vair and purple dyes;
11  Carve it in doves and pomegranates,
12      And peacocks with a hundred eyes;
13  Work it in gold and silver grapes,
14      In leaves and silver fleurs-de-lys;
15  Because the birthday of my life
16      Is come, my love is come to me.

a. Why do you think the speaker calls the event she describes a "birthday"?

b. How does Rossetti's use of anaphora and simile in the first eight lines and epistrophe in lines 8 and 16 work in this poem?

c. How does Rossetti use sensory details and imagery?

## Meeting at Night (1849)

by Robert Browning

### I

1 The grey sea and the long black land;
2 And the yellow half-moon large and low;
3 And the startled little waves that leap
4 In fiery ringlets from their sleep,
5 As I gain the cove with pushing prow,
6 And quench its speed i' the slushy sand.

### II

7 Then a mile of warm sea-scented beach;
8 Three fields to cross till a farm appears;
9 A tap at the pane, the quick sharp scratch
10 And blue spurt of a lighted match,
11 And a voice less loud, thro' its joys and fears,
12 Than the two hearts beating each to each!

d. What is the goal of the speaker's trip?

e. Describe the speaker's journey to reach his goal.

f. What senses are brought into play in the poem?

## The Negro Speaks of Rivers (1922)

by Langston Hughes

1 I've known rivers:
2 I've known rivers ancient as the world and older than the flow of human blood in human veins.
3 My soul has grown deep like the rivers.
4 I bathed in the Euphrates when dawns were young.
5 I built my hut near the Congo and it lulled me to sleep.
6 I looked upon the Nile and raised the pyramids above it.
7 I heard the singing of the Mississippi when Abe Lincoln went down to New Orleans, and I've seen its muddy bosom turn all golden in the sunset.
8 I've known rivers:
9 Ancient, dusky rivers.
10 My soul has grown deep like the rivers.

g. Who is the speaker in this poem?

h. Explain how the use of asyndeton and anaphora work in the poem.

i. To which senses do the sensory details appeal?

2. Reread "October" (page 130) and read the following poem. Both are about the end of summer, though they were written nearly a hundred years apart. Answer the questions.

## Eve Among the Perennials* (1999)
### by John Engels

1  These perennials,
2  unweeded, unthinned,
3  and left to go wild,

4  have won out this year,
5  have strangled everything
6  that shouldn't be here.

7  The earth is choked with growth!
8  Long ago I had foreseen
9  this bright day, this empty place.

10  Well, all to the good. Let the house plants
11  burst their pots, let them make it
12  or not. Let the garden grow

13  and seed and grow and seed
14  dry up, collapse under the fall
15  leaves, let the composts

16  commence their rich
17  fever, let the dead leaves
18  of the geraniums go

19  unpicked, let pansies seed,
20  let leaves and petals blow
21  into the neighbor's yard

22  and make colorful drifts
23  at the roots of his fences.
24  Nor will I prune the grape vine:

25  but let it tangle and hood the little
26  wild apple at the end of the porch, let it
27  climb as high as it likes, and stop

---

* This poem is from a sequence of poems about Adam and Eve after they left the Garden of Eden. In this poet's imagination, they now have a house and garden in Vermont.

28   where it likes. I've decided
29   the gardener's duty
30   is to wildness. I'm the only one

31   who knows how to follow the flagstones,
32   having placed them there
33   and for eight years,

34   watched them slowly
35   grown over by
36   the ravenous borders.

a. Both poems appeal primarily to the sense of sight. In what ways do the uses of sensory detail and imagery differ?

b. Compare the diction of the two poems. What do you find?

c. Read the first chapter of Genesis in any Bible. What light does it shed on your reading of *Eve Among the Perennials*?

d. How does Engels' use of asyndeton and polysyndeton contribute to the poem?

3. Write a poem that appeals to at least two senses and uses sensory detail to create an image. If a topic does not immediately come to you, consider one of the following:

a. Describe the most striking scene you've ever seen.

b. Highlight a crucial moment in history (famous or not).

c. Recall your first experience of a favorite work of visual art.

d. Retell an encounter with an animal of any kind (from a mosquito to a fossilized saber-toothed cat).

(Answers are on page 167.)

# LEVELS OF MEANING

## What cannot be said

People struggle with the inadequacy of language to express their experience. Our experience may be too wonderful, too painful, too fleeting to capture in words. Or, we may struggle to discover a way of saying something that will elicit the reaction we desire.

## Multiple examples

The speaker in this poem has a problem with finding language inadequate. Prufrock tries **multiple examples** to convey his meaning. (Be sure to check the allusion to Lazarus, a New Testament figure.)

### The Love Song of J. Alfred Prufrock (1915)
by T. S. Eliot (excerpt)

87    And would it have been worth it, after all,
88    After the cups, the marmalade, the tea,
89    Among the porcelain, among some talk of you and me,
90    Would it have been worth while,
91    To have bitten off the matter with a smile,
92    To have squeezed the universe into a ball
93    To roll it toward some overwhelming question,
94    To say: "I am Lazarus, come from the dead,
95    Come back to tell you all, I shall tell you all"—
96    If one, settling a pillow by her head,
97      Should say: "That is not what I meant at all.
98      That is not it, at all."

99      And would it have been worth it, after all,
100   Would it have been worth while,
101   After the sunsets and the dooryards and the sprinkled streets,
102   After the novels, after the teacups, after the skirts that trail along the floor—
103   And this, and so much more?—
104   It is impossible to say just what I mean!
105   But as if a magic lantern threw the nerves in patterns on a screen:
106   Would it have been worth while
107   If one, settling a pillow or throwing off a shawl,
108   And turning toward the window, should say:
109     "That is not it at all,
110     That is not what I meant, at all."

Prufrock asks five times (lines 87, 90, 99, 100, and 106) "would it have been worth" it for him to make the effort to explain himself, each time imagining that his communication fails and that he is misunderstood. He fears that what he wants to say cannot ever be adequately expressed. By giving several examples instead of only one, he increases our understanding of his dilemma and his frustration.

## Ellipsis

The technique of leaving out words is a rhetorical figure called **ellipsis**. There are two main forms: 1. Using ellipsis marks (. . .), dashes (—), or just empty space shows the pauses and gaps we hear when someone cannot get their words out smoothly. When material is left out like this, it remains unknown to the reader, although enough context clues may make inference possible. 2. *Ellipsis* also names the technique of omitting something after establishing a grammatical pattern so that the reader can easily infer the missing material. Often, the missing words are replaced by a comma: I have known Ann for seven years, Tanya for four; Lynn, one. We don't need to repeat "have known . . . for . . . years" three times: The first clause gives the reader the pattern. This kind of ellipsis assumes understanding between writer and reader.

In this poem, the poet shows the speaker stumbling in his speech, failing to find the words, and finally changing the subject using ellipsis.

### Then and Now (c. 1200 C.E.)
by Xin Qi-Ji, translated by Runxia Ye (1998)

1  When I was young,
2  I didn't know the taste of grief,
3  I loved to climb the storied tower;
4  I used to climb the storied tower,
5  To make new rhymes and in my songs
6  I pretended to feel the pain too.

7  Now that I know all the tastes of sorrow,
8  I must say, . . . but no . . . ;
9  I could say, . . . but no . . . ,
10  Feeling the chill, I shall just say:
11  "Oh, what a fine, cold autumn day!"

## BRAIN TICKLERS
### Set # 28

Look back at the poem "Then and Now."
How has the speaker changed from "then" to
"now"?

(Answers are on page 170.)

## Analogy

**Analogy** is a rhetorical figure, but it is also a structural
technique used to shape entire poems. Whereas simile
compares two dissimilar things for effect, analogy compares
two things that have multiple similarities. Similes are usually a
brief figure that may appeal to the senses; analogies explain at
length, and in this they resemble extended metaphor. Analogy
can help us move from the known to the unknown, from what
can be stated to what cannot.

### **Sympathy** (1899)
#### by Paul Laurence Dunbar

1   I know what the caged bird feels, alas!
2       When the sun is bright on the upland slopes;
3   When the wind stirs soft through the springing grass,
4   And the river flows like a stream of glass;
5       When the first bird sings and the first bud opes,*
6   And the faint perfume from its chalice steals—
7   I know what the caged bird feels!

---

\* opens.

8    I know why the caged bird beats his wing

9    Till its blood is red on the cruel bars;

10    For he must fly back to his perch and cling

11    When he fain would be on the bough a-swing;

12    And a pain still throbs in the old, old scars

13    And they pulse again with a keener sting—

14    I know why he beats his wing!

15    I know why the caged bird sings, ah me,

16    When his wing is bruised and his bosom sore,—

17    When he beats his bars and he would be free;

18    It is not a carol of joy or glee,

19    But a prayer that he sends from his heart's deep core,

20    But a plea, that upward to Heaven he flings—

21    I know why the caged bird sings!

The speaker begins by telling us that he has a special understanding of the caged bird. In the first seven lines, he describes the bird's longing for freedom and enjoyment of natural beauty, beginning and ending by saying that he understands this longing. In the next seven lines, he describes the bird's futile attempts to escape, which he understands. And in the final seven lines, he describes the bird's choice to sing in its imprisonment, which he also understands.

Who is the speaker? We know his situation only by analogy. From the poem alone, we might gather that he was a prisoner, trying to share with us an understanding of the **paradox** of singing in captivity. A paradox is a rhetorical device in which what is proposed seems to contradict itself. If we allow ourselves to extend the analogy, we might also gather that, like the caged bird, the speaker has done nothing to deserve his imprisonment but is a captive because of his owner's whim. If we know that Dunbar was the son of escaped slaves, we might conclude that the speaker is a slave, rather than a prisoner in jail, which fits very well with the rest of the poem.

# BRAIN TICKLERS
## Set # 29

Read these poems in which the poet uses analogy. Then answer the questions.

### A Noiseless Patient Spider (1868)
#### by Walt Whitman

1 A noiseless patient spider,
2 I mark'd where on a little promontory it stood isolated,
3 Mark'd how to explore the vacant vast surrounding,
4 It launch'd forth filament, filament, filament, out of itself,
5 Ever unreeling them, ever tirelessly speeding them.

6 And you O my soul where you stand,
7 Surrounded, detached, in measureless oceans of space,
8 Ceaselessly musing, venturing, throwing, seeking the spheres to connect them,
9 Till the bridge you will need be form'd, till the ductile anchor hold,
10 Till the gossamer thread you fling catch somewhere, O my soul.

1. What are the two things being compared?
2. How are they similar?
3. How does analogy help Whitman's communication?

### Hen and Egg (1996)
#### by Vladimir Levchev,
#### translated by Vladimir Levchev and Henry Taylor (1999)

1 The hen has hatched
2 goose-eggs.
3 She leads her chicks
4 down by the river.
5 Suddenly they jump in
6 and they swim.
7 The hen flutters and clucks
8 in terror by the river.
9 At night you walk on water,

10 or sink in a bog,
11 or jump from the 15th floor
12 sweating, terrified by your own self.
13 What you are in your dream
14 is not yours.
15 It jumps in the river and swims away
16 talking in an unknown language.

4. What elements of the poem show you that analogy is being used?
5. What is being compared and what are the similarities?

## A Mirror (1937)
by Atanas Dalchev, translated by Vladimir Levchev (1998)

1 You've been expecting it for many years,
2 but the miracle is here every hour.
3 Look at the mover passing by your house
4 with a heavy mirror!
5 As he walks, the streets, the buildings,
6 and the fences zoom,
7 people come up from the shining bottom,
8 cars fly out in rage like birds from a cage.
9 Town squares and trees begin to sway,
10 roofs and balconies fall down,
11 blue skies flash . . .
12 You don't need to wonder why the mover
13 stoops and makes so slowly every step:
14 He is holding in his human hands
15 a new and amazing world.

6. How is looking into the mirror moving down the street like a miracle?
7. This poem is written in second person, speaking of *you* and your actions. Your action just now has been reading this poem. So suppose, for a moment, that there is another level of analogy going on here. In what ways is reading a poem like watching a mirror moving down the street? How is it like a miracle?

(Answers are on page 170.)

149

## Irony

With some rhetorical devices under our belts, we can gain deeper understanding of irony. Sometimes writers use irony to spark interest, sometimes to create surprise. However it is used, irony always helps writers share with their readers an understanding that goes beyond the words on the page. Irony is classified differently by different theorists. For our purposes, we will consider three types: verbal irony, dramatic irony, and situational irony.

### Verbal irony

**Verbal irony** occurs when what is said is not what is meant. There are at least two types of verbal irony. First, there are situations in which the speaker wants the listener to understand the real import of the message. In other situations, the speaker uses a double meaning and, though technically not lying, counts on being misunderstood. This second kind of verbal irony is called **equivocation**.

Verbal irony, hyperbole, and paraprosdokian are often coupled: The surprise ending can reveal the irony. This was true of Parker's poem *Comment*, which we analyzed in our examination of tone (page 56).

1   Oh, life is a glorious cycle of song,
2   A medley of extemporanea;
3   And love is a thing that can never go wrong;
4   And I am Marie of Roumania.

The first three lines are hyperbole. The paraprosdokian in line 4 reveals that lines 1–3 are ironic.

# BRAIN TICKLERS
### Set # 30

Read another poem by Dorothy Parker.
Explain the use of verbal irony and
paraprosdokian in the poem.

### Finis (1923)
by Dorothy Parker

1  Now it's over, and now it's done;
2      Why does everything look the same?
3  Just as bright, the unheeding sun,—
4      Can't it see that the parting came?
5  People hurry and work and swear,
6      Laugh and grumble and die and wed,
7  Ponder what they will eat and wear,—
8      Don't they know that our love is dead?

9  Just as busy, the crowded street;
10     Cars and wagons go rolling on,
11  Children chuckle, and lovers meet,—
12     Don't they know that our love is gone?
13  No one pauses to pay a tear;
14     None walks slow, for the love that's through,—
15  I might mention, my recent dear,
16     I've reverted to normal, too.

(Answers are on page 171.)

### Dramatic irony

In **dramatic irony**, the poet and reader (and sometimes some
characters) share an understanding that one or more characters
do not. In "Ozymandias," Shelley, the speaker, the traveler, and
the reader all know that Ozymandias's expectation to influence
history and be remembered forever actually came to little: his
empire is gone; his enemies (who might have recollected his
greatness) have disappeared off the face of the earth; even his
statue is broken and will soon be buried in the desert sands.

# BRAIN TICKLERS
## Set # 31

Read this poem. Then answer the questions.

### The Children and Sir Nameless (1922)
by Thomas Hardy

1 Sir Nameless, once of Athelhall, declared:
2 "These wretched children romping in my park
3 Trample the herbage till the soil is bared,
4 And yap and yell from early morn till dark!
5 Go keep them harnessed to their set routines:
6 Thank God I've none to hasten my decay;
7 For green remembrance there are better means
8 Than offspring, who but wish their sires away."

9 Sir Nameless of that mansion said anon:
10 "To be perpetuate for my mightiness
11 Sculpture must image me when I am gone."
12 —He forthwith summoned carvers there express
13 To shape a figure stretching seven-odd feet
14 (For he was tall) in alabaster stone,
15 With shield, and crest, and casque, and sword complete:
16 When done a statelier work was never known.

17 Three hundred years hied; Church-restorers came,
18 And, no one of his lineage being traced,
19 They thought an effigy so large in frame
20 Best fitted for the floor. There it was placed,
21 Under the seats for schoolchildren. And they
22 Kicked out his name, and hobnailed off his nose;
23 And, as they yawn through sermon-time, they say,
24 "Who was this old stone man beneath our toes?"

1. Explain the use of dramatic irony in the poem. How does the title work in communicating what Hardy is doing?
2. How does the use of polysyndeton in line 15 help to characterize Sir Nameless?
3. Compare and contrast this poem's meaning and approach with that of "Ozymandias."

(Answers are on page 172.)

### Situational irony

With **situational irony**, the poet plays with expectations—those of the reader, of the characters, or both—by building a strong expectation of a specific occurrence or result that never occurs.

Read this poem, and see what you can make of it. Try to discover the meaning of the allusion used in line 11.

### My prime of youth is but a frost of cares (1586)
#### by Chidiock Tichborne

1  My prime of youth is but a frost of cares,
2  My feast of joy is but a dish of pain,
3  My crop of corn is but a field of tares,
4  And all my good is but vain hope of gain.
5  The day is gone and yet I saw no sun,
6  And now I live, and now my life is done.

7  The spring is past, and yet it hath not sprung,
8  The fruit is dead, and yet the leaves are green,
9  My youth is gone, and yet I am but young,
10  I saw the world, and yet I was not seen,
11  My thread is cut, and yet it was not spun,
12  And now I live, and now my life is done.

13  I sought my death and found it in my womb,
14  I lookt for life and saw it was a shade,
15  I trode the earth and knew it was my tomb,
16  And now I die, and now I am but made.
17  The glass is full, and now the glass is run,
18  And now I live, and now my life is done.

The poem is a series of propositions that all seem to be self-contradictory: How can joy be pain, corn be weeds, and so on? These statements are examples of the rhetorical figure **paradox**. Sometimes paradox can be used to create humor, but here it is ironic. We do not expect joy to be painful; we do not expect to plant corn and reap weeds. How can this be understood?

We can begin to find the answer in the allusion in Line 11. By mentioning "my thread" that is cut, Tichborne is evoking the three Fates from Greek mythology who are pictured as spinners: Clotho spins the thread of life, Lachesis measures out the thread for each individual, arid Atropos severs the thread at the time appointed for death. Line 11 can then be interpreted: I am going to die while I am still young. Line 16 echoes this, as does the refrain, and this understanding floods the rest of the poem with meaning. A person who knows that his or her life will be cut short in youth finds all expectations turned on their heads. In fact, Tichborne was involved in a plot to murder Queen Elizabeth I of England. He was caught, found guilty, and condemned to death. This poem was written within a few days of his execution at the age of twenty-six or twenty-seven. Do you think it likely that he is the speaker?

# BRAIN TICKLERS
## Set # 32

Read this poem aloud and explain the situational irony.

### The Golf Links (c. 1900)
by Sarah Norcliffe Cleghorn

1   The golf links lie so near the mill
2       That almost every day
3   The laboring children can look out
4       And see the men at play.

(Answers are on page 172).

## Symbolism

**Symbolism** is a technique in which one item is used to represent another. Symbols, like allusions, allow the poet to call a whole array of thoughts to a reader's mind with a brief reference. A symbol may have a long tradition and be well accepted in a culture or may be unique to the individual poet. Following are some examples of cultural symbols.

| | |
|---|---|
| for a country | eagle/Statue of Liberty for USA |
| for a political party | donkey for Democrats; elephant for Republicans |
| for a religion | cross for Christianity; Star of David for Judaism |
| for character trait | peacock for pride; owl for wisdom |
| for an emotion | flowers (rose for love); colors (white for purity) |
| for birthdates | zodiac symbols (Aries); birthstones (Topaz) |

There are also specifically literary symbols that have been used by many authors:

- A *journey underground* and return to earth for an internal struggle or trip into the unconscious, death and rebirth of the individual, or a spiritual experience;
- *forests* for confusion;
- *ugliness* for evil; and
- *beauty* for goodness.

  As was pointed out earlier, using sleep to represent death is a well-known literary convention. Characters, too, may be symbolic—when they are, they often have names that indicate their roles—and works that use this technique are called **allegories**.

Read this Australian poem. What do you think the pelican's nest symbolizes?

## Where the Pelican Builds (1881)

### by Mary Hannay Foott

1 The horses were ready, the rails were down,
2     But the riders lingered still,—
3         One had a parting word to say,
4     And one had his pipe to fill.
5 Then they mounted, one with a granted prayer,
6     And one with a grief unguessed.
7         "We are going" they said, as they rode away—
8     "Where the pelican builds her nest!"

9 They had told us of pastures wide and green,
10     To be sought past the sunset's glow;
11         Of rifts in the ranges by opal lit,
12     And gold 'neath the river's flow.
13 And thirst and hunger were banished words
14     When they spoke of that unknown West;
15         No drought they dreaded, no flood they feared,
16 Where the pelican builds her nest!

17 The creek at the ford was but fetlock deep
18     When we watched them crossing there;
19         The rains have replenished it thrice since then
20     And thrice has the rock lain bare.
21 But the waters of Hope have flowed and fled,
22     And never from blue hill's breast
23         Come back—by the sun and the sands devoured—
24     Where the pelican builds her nest!

What can we make of this? In lines 1–8, two riders leave on a quest, heading to a location known only as "Where the pelican builds her nest." Their description of it in lines 9–16 sounds too good to be true. The speakers have waited for the riders' return for three years, but they have never returned and are now presumed dead (line 23). Thus "Where the pelican builds her nest" is a symbol of paradise-on-earth, like Shangri-la; it is a utopia that doesn't exist. This interpretation is confirmed by a note from the poet. The note says that the expression comes from the bushmen of Western Queensland. As far as she knows, the pelican's nest "is seldom, if ever found." By using symbols, Foott expands the world of the poem, from the story of an ill-fated trip taken by two particular men in Australia to a recounting of the universal story of the explorer seeking the perfect haven.

## BRAIN TICKLERS
### Set # 33

1. Read the following poems. Then answer the questions.

**So Much Depends** (1923)
by William Carlos Williams

1 so much depends
2 upon

3 a red wheel
4 barrow

5 glazed with rain
6 water

7 beside the white
8 chickens

a. Williams does not use standard symbols, so all we have is the poem and our personal experience and background knowledge with which to make meaning.

What is the setting? What role does each item mentioned in the poem play in the setting?

b. What "depends upon" the things Williams mentions?

c. Why do you think Williams put the poem on the page the way he did? Think of an answer first. Then try this experiment: Copy the first two lines of the poem on a separate piece of paper, just as it is printed here but leave out the line numbers. Draw a curved line outlining the group of two lines. Then draw a small circle centered under the even-numbered line. What do you see?

### The Road Not Taken (1916)
#### by Robert Frost

1 Two roads diverged in a yellow wood,
2 And sorry I could not travel both
3 And be one traveler, long I stood
4 And looked down one as far as I could
5 To where it bent in the undergrowth;

6 Then took the other, as just as fair,
7 And having perhaps the better claim,
8 Because it was grassy and wanted wear;
9 Though as for that the passing there
10 Had worn them really about the same,

11 And both that morning equally lay
12 In leaves no step had trodden black.
13 Oh, I kept the first for another day!
14 Yet knowing how way leads on to way,
15 I doubted if I should ever come back.

16 I shall be telling this with a sigh
17 Somewhere ages and ages hence:
18 Two roads diverged in a wood, and I—
19 I took the one less traveled by,
20 And that has made all the difference.

d. What differences are there between the two roads?

e. What cues the reader that this poem is about something more than a particular day's excursion in the woods?

f. Does the speaker regret his choice? Would he choose differently if he had to do it over?

g. Is this poem ironic? Explain why you think as you do.

2. Write a poem in which you use at least one of these techniques—examples, ellipsis, analogy, irony, paradox, and/or symbolism—to express something that is difficult to express or explain. See page 158 for some topic ideas. What clues and hints are you providing to help your reader reach a deeper level of meaning than your words convey on the surface?

Here are some topic ideas:
a. A season of the year
b. The oldest or youngest person you know
c. An argument
d. The most beautiful thing you've ever seen in your life

(Answers are on page 173.)

# BRAIN TICKLERS—THE ANSWERS

## Set # 14, page 90

**Possible responses:**

1. The phrases *host of golden daffodils* and *bliss of solitude* stood out for me.

2. I noticed that he used some synonyms (*crowd/host/ company; shine/twinkle/sparkling; gay/jocund*).

3. An example of simile is the comparison "lonely as a cloud"; an example of personification is "Tossing their heads in sprightly dance."

4. The appeal is almost entirely to the sense of sight.

5. The experience is powerful when we have it, but it gains even more power as it lives in our recollection.

## Set # 15, page 96

**Possible responses:**

1. I notice the repetition of the first two words of line 1 in lines 2 and 3.

2. The poem has some visual/sound jokes. When you say the words *was he*, it sounds just the same as when you say the word *Wuzzy*. *Bare* and *bear* are homophones. I never heard

the last line before. The poem as I knew it ended with the third line, which sounds complete because of the rhyme, even though it's short. There's also humor in a bear called Fuzzy being hairless, and the last line reemphasizes that part of the joke.

## Set # 16, page 98

**Possible responses:**

1. I didn't understand the first poem until I paraphrased the first sentence: "Love makes the swift person and the slow person equal." The second poem engaged my imagination. I could picture the darkening that makes it impossible to distinguish things that are easily separated in the light. The visual similarity of *on* and *one* also caught my attention. I wondered if lines 6–8 refer to a particular person.

2. a. scent, stench, odor, furry, striped, persuasion, plea
   b. unexpected, neglected, affected, telescope, hope, gift, present

   > Dear Aunt Mabel and Uncle Bob,
   > I had actually given up hope
   > of ever owning a telescope.
   > Your present was completely unexpected.
   > When I saw what it was, I was very affected.
   > I would be rude if I neglected to say,
   > "THANK YOU SO MUCH FOR THE GIFT!!!!!!!"
   >
   > Love,
   > Patty

   c. freedom, honor, growing, values, becoming, mature, integrity
   d. shepherd's pie, potatoes, cheese, please, slice, knife, serve
   e. Mars, stars, threat, beset, alphabet, etiquette, silhouette

## Set # 17, page 103

The number of pronunciations will vary, and your pronunciations may or may not match the dictionary's first choice. Possible responses for number of pronunciations (from *American Heritage Dictionary*):

1. February 2
2. jewelry 1 (*Merriam-Webster's* has 3)
3. Wednesday 2
4. garage 4
5. often 2
6. dog 2
7. coyote 2
8. rodeo 2
9. taut 1
10. tot 1

## Set # 18, page 104

LIST 1:

*that*, subordinating conjunction; demonstrative pronoun; relative pronoun
*instead*, adverb
*which*, relative pronoun; interrogative pronoun
*but*, coordinating conjunction
*sometimes*, adverb
*when*, subordinating conjunction; adverb; noun
*him*, pronoun
*rather*, adverb
*over*, preposition; adverb; adjective

LIST 2:

*Moon*, proper noun
*peacock*, common noun
*Tibet*, proper noun
*music*, common noun
*firelight*, common noun
*temple*, common noun
*danced*, past tense verb
*joy*, abstract noun

**Possible conclusion:** Nouns and verbs do more to create pictures in the mind than words like adverbs, prepositions, conjunctions, and pronouns, the purpose of which is to replace nouns and to connect sentence elements.

2. Sentence 1. simple, interrogative
   Sentence 2. complex (*that* introducing subordinate clause is omitted), declarative
   Sentence 3. simple, interrogative (conjunctions missing between objects of the verb *saw*)
   Sentence 4. simple, interrogative
   Sentence 5. complex, declarative
   Sentence 6. simple, declarative
   Sentence 7. compound, declarative
   Sentence 8. compound-complex, exclamatory
   Sentence 9. complex, declarative
   Sentence 10. simple, declarative
   Sentence 11. compound, interrogative (with verb *have been* omitted from second independent clause)
   Sentence 12. simple, declarative
   Sentence 13. simple, declarative
   Sentence 14. compound, declarative

3. **Possible response:**

*A Poet's Suffering*

*You think that YOU had a bad day?*
*I'll bet it was nothing to mine.*
*My adverbs just sulked in a corner.*
*Those pronouns did nothing but whine.*

*It wasn't quite ten in the morning*
*When th' insufferable nouns went on strike;*
*The adjectives left and played hooky;*
*And verbs always do what they like.*

*But at last I conjunctioned them all,*
*A picture of utter defiance.*
*Then I sent in a huge interjection —*
*Oh! he bullied them into compliance.*

*For today I have finished my writing,*
*But I don't know if I'll write again.*
*For now that the words are in order,*
*I've run out of ink in my pen*

[original]

Set # 19, page 112

1. **Possible responses:**
   **The Football Match**
   The excerpt from "The Football Match" is a jumble of
   different dictions, possibly chosen by the poet to represent
   both the lofty and the unpretentious ancestry of the sport
   of football (mixing the traditions of heroic battle and of the
   fist fight). Words like *kaleidoscopic, panorama,*
   *protuberant, thews, insertion, élan, Homeric, ferocity,* and
   *abraded* are rather formal, but words like *tussling, tugging,*
   *thumping, wormlike, wallowing, rowdyism,* and *muddy*
   are informal. *Jaculatory* is now rare, but *wriggleness*
   appears to be a neologism. The first 6 lines are
   characterized by longish words, whereas line 7 in particular
   has mostly one-syllable words. The phrase *cowboy Homeric*
   *ferocity* is typical of the diction as a whole—joining the
   new (Canadian cowboys) with the old (a Greek epic poet),
   the formal with the informal, to create an image of the
   football players as heirs of all traditions of manly work and
   combat.

   **The Land of Nod**
   The diction of "The Land of Nod" is consistently the
   simple, straightforward speech of a child, but it is rather
   formal for a child, with neither contractions nor slang. The
   words are ordinary: no unusual origin, rare or obsolete
   words, or neologisms. Most are only one syllable; only
   three (*mountain-side, remember,* and *curious*) have three
   syllables, but *frightening* is probably pronounced as two to
   fit the meter. The multisyllabic words call attention to the
   parts of the poem where they are found: *mountain-sides of*
   *dreams* and *curious music* seem to be the most important
   phrases in the poem. Although the words are simple, and
   there is little detail to support them, both phrases carry
   connotations of the wondrous, lovely, mysterious quality
   of our dreamlife.

   **The Rubáiyát of Omar Khayyám**
   This verse from "The Rubáiyát" is about the transformation
   of wilderness from barren sterility to a paradise by
   means of a few simple things. The words are almost all

one-syllable, except for the two three-syllable words that show the contrast: *wilderness* and *paradise*. *Enow*, which is archaic now, is a variation of *enough*, and was not uncommon when Fitzgerald wrote. The capitalization of the words seems to emphasize their connotations by lending them unusual importance and encouraging the reader to make the most of each.

2. **Possible response:** *Crannied*

### The Berry Patch

Looking up from underneath finds berries others missed.
Not because they were not looking. Only that they
looked the way they always look and didn't try new
ways of looking: hooked and nooked and cornered, crannied
vision. Looking looks that breach bold thorns and sneak and
peek beneath green, capelike leaves can find what's hidden
from straight stares.

[original]

## Set # 20, page 116

**Possible responses:**

1. John Milton used anaphora here in line 17 to line 18 to further explain the idea in line 17 that Samson can only find partial ease.

2. Anaphora is used at the beginning of lines 1, 5, 9, and 13 in the poem, but the more it is repeated, the less I believe it.

3. The poem does not have a set rhyme scheme, so the repeated sound of *home* in lines 117 and 118 is both notable, and works with the use of *home* in lines 116 and 122 to really draw the reader's attention to the word.

## Set # 21, page 119

1. In this excerpt from T. S. Eliot's poem, the speaker questions how he might begin to reveal himself and offers a tentative proposal, employing aporia in lines 68 and 69.

2. In this sentence, Homer uses apostrophe in invoking the muse to help him tell the story of Odysseus.

3. This is a humorous poem, and the humor is mainly from punning use of the names of the various fish, but the title itself is also a pun involving *see* and *sea*. Other puns appear in lines 2, 3, 4–5, 6, 7, 8, 9, 10, 12, 13, 14, 15, 16, 17, and 18.

## Set # 22, page 122

**Possible responses:**

1. Maya Angelou uses asyndeton in lines 63–66 of her inaugural poem for former president Clinton, to indicate that the nationalities listed are representative of the many, many nations from which immigrants came to America.

2. Shakespeare uses polysyndeton in lines 14–17 to emphasize the sheer number and unappetizing nature of the ingredients the weird sisters are adding to their brew.

3. In line 165 of "Lycidas," Milton uses epanalepsis to express a desire to console.

## Set # 23, page 125

**Possible responses:**

1. Hillaire Belloc uses epithets for the frog in lines 3–6 to create humor.

2. Tennyson uses epizeuxis in the speaker's apostrophe to the sea at the beginning and end of this poem (lines 1 and 13,

respectively). The repetition adds to the emotion we feel in the speaker's cry, and may suggest that in addition to the waves breaking on the rocks, his heart is breaking.

3. Marvell's speaker emphasizes, in lines 13–14, his desire to admire his lady by telling how he would woo her if time were infinite, employing hyperbole.

## Set # 24, page 128

**Possible responses:**

1. Burns's speaker evokes the depth of his love with several similes in lines 1–2 and 3–4. Burns wrote in the Scottish dialect (we saw an example on page 101), and that is the reason for the unusual spelling of some words, like *love*, *melody*, etc. I also noticed the use of hyperbole in lines 8–10, 12, and 16, as well as the use of anaphora and epistrophe.

2. Macbeth, the main character in the play, uses three metaphors to convey how terrible life has become for him (Life's but a walking shadow, line 1; a poor player, lines 1–2; and a tale told by an idiot, lines 26–27). The comparison of life and an actor is personification.

3. The speaker in Frost's poem creates a character foil (a character who serves as a contrast) for himself by acting as if his horse had views contrary to his own in lines 5–8 and 9–10.

4. Dunbar combines extended metaphor and personification throughout the entire poem to characterize October. I noticed that he uses asyndeton in line 21 and anaphora in lines 11 and 12.

## Set # 25, page 133

**Possible responses:**

1. In this excerpt, *earth* is substituted for *people*, creating metonymy. The King James Version on page 54 has *land*. In both cases, the metonymy results in personification.

2. That the owl is alive and was alive, as indicated by line 70 and following, was a surprise both to the young man and to me, and therefore an example of paraprosdokian.

3. This apostrophe to Love, which is personified, has repeated independent clauses in lines 399 to 400 and 407–408, creating parataxis. I noticed the use of anaphora as well.

4. In lines 2–4, Sidney mixes polyptoton with epanalepsis to create a chain, jumping from *love* to *pleasure* to *read/ reading* to *know/knowledge* to *pity*.

## Set # 26, page 137

1. The first example of each type of figure is noted:

**Robin Hood**

| line 2 | personification | line 7 | epithets |
|---|---|---|---|
| lines 2–3 | anaphora | lines 11–12 | epistrophe |
| lines 5–6 | epanalepsis | lines 33–36 | asyndeton |

**America the Beautiful**

| lines 1–3 | asyndeton | line 7 | personification |
|---|---|---|---|
| lines 1–4 | epithets | line 8 | epanalepsis |
| lines 1–4 | apostrophe | lines 1 and 9 | anaphora |
| line 5 | epizeuxis | lines 25–28 | hyperbole |

2. **Possible response:**

(metaphor, line 2; anadiplosis, lines 1–2; epanalepsis, line 10)

### Window Washing (2010)
#### by India Douglas

Every Sunday, I take time out of my hectic week to wash my windows.
Windows are the one pair of eyes people can't escape from.
They know all your secrets, and they see all your turmoil.
If you clean them well, windows can shine the sunlight on your face.
Windows let you see into the movie of life.
Rain and snow are like a moving piece of art.

Every day feels like anticipation of what the windows will show next.
My windows and I watch people in their natural state.
Every Sunday, the more I scrub, the more I can see into the world's soul.
I wash and I wash, but my windows are never clean enough
To let me see into the souls of my peers.

## Set # 27, page 140

**Possible responses:**
1. a. The appearance (or discovery) of her love has begun a whole new era in her life, and it is as if she is born anew.
   b. The three comparisons and summary in lines 1–8 describing the speaker's heart reveal that her feelings are beyond the description of the most profound feelings of fulfillment that she can imagine. The use of epistrophe also emphasizes the speaker's sense of fulfillment and completion with the arrival of her love.
   c. Sensory details appealing to the senses of hearing and sight are used in the first eight lines in similes in a vain attempt to describe how the speaker's heart feels. In the second eight lines, the sensory details are used to create an image of the glorious and rich decorations that would befit the celebration of the coming of her love.
   d. He is going home or to the home of the important woman in his life.
   e. He comes toward land from the open sea, into a cove, and runs his boat onto the sand. Then he crosses a mile of beach and three fields to reach the farmhouse that is the goal of his journey.

    f.  Lines 1–10 appeal to sight. Line 6 appeals to touch. Line 7 appeals to smell. Lines 3 and 9–12 appeal to hearing.

    g.  Hughes' speaker seems to be an embodiment of the Negro race throughout history.

    h.  The repetition of the observations of the speaker beginning with *I* or *I've* and the series without conjunctions both emphasize the long and deep experience of the ancient speaker.

    i.  The details appeal to sight and hearing.

2. a.  Dunbar's extended metaphor and sensory detail (with personification of October, the Sun, Nature, and Frost) and many specific nouns and adjectives build an image of carefree and generous bounty, joyous living that is quenched neither by theft nor by aging and the prospect of death. Engels, in lines 1–9, builds up an image by description that is far more open-ended than Dunbar's, and invites the reader to build up an idea primarily from adjectives and verbs: *unweeded, unthinned, wild, strangled, choked.* With line 10, he begins to fill in the picture, but with general statements about what the speaker will allow to happen in the future. Lines 22–28 refer to more specific outcomes from the speaker's purposeful neglect of the garden. Lines 30–36 create a negative image in that they focus on the loss of the ability to see a particular feature of the garden.

    b.  Dunbar's diction is somewhat elegant, as fits his subject: *bounty, coffers, lavishness, decks, jewels, princely fortunes*—but it is also grounded by words that name simple fundamental things: *months, fields, orchards, hours, sky, breezes, woodland, dew, Nature, Sun, Frost.* Engels uses a notable number of negative words beginning with the prefix *un-* and other words related to the concept of wildness and encroaching and choking. He relies heavily on verbs, as already mentioned. Even when specific nouns (*house plants, garden, composts, dead leaves of the geraniums, pansies, grape vine*) are mentioned, the emphasis is on the verbs that follow them. The language is very plain, with many simple, fundamental one-syllable words emphasizing the fundamental struggle between the powers of order and chaos, and the speaker's refusal to intervene.

c. In the mythology of Genesis, Adam and Eve were given the care of the earth and all living things, including the plants, as part of the ordering of creation. Eve is refusing to be a gardener, recalling that disobedience is what lost the first Garden. It seems that she will lose this garden, too—though in a different way.

d. The use of asyndeton contributes to the sense of disorder, of chaos taking over and nature taking off without the arrangement and intervention of a person. The use of polysyndeton emphasizes Eve's determination to abandon the garden forever: "Let the garden grow and seed and grow and seed" suggests cycle after cycle of neglect, year after year of uncontrolled growth.

3. **Possible response:** Appeals to sight, sound, smell.

### Flowers of the Night

We have invented many things
to set beside those we found when we appeared—
columbine, fuchsia,
swallow, peregrine,
granite, garnet,
boulder, glacier—
some indifferent, some of no worth, some profound;
some that do harm, some that do no good, some almost miracles.

But how can one condemn the noise, smell, danger,
when the fountain of fire flames over our heads
and the world seems graced
by falling stars of our own creation,
that shower upon us at our will,
and make us believe that we, somehow, are more than just creatures of Earth?

[original]

Set # 28, page 146

**Possible responses:**

1. The poet as a youth was not afraid to glibly write poems and songs about experiences beyond his understanding, pretending to share a pain that he didn't feel. Now that he is older and has experienced great sorrows, he is no longer glib and admits that he cannot find the words to communicate the realities of suffering. Instead, he speaks of something less personal—the weather.

Set # 29, page 148

**Possible responses:**

1. The spider and the speaker's soul are being compared.

2. The spider and the soul are both noiseless, though Whitman only uses the word to describe the spider. They are each alone (*isolated, detached*), both searching their surroundings (*explore, venturing/seeking*) to make connections. The spider has already found a place to attach its filaments; the soul is still seeking.

3. The soul is hard to imagine in and of itself, having no substance, and its relationship to the world is also hard to understand. By drawing an analogy with the spider, Whitman gives readers a means by which to imagine the soul's situation and activity.

4. The parallel between the terror felt by *you* and the hen in lines 8 and 12 and between the chicks she thought were hers and the dream-self you thought was yours both jumping in the water and swimming away (lines 5–6 and 15) direct the reader's attention to a relationship of analogy.

5. The hen's experience and her reaction to it are compared to the reader's. The hen nurtures and cares for some chicks as usual until they do something no chicken ever did. It is not clear at first whether her terror (she is personified here)

stems from the surprise and disruption of her expectations, her inability to grasp the reality of the situation, and/or her fear for her chicks' safety. But in lines 9–12, the actions that the dream-self takes and the reaction of *you*, the waking self, indicates that all three feelings are felt by *you* and are also combined in the hen's terror. Just as the chicks startle the hen, we can startle ourselves by our choices and actions.

6. A miracle is a sudden divine intervention in the ordinary world, which *you* have been awaiting. When the mirror moves by, the ordinary world suddenly becomes extraordinary.

7. Reading a poem is like watching the world in the mirror because a poem presents things from a new angle and perspective that we share when we read. It is like a miracle in that it is a revelation of the freshness and wonder of the world.

## Set # 30, page 151

**Possible response:** The title suggests that the poem is about an ending. The use of Latin may suggest that it is a lofty topic. The repetition in the first line assures me that whatever it is truly *is* finished. In lines 2–8, the speaker seems to be questioning why the cold and uncaring universe has not reacted to and shared in the trauma of the end of her relationship. In lines 9–14, she points out a number of things that haven't changed their normal patterns at all, again, seeming to be wondering at the lack of impact her sorrow has had on the world, but surprising me by adding (lines 15–16) that she shares in their indifference. The paraprosdokian in lines 15–16 makes me realize that Parker was leading readers on (as usual).

## Set # 31, page 152

**Possible responses:**

1. The title suggests that the poem is about a person who was once important (indicated by his having been knighted) but is now forgotten (hence nameless). Dramatic irony is evident in that we read the whole poem with the knowledge that Sir Nameless, who thinks himself so important, will end up an unknown. When Sir Nameless says of children, "Thank God I've none to hasten my decay" we are alerted to the possibility of more irony because the title mentions children. The irony is delivered when we find out that the children do "hasten the decay" of the entire legacy that is left of Sir Nameless—his statue.

2. The possessions that he chooses to be sculpted with him are listed in a way that seems pompous because each one receives so much emphasis.

3. The theme of the mighty being brought low is very similar, but in "The Children and Sir Nameless" there is an element of poetic justice. In Hardy's poem, it is children—whom Sir Nameless found so distasteful that he didn't want any around and hence had no heirs (which is probably why no one remembers him)—who destroy his statue as they kick it. In "Ozymandias," the great king is lost to our knowledge by the greater workings of history and the sands of time—there is no retribution evident; nature, fate, and history are what bring Ozymandias low.

## Set # 32, page 154

**Possible response:** When I saw a poem called "Golf Links," I expected it to be about recreation and enjoyment. Reading the first line, I thought the speaker was going to tell of some advantage to the location of the links—that the men at the mill could play after work, or something like that. The second line didn't change my view. When I reached line 3, I realized that the poem was social commentary, and the poet was pointing out the irony of children working (and from what I know, conditions were harsh, hours long, and pay poor in the mills) with adults playing. I think the poet is suggesting that the men should be looking at the children and doing something about the situation.

## Set # 33, page 156

**Possible responses:**

1. a. The wheelbarrow sitting out and the chicken suggest a farm setting. Wheelbarrows move things—take weeds away from the garden, perhaps bring feed to the chickens and other farm animals, and take care of other small to medium-sized moving tasks. Chickens may be the farmer's livelihood, food for himself and his family, or both. The rain water may provide water for bathing, watering the animals, and drinking.
   b. If it is a farm, the farmer and his family depend on those items. In addition, the local economy, the people who buy the food the farmer grows, and ultimately the world also depend on them.

   c. Each set of two lines looks like the handle and basin of a wheelbarrow. The poet has visually reinforced his message.
   d. The only certain difference between the two roads is that they go in different directions. The words *just as fair, worn them really about the same,* and *and both that morning equally lay* suggest little actual difference that can form the grounds of a choice between them.
   e. The speaker is very serious about the choice of paths in a wood for someone just going on a walk. His sorrow at having to choose only one (line 2), the length of time he takes to decide (lines 3–12), the going back and forth

weighing the possibilities (lines 3–12), his near certainty of having no opportunity to return and explore the "road not taken" (lines 14–15), and the prediction that the choice will be of momentous importance (lines 16–20)—all these point to the choice as a symbolic and important one: one of the "deciding moments" in life.

f. The speaker doesn't regret the specific choice of one road over the other so much as the need to make choices that rule out other possibilities and set one's life on a course. He's sorry that he must make decisions and leave "just as fair" possibilities behind. Given the way I read this, I don't know that he would choose differently.

g. Some people might think it's ironic that, after showing the roads to be about equally traveled in lines 9–10 and both good choices, he imagines himself in the future stating that he "took the one less traveled by" and that made "all the difference." But if you look closely at lines 7–10, you can see that he was looking for the less worn road: he says the second "had a better claim because . . . it wanted wear." Even though they were worn "about the same," apparently there was enough difference that he did finally choose the second. The explanation, I think, is that important choices that have small differences at the beginning, when pursued for a lifetime, end up in very different places. Again, he is regretting the necessity of choosing more than the specific choice.

2. **Possible response:** (analogy; something beautiful)

> I walk a green path
> strewn lightly with white blossoms
> while birds strew the air with song.
>
> [original]

# CHAPTER FOUR

# Vachel We Say About Sound?

Prose is shaped by meaning units: paragraphs, sections, and chapters. But it is primarily sound that gives a poem its shape. In poetry, **lines**, **stanzas**, and space are the essential organizing features. In this chapter, we'll explore poetic structure. Then we'll look at poetic sound effects—first meters, then rhyme, then other sound devices.

To get us started, we'll look at a poem by Vachel Lindsay. When the poem first appeared, there was a note above it that said, "War. September 1, 1914. Intended to be Read Aloud."

# BRAIN TICKLERS
## *Set # 34*

Read the poem aloud. Then answer the questions.

### Abraham Lincoln Walks at Midnight
(1914)

by Vachel Lindsay (*In Springfield, Illinois*)

1  It is portentous, and a thing of state
2  That here at midnight, in our little town
3  A mourning figure walks, and will not rest,
4  Near the old court-house pacing up and down.

5  Or by his homestead, or in shadowed yards
6  He lingers where his children used to play,
7  Or through the market, on the well-worn stones
8  He stalks until the dawn-stars burn away.

9  A bronzed, lank man! His suit of ancient black,
10  A famous high top-hat and plain worn shawl
11  Make him the quaint great figure that men love,
12  The prairie-lawyer, master of us all.

13  He cannot sleep upon his hillside now.
14  He is among us:—as in times before!
15  And we who toss and lie awake for long
16  Breathe deep, and start, to see him pass the door.

17  His head is bowed. He thinks on men and kings.
18  Yea, when the sick world cries, how can he sleep?
19  Too many peasants fight, they know not why,
20  Too many homesteads in black terror weep.

21  The sins of all the war-lords burn his heart.
22  He sees the dreadnaughts scouring every main.
23  He carries on his shawl-wrapped shoulders now
24  The bitterness, the folly and the pain.

25  He cannot rest until a spirit-dawn
26  Shall come;—the shining hope of Europe free:
27  The league of sober folk, the Workers' Earth,
28  Bringing long peace to Cornland, Alp and Sea.

29  It breaks his heart that kings must murder still,
30  That all his hours of travail here for men
31  Seem yet in vain. And who will bring white peace
32  That he may sleep upon his hill again?

1. What do you notice about Lindsay's diction?
2. List the rhetorical figures in this poem and tell how they're used.
3. Explore Lindsay's use of sensory detail and imagery.
4. How did Lindsay structure the poem?
5. What do you notice about the poem's sound as you read it aloud?
6. One copy of the poem available online has *Cornwall* instead of *Cornland*. Would this change your understanding? Explain.
7. There have been reports of Lincoln's ghost walking around Springfield since a few days after his death. What historical situation was, according to the poem, causing Lincoln's unrest in September of 1914? If you haven't checked the allusions, do so now.
8. What is this poem about? How would you state its theme? Does focusing on the two interrogative sentences in the poem help you answer? Explain.

(Answers are on page 241.)

# MOUTHFULS OF POETRY: PARTS OF A POEM

When we first look at a poem, we usually see the title, author attribution, and some kind of pattern (or at least a display) of type on the page. After we see the shape of the whole, we grasp a poem one line at a time. Let's begin by discussing lines.

## Line length

Lines can be short or long. The choice of line length immediately opens some possibilities and limits others. Short lines are more useful for expressing pithy observations and lend themselves to sentence fragments and elliptical expression. Long lines can handle intricate stories, philosophical discourses, and compound-complex sentences.

## BRAIN TICKLERS
### Set # 35

1. Read the following excerpt and complete poem. Then tell whether you think the line length was appropriately chosen for each poem. In your explanation, mention the diction and the meaning units.

### The Mahogany Tree (c. 1883)
by William Thackeray (excerpt)

| | | | |
|---|---|---|---|
| 1 | Christmas is here: | 9 | Once on the boughs |
| 2 | Winds whistle shrill, | 10 | Birds of rare plume |
| 3 | Icy and chill, | 11 | Sang, in its bloom; |
| 4 | Little care we: | 12 | Night-birds are we: |
| 5 | Little we fear | 13 | Here we carouse, |
| 6 | Weather without, | 14 | Singing like them, |
| 7 | Shelter about | 15 | Perched round the stem |
| 8 | The Mahogany Tree. | 16 | Of the jolly old tree. |

# Casey at the Bat (1888)

by Ernest Laurence Thayer

1 The outlook wasn't brilliant for the Mudville nine that day;
2 The score stood four to two, with but one inning more to play,
3 And so, when Cooney died at first, and Burrows did the same,
4 A sickly silence fell upon the patrons of the game.

5 A straggling few got up to go in deep despair. The rest
6 Clung to that hope which springs eternal in the human breast;
7 They thought, "If only Casey could but get a whack, at that,
8 They'd put up even money now, with Casey at the bat."

9 But Flynn preceded Casey, as did also Jimmy Blake,
10 And the former was a hoodoo, while the latter was a fake;
11 So upon that stricken multitude grim melancholy sat,
12 For there seemed but little chance of Casey getting to the bat.

13 But Flynn let drive a single, to the wonderment of all,
14 And Blake, the much despisèd, tore the cover off the ball;
15 And when the dust had lifted, and they saw what had occurred,
16 There was Jimmy safe at second, and Flynn a-hugging third.

17 Then from the gladdened multitude went up a joyous yell;
18 It bounded from the mountaintop, and rattled in the dell;
19 It struck upon the hillside, and recoiled upon the flat;
20 For Casey, mighty Casey, was advancing to the bat.

21 There was ease in Casey's manner as he stepped into his place;
22 There was pride in Casey's bearing, and a smile on Casey's face.
23 And when, responding to the cheers, he lightly doffed his hat,
24 No stranger in the crowd could doubt 'twas Casey at the bat.

25 Ten thousand eyes were on him as he rubbed his hands with dirt;
26 Five thousand tongues applauded when he wiped them on his shirt;
27 Then while the writhing pitcher ground the ball into his hip,
28 Defiance flashed in Casey's eye, a sneer curled Casey's lip.

29 And now the leather-covered sphere came hurtling through the air,
30 And Casey stood a-watching it in haughty grandeur there;
31 Close by the sturdy batsman the ball unheeded sped.
32 "That ain't my style," said Casey. "Strike one!" the umpire said.

33 From the benches, black with people, there went up a muffled roar,
34 Like the beating of the storm waves on a stern and distant shore;
35 "Kill him! Kill the umpire!" shouted some one on the stand;
36 And it's likely they'd have killed him had not Casey raised his hand.

37 With a smile of Christian charity great Casey's visage shone;
38 He stilled the rising tumult; he bade the game go on;
39 He signaled to the pitcher, and once more the spheroid flew;
40 But Casey still ignored it, and the umpire said, "Strike two!"

41  "Fraud!" cried the maddened thousands, and echo answered "Fraud!"
42  But one scornful look from Casey, and the audience was awed.
43  They saw his face grow stern and cold, they saw his muscles strain,
44  And they knew that Casey wouldn't let that ball go by again.

45  The sneer has fled from Casey's lip, his teeth are clenched in hate;
46  He pounds with cruel violence his bat upon the plate.
47  And now the pitcher holds the ball, and now he lets it go.
48  And now the air is shattered by the force of Casey's blow.

49  Oh! somewhere in this favored land the sun is shining bright;
50  The band is playing somewhere, and somewhere hearts are light;
51  And somewhere men are laughing, and somewhere children shout,
52  But there is no joy in Mudville—mighty Casey has struck out!

(Answers are on page 244.)

## Regular and irregular lines

Regular lines, whether short or long, have a certain feel to them that draws you at a fairly even pace through the material of the poem. But sometimes poems do not have lines of equal length. There are various reasons for this. A poet may choose an alternating pattern of longer and shorter lines, as in ballad meter (see page 193). Free verse, which is not metrical, also makes inventive use of varied line length. Look back at "The Love Song of J. Alfred Prufrock" on page 144. The irregular lines and occasional, but irregular, use of rhyme, convey Prufrock's uncertain fits and starts as he tries to express himself. In this case, the uneven lines fit the troubled speaker. (For more on free verse, see page 290.)

Translators sometimes convey the sense of the original in the identical form (see pages 271–272 for two translations of a Spanish sonnet into English). But sometimes, to preserve meaning, translators take liberties in rendering the form, another reason you may find uneven lines.

## Stanzas: groups of lines

Poems can have a single stanza, or many. And the stanzas of a single poem may or may not have identical numbers of lines. Sometimes we can identify subunits within a stanza—sets of two rhyming lines (called couplets), for example, can be the building blocks of a stanza. At other times, the stanza may be the primary unit in the poem.

Stanzas can take on different functions, depending on the needs of the poem. For example, they can be episodes in a story, examples of a single phenomenon, or alternating voices in a dialogue. The function will help determine the stanza length. Stanzas can range in length from two lines on up.

# BRAIN TICKLERS
## Set # 36

1. Read the following poems and excerpt. Then tell how the stanzas in each poem or excerpt work to make meaning.

### Death of an Old Carriage Horse
(before 1865)
by George Moses Horton

1   I was a harness horse,
2       Constrained to travel weak or strong,
3   With orders from oppressing force,
4       Push along, push along.

5   I had no space of rest,
6       And took at forks the roughest prong,
7   Still by the cruel driver pressed,
8       Push along, push along.

9   Vain strove the idle bird,
10      To charm me with her artless song,
11  But pleasure lingered from the word,
12      Push along, push along.

13  The order of the day
14      Was push, the peal of every tongue,
15  The only word was all the way,
16      Push along, push along.

17 Thus to my journey's end,
18    Had I to travel right or wrong,
19 'Till death my sweet and favored friend,
20    Bade me from life to push along.

## New England Boy's Song about Thanksgiving Day (1845)
### by Lydia Maria Child (excerpt)

1 Over the river, and through the wood,
2    To grandfather's house we go;
3       The horse knows the way,
4       To carry the sleigh,
5 Through the white and drifted snow.....

11 Over the river, and through the wood,
12    Oh, how the wind does blow!
13       It stings the toes,
14       And bites the nose,
15    As over the ground we go.

## When I Set Out for Lyonnesse (1870)
### by Thomas Hardy

1 When I set out for Lyonnesse,
2    A hundred miles away,
3    The rime was on the spray,
4 And starlight lit my lonesomeness
5 When I set out for Lyonnesse
6    A hundred miles away.

7 What would bechance at Lyonnesse
8    While I should sojourn there
9    No prophet durst declare,
10 Nor did the wisest wizard guess
11 What would bechance at Lyonnesse
12    While I should sojourn there.

13 When I came back from Lyonnesse
14    With magic in my eyes,
15    All marked with mute surmise
16 My radiance rare and fathomless,
17 When I came back from Lyonnesse
18    With magic in my eyes!

### (Answers are on page 245.)

## End-stops and enjambment

When a phrase, clause, or sentence concludes at a line-end, we have an **end-stopped line**. Often this coincides with a punctuation mark. **Enjambment** is the term for meaning units that run over the end of one line and into the next. Poets use these two possibilities in all kinds of ways and to create many different effects.

# BRAIN TICKLERS
### Set # 37

Read the following poem. Then answer the questions.

### Up-Hill (1858)
by Christina Rossetti

1  Does the road wind up-hill all the way?
2      Yes, to the very end.
3  Will the day's journey take the whole long day?
4      From morn to night, my friend.

5  But is there for the night a resting-place?
6      A roof for when the slow dark hours begin.
7  May not the darkness hide it from my face?
8      You cannot miss that inn.

9  Shall I meet other wayfarers at night?
10      Those who have gone before.
11  Then must I knock, or call when just in sight?
12      They will not keep you standing at that door.

13  Shall I find comfort, travel-sore and weak?
14      Of labour you shall find the sum.
15  Will there be beds for me and all who seek?
16      Yea, beds for all who come.

1. Tell how the use of end-stop is effective in the poem.
2. Is the journey in this poem real or symbolic? What elements of the poem support your interpretation?

(Answers are on page 246.)

## Refrains

Some poems, whether or not they are intended to be sung, have what in singing is called a **refrain**, a section of text repeated at intervals (sometimes with minor variations). A refrain may rhyme or not, and it may be any length between one word and an entire stanza. Sometimes a refrain recalls the reader to a focus, but sometimes the developments in the poem will cast new light on the meaning of a refrain, as in "Death of an Old Carriage Horse" (page 182). A poetic refrain may be *epistrophe* (see page 115).

## BRAIN TICKLERS
### Set # 38

Reread "The Owl Critic," page 134. What is the refrain? What purpose does the refrain serve?

(Answers are on page 246.)

## Titles

Titles of poems may serve a variety of functions. They may place the poem in a wider setting, such as a sequence (this is why Shakespeare's sonnets are titled with numbers, for example, "Sonnet CXXX"). They may name the subject or a character, hint at the theme, disclose an important plot element, give away the ending, signal irony, and so on. Titles are usually the first part of the poem we read, and often, if we return to them after we have finished our reading, we may find new insights into their meanings.

Sometimes, poets do not title a poem, in which case it is usually known by its first line, which is used to identify the poem in indexes and the like.

## BRAIN TICKLERS
### Set # 39

1. Cover the following poem and read only the title. Then read the poem and answer the questions.

### The Dream?

1  I dreamed that I went to a lake
2  And tussled with a slimy snake;
3  but when that snake I'd overcome,
4  I was assaulted by a glum
5  and vicious eel. I tied him up
6  in knots, and faced a school of scup.
7  When I eluded all those fish,
8  I only had a single wish:
9  to swim without one more attack.
10  But snapping turtles in a pack
11  were coming! I woke with a scream.
12  Thank goodness! It was just a dream.

13  But if it's just a dream, I said,
14  Why are there algae in my bed?
15  Why is there sand upon my sheet
16  and gritty dirt on both my feet?
17  And why is my face wan and white
18  as if I hadn't slept all night?

[original]

What is the function of the title of this poem? Tell your thoughts when you read only the title, and also after you finished the entire poem.

2. Reconsider the title of the poem "Abraham Lincoln Walks at Midnight." Also notice the use of lines, and stanzas. What further insights do you have into the art of that particular poem?

3. Choose one of the following to do:
   a. Write a poem that is hard to understand without its title.
   b. Write a poem with a refrain.
   c. Write a poem with very, very short or very, very long lines.
   d. Write a poem in which the first stanza has one line, the second has two, the third has three, and so on.

If you're stuck for a topic, here's a suggestion: Look back at the poems printed earlier in this book, and "steal" an idea.

(Answers are on page 247.)

# THE MUSIC OF POETRY

Try reading the following text in a whisper.

It's incredible! It's astonishing! Oh, it's unbelievable!

Now read the sentences as if "it" were very likely unsafe, possibly deadly. Finally, read the sentences as if "it" were the fulfillment of your dearest wish.

The human voice has great flexibility of expression. Subtle changes in the way we say words can change the meaning perceived by the listener. When we utter words out loud, we cannot help shaping them with our attitudes and emotions through our tone of voice. This process, called **intonation**, is a major element in creating the musicality of a poem. Written prose, because it is often not intended to be read aloud, may give us few cues to how it might be spoken. Poetry, on the other hand, is designed to be spoken and gives us many hints, to which we add our own shaping based on our interpretation. In order to understand the music of poetry, we're going to examine the elements that make up spoken sound and then examine how poetry gives us cues about how we might shape that sound.

## Spoken sound

Spoken sound has a number of different characteristics:

| Stress | the emphasis, or intensity we give to a syllable relative to other syllables in the same phrase. (It is not the same as loudness—words can be said softly but intensely—nor is it the same as regional or dialectical accent.) |
|---|---|
| Pitch | the note or sound frequency of the voice |
| Speed | the quickness or slowness, also called the *rate* at which sounds are produced |
| Timbre | the "personality" in your voice—the characteristics that make your voice uniquely yours (e.g., gruff, crisp, purring) |
| Loudness | the volume or amplitude of the sound you make |
| Content | the thoughts, ideas, and emotions contained in the words and sounds said and the meaning expressed |
| Tone of voice | the element of voice that reflects our attitude toward the content of what we are saying |
| Pauses | silence between sounds for breathing, creating meaning, rhythm, building suspense, etc. |

All these elements are involved whenever we speak, including when we speak poetry. We use all of them all the time, but when we perform (acting in a play, reading a poem, telling a story), we usually give them more thought and use more variety.

Poetry and prose differ in how they treat intonation. Both prose and poetry provide us with hints from which we can deduce mood, tone, characterization, and so on, all of which inform our reading. But poetry goes farther in giving us both cues and boundaries to guide us in how to intone its words. You have been able to read the prose sentences at the beginning of this section in very different ways, following my directions and at the same time keeping within the cues given by the language, punctuation, and structure. Poetry provides even more guidance.

## How does poetry influence sound?

### Orthography, typography, punctuation, and symbols

Some information about how to voice a poem can be gathered from its **orthography**, the representation of the words on the page in print. Orthography includes both standard spelling and changes that the poet has made to standard spelling. Poets frequently use apostrophes and spelling changes to indicate colloquial speech (like *gonna* for *going to*) and dialects. The spelling, whether standard or not, guides us in pronunciation and in identifying dialects, which helps us to understand character.

**Typography** that is unusual like *italics* and **boldface** may give us hints about words that require special emphasis. We may signal this emphasis by slowing down and speaking the marked word(s) with special intensity, pausing before and after, and raising the pitch.

**Punctuation** tells us many things about how to use our voices when we read poetry.

- End marks (periods, question marks, exclamation points) often indicate pitch shifts because we tend to raise pitch in questions and exclamations and lower it toward the end of statements. End marks also often indicate a place to pause and to breathe.
- Pauses of various lengths within sentences are indicated by the following marks (from longest pause to shortest): period, colon, semicolon, and comma. Ellipses are also used for pauses, as are rows of dashes or asterisks, and space on the page. The marks that indicate pauses may also indicate topic shifts.
- Brackets (including parentheses) and long dashes are used to separate material, either to subordinate it or to emphasize it. They usually signal a pause to gather attention and a pitch shift to indicate to the listener that there's been a change. For material that is set off because it is less important, we tend to lower the pitch.

- Apostrophes signal elision, the omission of a letter or syllable by dropping it or slurring it into the next.
- Double quotation marks indicate that a character other than the poem's speaker is speaking, shifting us into characterization. Our decisions about intonation when we see this will depend on the identify of that character.
- Single quotation marks usually indicate irony (standing for *so-called*), usually calling for an increase in intensity, an introductory pause to gather attention, and a pitch shift.

**Accent marks** are symbols that are specifically designed to inform us about pronunciation. They may signal a particular sound (like the German umlaut ••), which syllable of a word to stress, or indicate that an ordinarily silent vowel should be pronounced (like the grave accent that we discussed on page 24).

## Word order

**Word order** helps bring important words to our attention: Poets highlight words by placing them at the beginning and end of a poem as well as the beginnings and ends of individual lines and stanzas and by repeating them. Focusing on word placement can help us identify theme and overall meaning.

We have already discussed how some rhetorical devices place key words at the beginnings and/or endings of lines or repeat them. In the following poem, the use of line beginnings and endings is so carefully planned that you can probably guess quite a lot about the meaning, even though I've removed the middle of every line:

### A Marriage Ring (c. 1800)
by George Crabbe

1 The ring . . . behold,
2 So thin . . . of gold:
3 The passion . . . prove—
4 Worn . . . was love.

After you've considered it for a few minutes, take a look at the entire poem on page 218 and see how well you did in figuring out the meaning.

The following poem puts weighted words at the ends of the lines, and then draws our attention to them in several ways. One way is the rhymes. In Crabbe's poem, you may have noticed that Crabbe used couplets, sets of two rhyming lines. Forming stanzas of rhyming couplets like that is not uncommon. But in Wordsworth's poem, no two lines rhyme until we finish reading line 4, and by that time, our ear is hungry for a rhyme, so we're listening attentively to the final words. And it is in the final words of lines 3–5 that Wordsworth makes the point that joy in nature is joy for our whole lifetime.

### The Rainbow (1807)
by William Wordsworth

1 My heart leaps up when I behold
2   A rainbow in the sky:
3 So was it when my life began;
4 So is it now I am a man;
5 So be it when I shall grow old,
6   Or let me die!
7 The Child is father of the Man;
8 I could wish my days to be
9 Bound each to each by natural piety.

Some poems use the first line of a stanza as a topic sentence is used for a paragraph. In this example, you can read only the first lines of each stanza and capture the overall movement of the poem.

### Love's Secret (c. 1793)
by William Blake

1 **Never seek to tell thy love,**
2   Love that never told can be;
3 For the gentle wind doth move
4   Silently, invisibly.

5 **I told my love, I told my love,**
6   I told her all my heart,
7 Trembling, cold, in ghastly fears.
8   Ah! she did depart!

9 **Soon after she was gone from me,**
10   A traveller came by,
11 Silently, invisibly:
12   He took her with a sigh.

Sometimes poets use unusual word order to make words fall at the beginning or end of a line or stanza for the sake of meter or rhyme. In this excerpt, the poet makes several decisions about word order—also called *syntax*—that, at least to modern ears, are unusual. Read his version, and then read a version with word order as we might expect to find it in prose, paying attention to the placement of *long* (line 10), *first* (line 12), and *vain* (lines 16 and 17).

### An Account of the Greatest English Poets (1694)
by Joseph Addison (excerpt)

10   Long had our dull forefathers slept supine,
11   Nor felt the raptures of the tuneful Nine;
12   Till Chaucer first, the merry bard, arose,
13   And many a story told in rhyme and prose.
14   But age has rusted what the poet writ,
15   Worn out his language, and obscur'd his wit;
16   In vain he jests in his unpolish'd strain,
17   And tries to make his readers laugh, in vain.

Modernized word order:

10   Our dull forefathers had long slept supine,
11   nor felt the raptures of the tuneful Nine;
12   Till Chaucer, the merry bard, first arose,
13   And told many a story in rhyme and prose.
14   But age has rusted what the poet writ,
15   Worn out his language, and obscur'd his wit;
16   He jests in vain in his unpolish'd strain,
17   And tries in vain to make his readers laugh.

## Structure

Finally, there is the **structure** of the poem from the broadest to the smallest level. Overarching all is the poetic form, which generally determines the type of stanza and which we will explore more deeply in Chapter Five. Other elements of poetic structure include lines, feet, words, stressed and unstressed syllables, individual sounds, and the patterns formed by these. Through all these levels of structure the poem's meaning is revealed and its performance is cued.

## *What's my line?*

Lines can be composed in several ways, and there are standard names for the five most common ways of constructing lines.

| Criteria for setting line length | Name of verse type |
| --- | --- |
| both number of stresses and number of syllables | accentual-syllabic verse |
| number of stresses only | accentual verse |
| number of syllables only | syllabic verse |
| number of words | didactic (teaching) verse |
| neither number of stresses nor number of syllables | free verse |

Did you notice the word *accentual*? Although so far in this book, we have been using the word *stress* for emphasis and saving *accent* for pronunciations, used by non-native speakers or speakers using different dialects, here *accentual* is used to mean *stressed*. Since it is a standard term, we will use it. **Accentual-syllabic verse** is characterized by having an underlying **meter**, from which its rhythms are drawn. **Accentual verse**, since syllables are not counted, is very flexible, being able to accept extra syllables into lines very easily. Accentual verse includes:

- ballads—narrative poems meant to be sung and characterized by four stresses in the odd lines and three in the even lines.
- limericks, coming up on page 275,
- nursery rhymes. These are all primarily "folk" rather than "literary" efforts.

**Syllabic verse** is treated beginning on page 279, **didactic verse** beginning on page 285, and **free verse** beginning on page 290. Accentual and accentual-syllabic verse are our topic for the rest of this chapter.

# RHYTHM AND METER

Most of the poetry you've read so far in this book is accentual-syllabic verse. Now let's take a close look at an excerpt from a famous accentual poem so we can see how accentual verse and accentual-syllabic verse differ.

### The Highwayman (1907)
by Alfred Noyes (excerpt)

1   The wind was a torrent of darkness among the gusty trees,
2   The moon was a ghostly galleon tossed upon cloudy seas,
3   The road was a ribbon of moonlight looping the purple moor,
4   And the highwayman came riding—
5   Riding—riding—
6   The highwayman came riding, up to the old inn door.

7   He'd a French cocked hat on his forehead, a bunch of lace at
        his chin;
8   He'd a coat of the claret velvet, and breeches of brown doe-skin.
9   They fitted with never a wrinkle; his boots were up to the thigh!
10  And he rode with a jeweled twinkle—
11  His rapier hilt a-twinkle—
12  His pistol butts a-twinkle, under the jeweled sky.

13  Over the cobbles he clattered and clashed in the dark inn-yard,
14  He tapped with his whip on the shutters, but all was locked and barred;
15  He whistled a tune to the window, and who should be waiting there
16  But the landlord's black-eyed daughter—
17  Bess, the landlord's daughter—
18  Plaiting a dark red love-knot into her long black hair.

19  Dark in the dark old inn-yard a stable-wicket creaked
20  Where Tim, the ostler listened—his face was white and peaked—
21  His eyes were hollows of madness, his hair like mouldy hay,
22  But he loved the landlord's daughter—
23  The landlord's black-eyed daughter,
24  Dumb as a dog he listened, and he heard the robber say:

25  "One kiss, my bonny sweetheart; I'm after a prize tonight,
26  But I shall be back with the yellow gold before the morning light.
27  Yet if they press me sharply, and harry me through the day,
28  Then look for me by moonlight,
29  Watch for me by moonlight,
30  I'll come to thee by moonlight, though hell should bar the way."

The number of stresses per line is very consistent. The first three lines in each stanza, as well as the final line, all have six accents (except for lines 25, 26, and 31, which have seven). But the number of syllables per line varies from thirteen syllables to eighteen syllables, with no one syllable count per line predominating. Here is a marked stanza to help clarify. Each stressed syllable has a little line over it.

31  He stood upright in the stirrups; he scarce could reach her hand,

32  But she loosened her hair in the casement! His face burned like a brand

33  As the sweet black waves of perfume came tumbling o'er his breast,

34  Then he kissed its waves in the moonlight

35  (O sweet black waves in the moonlight!),

36  And he tugged at his reins in the moonlight, and galloped away to the west.

The pretty consistent number of stresses combined with the wide variation of the syllable count suggests that "The Highwayman" is accentual verse.

## Meter

**Meter** is the basic underlying pattern of stresses in the lines of a poem. If you have ever tapped your foot to music, you were tapping the meter. The **rhythm** is how the words fit into the meter in any particular line (in poetry) or any particular measure (in music). It is the way a poet has played out the meter in the particular context of a particular poem. Just as in the musical meter of, say, $\frac{3}{4}$ (three beats to a measure and a quarter note gets one beat), not every measure consists of three quarter notes, so in poetry, not every foot in a line will match the poetic meter.

Meter means "measurement," and in poetry the unit of measurement is called a **foot**. A foot is a set of syllables, usually two or three, of which (in English) usually only one is strongly stressed.* The stronger stress is shown by an **ictus** ´,

---

*Notice that I said that "usually only one is strongly stressed." This does not mean that the others are **un**stressed, but that they are stressed **less**. In speaking, we have (according to linguistic research) four levels of stress. In metrics, there are only two. It's helpful to keep that in mind.

the weaker one(s) with a **breve** ˘. Each foot has a name and the feet names, like other terminology coming up, may be new to you. As with new terms in any subject, these words will help you to think about the subject and communicate about it with others. The more you use them, the sooner they will become familiar.

This chart describes the main poetic feet, telling how many syllables they have, their names, the adjective form of their names, their stress patterns, and an example for each.

| Number of syllables | Stress on first syllable | Stress on last syllable | Stress on first and last syllables |
|---|---|---|---|
| 2 | trochee (trochaic) strong/weak ˊ ˘ urgent | iamb (iambic) weak/strong ˘ ˊ persuade | spondee (spondaic) strong/strong ˊ ˊ true–blue |
| 3 | dactyl (dactylic) strong/ weak/weak ˊ ˘ ˘ happily | anapest (anapestic) weak/weak/ strong ˘ ˘ ˊ guarantee | amphimacer (amphimaceric) strong/weak/ strong ˊ ˘ ˊ first and last |

To help you fix this terminology in your mind, read (and memorize if you wish) this excerpt from a poem written by a poet to teach his young sons the poetic terms that you're just learning. The feet are separated with this symbol |.

### Metrical Feet: Lesson for a Boy (c. 1800)
by Samuel Taylor Coleridge (excerpt)

1 Trochee | trips from | long to | short;
2 From long | to long | in sol | emn sort
3 Slow Spon | dee stalks; | strong foot, | yet ill | able
4 Ever to | come up with | Dactyl tri | syllable
5 Iam | bics march | from short | to long;
6 With a leap | and a bound | the swift An | apests throng.

In naming the meter, you first give the name of the primary foot, and then the number of feet in a line, using the words in this chart.

| Number of feet | Name for it | Number of feet | Name for it |
|---|---|---|---|
| 1 | monometer | 6 | hexameter |
| 2 | dimeter | 7 | heptameter |
| 3 | trimeter | 8 | octameter |
| 4 | tetrameter | 9 | nonameter |
| 5 | pentameter | 10 | decameter |

So a line with five iambic feet is iambic pentameter, and a line with three anapests is anapestic trimeter. Knowing the meter is useful because it gives you a starting point for analysis.

## Helpful hints

1. Almost all accentual-syllabic verse poems have only one meter, and most of the feet will be the same. In English poetry, the most common feet are iamb, trochee, dactyl, anapest, and spondee, and the metric foot is nearly always one of the first four.
2. Most English two-syllable words are trochees (stressed on the first syllable). The words that are iambic are often from another language. Yet, the iamb is the most common foot in English meter. Trochaic words can be fit into iambic lines by slipping in an unstressed one-syllable word ahead of them.

   Trochee | trips from | long to | short

   A tro | chee trips |

   from long | to short

   One-syllable verbs and nouns usually are stressed. But articles, prepositions, conjunctions, and pronouns (except demonstrative pronouns because they are used for emphasis) are usually not stressed.

   Look at the first word in each line of this excerpt from a poem in iambic tetrameter. Notice how conjunctions, pronouns, prepositions, and articles can be followed by a trochaic word to make an iambic foot.

| Conjunction + trochee | line 2, *As, restless* line 17, *But swinging* |
|---|---|
| Pronoun + trochee | line 7, *She fashions* line 13, *My daily* |
| Preposition + trochee | line 8, *By instinct's* |
| Article + trochee | line 32, *A sheltered* |

## Arachne (before 1888)
### by Rose Terry Cooke (excerpt)

1   I watch her in the corner there,
2   As, restless, bold, and unafraid,
3   She slips and floats along the air
4   Till all her subtile house is made.

5   Her home, her bed, her daily food
6   All from that hidden store she draws;
7   She fashions it and knows it good,
8   By instinct's strong and sacred laws. . . .

21   Poor sister of the spinster clan!
22   I too from out my store within
23   My daily life and living plan,
24   My home, my rest, my pleasure spin.

25   I know thy heart when heartless hands
26   Sweep all that hard-earned web away:
27   Destroy its pearled and glittering bands,
28   And leave thee homeless by the way,

29   I know thy peace when all is done,
30   Each anchored thread, each tiny knot,
31   Soft shining in the autumn sun;
32   A sheltered, silent, tranquil lot.

33   I know what thou hast never known,
34   —Sad presage to a soul allowed;—
35   That not for life I spin, alone.
36   But day by day I spin my shroud.

3. English words are not usually anapestic. So anapests often have prepositional phrases or other groups of function words to fill the unstressed positions. You can see some examples in this humorous poem.

### The Legatee (before 1892)
#### by Ambrose Gwinnet Bierce

1   In fair San Francisco a good man did dwell,
2   And he wrote out a will, for he didn't feel well.
3   Said he: "It is proper, when making a gift,
4   To stimulate virtue by comforting thrift."

5   So he left all his property, legal and straight,
6   To "the cursedest rascal in all of the State."
7   But the name he refused to insert, for, said he:
8   "Let each man consider himself legatee."

9   In due course of time that philanthropist died,
10   And all San Francisco, and Oakland beside—
11   Save only the lawyers—came each with his claim,
12   The lawyers preferring to manage the same.

13   The cases were tried in Department Thirteen,
14   Judge Murphy presided, sedate and serene,
15   But couldn't quite specify, legal and straight,
16   The cursedest rascal in all of the State,

17   And so he remarked to them, little and big—
18   To claimants: "You skip!" and to lawyers: "You dig!"
19   They tumbled, tumultuous, out of his court
20   And left him victorious, holding the fort.

21   'Twas then that he said: "It is plain to my mind
22   This property's ownerless—how can I find
23   The cursedest rascal in all of the State?"
24   So he took it himself, which was legal and straight.

Did you notice these phrases: "of the State," "and he wrote," "out a will," "so he left," "of his court," "it is plain," and "to my mind"?

## Ways to vary meter when creating rhythm

Sticking to the meter throughout an entire poem could be very monotonous. It would also limit word choice. For these reasons, meters have developed standard substitutions. This flexibility gives poets some room to play with the sound in order to make as much sense as possible. There are a variety of acceptable ways to vary rhythm to avoid monotony and marry sound and sense.

**Foot substitution.** It is possible to replace one foot with another. This changes the rhythm without changing the meter. For example, an iamb can be replaced by a trochee, spondee, dactyl, or anapest. The beginning of this Shakespeare play shows substitutions with trochees and spondees. The meter is iambic pentameter, five iambic feet in each line, but there are several substitutions.

### The Tragedy of Julius Caesar (1599)
by William Shakespeare

1 Flavius. Hence! home, you idle creatures, get you home:

2 Is this a holiday? What! Know you not,

3 Being mechanical, you ought not walk

4 Upon a labouring* day without the sign

5 Of your profession? Speak, what trade art thou?

1 spondee iamb iamb iamb iamb
2 iamb iamb iamb spondee iamb
3 trochee iamb iamb iamb iamb
4 iamb iamb iamb iamb iamb
5 iamb iamb iamb spondee iamb

---

\* *labouring* is pronounced as two syllables: (LAY bring).

## Syllabic additions or deletions at the beginning

**or end.** Lines may also be altered by addition or deletion of syllables at the beginning or end. Here are the possibilities, their names, and the adjective form in parentheses. Notice that only unstressed syllables are added and subtracted.

| Name | Effect on line | Where? |
|------|----------------|--------|
| catalexis—tailless (catalectic) | subtract one unstressed syllable | end |
| brachycatalexis (brachycatalectic) | subtract more than one unstressed syllable | end |
| hypercatalexis (hypercatalectic) | add one unstressed syllable | end |
| acephalexis— headless (acephalectic) | subtract one or more unstressed syllables | beginning |
| anacrusis (anacrustic) | add one or more unstressed syllables | beginning |

A perfect and complete line of the chosen meter is called **acatalectic**. You're not likely to need these words often but if you ever need them, you can just flip to this chart. And if you find extra or missing syllables in accentual-syllabic verse— knowing about the possibilities—you won't be thrown off.

**Pauses.** Pauses are another way of varying lines. We have already discussed the punctuation marks that indicate pauses necessitated by meaning, but sometimes there are pauses not indicated by punctuation (for example, before subordinate clauses). Either of these types of pause is designated in scansion by the caesura ‖. A line may have no caesura, or several. One per line is typical of much verse. The placing of the caesura(s) varies the sound of the line.

There may also be very small pauses between feet. If we are interested in those pauses, we can mark them in our scansion with a single vertical line |, as was done in *Metrical Feet*, p. 196.

Some literary theorists also recognize metrical pauses—units of time that replace missing syllables in, for example, catalectic lines, or may feel right after extra syllables.

## Scanning a poem

**Scanning** is the process by which we discover, understand, and/or analyze the rhythm of an accentual-syllabic poem, or test a poem to see if it is accentual-syllabic. There are four steps to scanning, and worked examples appear on pages 205–211. This process presumes that you have already read the poem and have some ideas about meaning. Use a pencil, not a pen. You may want to reconsider and erase.

1. Count and note the number of syllables in each line.
2. Figure out the meter of the poem, if you haven't recognized it right off. You may need to test a number of lines to do this. Remember that meter is the pattern on which the poet is drawing, not the rhythm of every part of the poem. Looking at multisyllabic words can help you. Often (not always), the primary stress in the word will be a stressed syllable in the poem. And often (though not always) function words, especially short ones, will be unstressed. Most often, one-syllable nouns and verbs will be stressed. Underline words if the natural stress contradicts the meter or if a "little" word appears to get undeserved stress.
3. Read each line as if it were prose with as much meaning as you can give it but don't be melodramatic. Just think about where the stresses would fall in natural speech. If there's no end-stop, continue into the next line to see how the continuity works. Listen to yourself. Try reading it different ways and settle on what seems best. Write it above the line, using ictuses and breves, above or below the meter.
4. Look at the two scansions—the prose/meaning scansion and the metric scansion. Where there are differences, compare the two readings offered by saying them aloud. How do sound and sense work together in each possible reading? Which meaning fits better with your understanding of the poem from all the other information you have already gathered? Which is more interesting? When you have thoroughly considered the matter, make necessary

modifications in your prose reading to make it work poetically, or keep both readings in mind as being worthwhile (or talk to someone else about it, if you can't decide). What insights have you gained into the poem's meaning?

Because it takes into account nuances of expression and interpretation, scansion is not a strictly mathematical process. My scansion and yours may not be precisely alike. A person can scan a poem in an unorthodox way and still come to a deep understanding of it. Just follow this guideline: Every time your scansion departs from the meter, have a good explanation based on meaning, interpretation, and/or pronunciation, if applicable, for your choice.

When you start the scansion process, glance at the first word of each line. If you see a lot of function words like *the*, *a*, *an*, *to*, *at*, *if*, *but*, the first syllable is very likely unstressed in the meter even though it may still be stressed in some lines in the rhythm.

## BRAIN TICKLERS
### *Set # 40*

Alexander Pope wrote advice for poets in this poem that he started writing in 1708, when he was about twenty. Explain each of his four points and tell whether you agree or disagree with him and why.

# An Essay on Criticism Part 2 (1708)

by Alexander Pope (excerpts)

1.

245  'Tis not a lip, or eye, we beauty call,
246  But the joint force and full result of all.
247  Thus when we view some well-proportioned dome,
248  (The world's just wonder, and even thine, O Rome!)
249  No single parts unequally surprise;
250  All comes united to the admiring eyes . . .

2.

337  But most by numbers judge a poet's song . . .

3.

347  And ten low words oft creep in one dull line,
348  While they ring round the same unvaried chimes,
349  With sure returns of still expected rhymes.
350  Where'er you find "the cooling western breeze,"
351  In the next line, it "whispers through the trees";
352  If "crystal streams with pleasing murmurs creep,"
353  The reader's threatened (not in vain) with "sleep";
354  Then, at the last and only couplet fraught
355  With some unmeaning thing they call a thought,
356  A needless Alexandrine ends the song
357  That, like a wounded snake, drags its slow length along.
358  Leave such to tune their own dull rhymes, and know
359  What's roundly smooth, or languishingly slow . . .

4.

364  'Tis not enough no harshness gives offense,
365  The sound must seem an echo to the sense.

(Answers are on page 248.)

Scanning involves a lot of choices and decisions. I'm going to model the process of scanning a few poems to show how this type of analysis works. First we'll return to "Sonnet CXXX" by Shakespeare. To begin, I count the syllables/line and write in the metric scansion. I already know that English sonnets are written in iambic pentameter, which stresses every even-numbered syllable, so it's easy to write in the metric scansion.

### Metric Scansion—Iambic Pentameter

1  ˘ ´ ˘ ´ ˘ ´ ˘ ´ ˘ ´
   My mistress' eyes are nothing like the sun;   10 syllables

2  ˘ ´ ˘ ´ ˘ ´ ˘ ´ ˘ ´
   <u>Coral</u> is far more red than her lips' red:   10

3  ˘ ´ ˘ ´ ˘ ´ ˘ ´ ˘ ´
   If snow be white, why then her breasts are dun;   10

4  ˘ ´ ˘ ´ ˘ ´ ˘ ´ ˘ ´
   If hairs be wires, black wires grow on her head.   10

5  ˘ ´ ˘ ´ ˘ ´ ˘ ´ ˘ ´
   I have seen roses damask'd, red and white,   10

6  ˘ ´ ˘ ´ ˘ ´ ˘ ´ ˘ ´
   But no such roses see I in her cheeks;   10

7  ˘ ´ ˘ ´ ˘ ´ ˘ ´ ˘ ´
   And in some perfumes is there more delight   10

8  ˘ ´ ˘ ´ ˘ ´ ˘ ´ ˘ ´
   Than in the breath that from my mistress reeks.   10

9  ˘ ´ ˘ ´ ˘ ´ ˘ ´ ˘ ´
   I love to hear her speak, yet well I know   10

10  ˘ ´ ˘ ´ ˘ ´ ˘ ´ ˘ ´
   That music hath a far more pleasing sound.   10

11  ˘ ´ ˘ ´ ˘ ´ ˘ ´ ˘ ´
   I grant I never saw a goddess go:   10

12  ´ ´ ˘ ´ ˘ ´ ˘ ´ ˘ ´
   My mistress, when she walks <u>treads</u> <u>on</u> the ground. 10

13  ˘ ´ ˘ ´ ˘ ´ ˘ ´ ˘ ´
   And yet, by heaven, I think my love as rare   10

14  ˘ ´ ˘ ˘ ´ ˘ ´ ˘ ´ ´
   As any she belied with false compare.   10

Look at the underlined words in lines 2 and 12. *Coral* is naturally stressed on the first syllable. *Treads* seems to deserve a stress, while the preposition *on* does not.

I then complete my prose scansion, compare the two scansions, and settle on this:

1. My mistress' eyes are nothing like the sun;

2. Coral is far more red than her lips' red:

3. If snow be white, ‖ why then her breasts are dun;

4. If hairs be wires, ‖ black wires grow on her head.

5. I have seen roses damask'd, ‖ red and white,

6. But no such roses see I in her cheeks;

7. And in some perfumes is there more delight

8. Than in the breath that from my mistress reeks.

9. I love to hear her speak, ‖ yet well I know

10. That music hath a far more pleasing sound.

11. I grant I never saw a goddess go:

12. My mistress, ‖ when she walks, ‖ treads on the ground.

13. And yet, ‖ by heaven, ‖ I think my love as rare

14. As any she belied with false compare.

You will notice that for some half of the lines (5, 7, 9, 10, 11, 13, 14) I've left the scansion as straight iambs. The others have substitutions. Let's go through my reasoning for each line.

Line 1: The way I read the poem, Shakespeare is describing his mistress realistically, unlike other poets whose mistresses—if their hyperbole is to be believed—are out of this world, hence the unusual emphasis on the pronoun *My*. Notice that this makes the first syllable of *mistress'* (the stressed syllable in the word), the less stressed syllable in the foot. In the second foot, there is no reason not to return to iambs, since we would want to emphasize the part of her that is being compared. So the entire word *mistress'* ends up without a stress. That's okay. Scansion is not just about the stresses in pronouncing single words; it's about which word has relatively more stress in each particular foot.

Line 2: The word *coral* is stressed on the first syllable. Therefore, Shakespeare must have substituted a trochee in the first foot. The rest is iambic.

Line 3: Making the fourth foot a trochee keeps the emphasis on the pronoun relating to the speaker's mistress, a continuing way of marking the contrast. Notice that I've chosen to stress a function word rather than a noun.

Line 4: The focal point in this line is the idea of wires growing out of a head. I've given both *black* and *wires* stress with a spondee, and I've shown a trochee in foot 4 to emphasize *grow*.

Line 6: I've scanned a spondee in foot 5 to emphasize the pronoun *her* to continue the contrast between the speaker's mistress and the others and *cheeks* because it should receive as much stress as *her*.

Line 8: Stress on *than* highlights the comparison; stress on *my* continues the contrast (trochees in 1 and 4).

Line 12: *My* is stressed, as before. I've stressed *treads* because it is the contrast word and because it makes the line sound like a heavy tread with trochees in feet 1 and 4, as opposed to the goddess line (11) that trips neatly along in iambs.

Line 13: I'm assuming that *heaven* is being pronounced as one syllable (sometimes written *heav'n*).

Notice that in my scansion the lines that refer to the ideal (lines 5, 10, and 11) are perfect iambic pentameter, while the lines that refer to the supposed defects of the speaker's mistress have metrical variations that "fall off" from the norm—until the end, when, we could say, the use of strict iambic pentameter for his mistress in line 14 shows her to be of the highest measure (pun intended) despite the speaker's refusal to speak of her in wild hyperbole.

Here's a poem with shorter lines. I have to go past the first line to discover that it's an octave of iambic trimeter with no caesuras. Here's my metric scansion.

## Nothing Gold Can Stay (before 1923)
### by Robert Frost

1 <u>Nature's</u> first green is gold,       6 syllables

2 Her hardest hue to hold.       6

3 Her early leaf's a flower;       6

4 But only so an hour.       6

5 Then leaf subsides to leaf.       6

6 So Eden sank to grief,       6

7 So dawn goes down to day.       6

8 <u>Nothing gold can stay.</u>       5

This is what I came up with after considering both metrics and prose:

## Nothing Gold Can Stay (before 1923)
### by Robert Frost

1 Nature's first green is gold,

2 Her hardest hue to hold.

3 Her early leaf's a flower;

4 But only so an hour.

5 Then leaf subsides to leaf.

6 So Eden sank to grief,

7 So dawn goes down to day.

8 Nothing gold can stay.

Read the second scansion aloud. Do you hear the metrical pauses at the end of Frost's lines?

Line 1: *Nature* has to be a trochee, but the contrast between *green* and *gold* lets me know that both those words need emphasis—the line turns iambic.

Lines 2–7: The movement from unstressed to stressed in most lines emphasizes what we could call the "falling off" from the ideal—everything decays. The sound and sense are particularly well connected in lines 5–7, with the iambs mirroring the meaning of *subsides, sank,* and *goes down.*

Line 3: The rhyme *flower/hour* and the very consistent syllable count up to this point help me decide that Frost intends *flower* to be pronounced as one syllable here.

Line 8: *Nothing* is a trochaic word, but the return of *gold* from line 1 must be emphasized and so must *stay.* The line is missing a syllable. What now? There are two possible explanations: An iambic line missing its first syllable (acephalexis) or a trochaic line with catalexis. In either case, the meaning is appealing because of the sense of loss conveyed by the poem. Like Shakespeare, Frost has used rhythm to reinforce sense. If we take iambic lines to represent the ideal because they match the meter, we can understand why, in his summary statement in which he says the ideal must be lost, we lose the flow of the iambs: "Nothing gold can stay."

Keep in mind that, on paper, we can have multiple choices for how to interpret a poem: There's no need to choose between interpretations. But what may remain ambiguous on the page must be decided in sound. So if we read or recite a poem, it's a good idea to plan ahead, give ourselves time to practice, and (if necessary) scan.

## Caution—Major Mistake Territory!

Scansion is not meant to give *the* answer. For example, you might not agree with my scansion of the last line of Frost's poem. That's okay. Just make sure you have good reasons for the choices you make.

The next poem we'll look at clearly has lines with varying numbers of syllables, and it's very hard to assign a meter to it. For this reason. I just went with a prose reading.

## My Star (1855)
### by Robert Browning

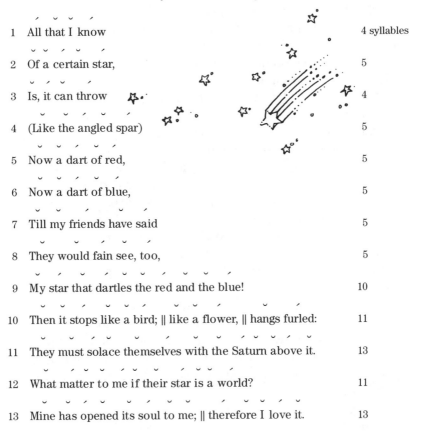

|   |   |   |
|---|---|---|
| 1 | All that I know | 4 syllables |
| 2 | Of a certain star, | 5 |
| 3 | Is, it can throw | 4 |
| 4 | (Like the angled spar) | 5 |
| 5 | Now a dart of red, | 5 |
| 6 | Now a dart of blue, | 5 |
| 7 | Till my friends have said | 5 |
| 8 | They would fain see, too, | 5 |
| 9 | My star that dartles the red and the blue! | 10 |
| 10 | Then it stops like a bird; ‖ like a flower, ‖ hangs furled: | 11 |
| 11 | They must solace themselves with the Saturn above it. | 13 |
| 12 | What matter to me if their star is a world? | 11 |
| 13 | Mine has opened its soul to me; ‖ therefore I love it. | 13 |

The first problem here is to figure out the meaning. First, I take the subject of the poem to be, not a real star, but a person—stars do not have souls. After looking up *dartle*, I think it might represent a sparkling personality, and this, perhaps, is what is reflected in the difficult-to-graph meter. It looks like Browning has divided the first four lines in half to emphasize the rhyme within the lines. I'm going to group them by twos and see what I can make of it that way. By now, I'm wondering if this is accentual rather than accentual-syllabic verse.

1.  All that I know of a certain star,  9 syllables

2.  Is, it can throw ‖ (like the angled spar)  9

3.  Now a dart of red, ‖ now a dart of blue,  10

4.  Till my friends have said they would fain see, too,  10

5.  My star that dartles the red and the blue!  10

6.  Then it stops like a bird; ‖ like a flower, ‖ hangs furled:  11

7.  They must solace themselves with the Saturn above it.  13

8.  What matter to me if their star is a world?  11

9.  Mine has opened its soul to me; ‖ therefore I love it.  13

The poem now seems to be primarily anapests, with four stresses per line (anapestic tetrameter). It has between 9 and 13 syllables per line. Is this from metrical variation, or is this accentual verse? If I analyze it as accentual-syllabic verse, I'll have to acknowledge about one-third substituted feet, and nearly half the lines dropping at least one unstressed syllable. I don't think it bears any more analysis: I think we can just call it four-stress accentual verse.

Keep in mind that you need not scan every poem you read all the way through. Scansion is a tool to help you when there is a need for it—say, for understanding a particular line. Opinions vary on this matter, but I recommend that you never, never read a poem guided by meter alone: You will end up with a wooden, sing-song reading.

# BRAIN TICKLERS
## Set # 41

1. Read the following poems and excerpts. Then identify the meter of each. But don't stop there! Make a comment about how some aspect of the rhythm fits the interpretation of the poem.

### Paul Revere's Ride (1860)
by Henry Wadsworth Longfellow (excerpt)

1 Listen, my children, and you shall hear
2 Of the midnight ride of Paul Revere,
3 On the eighteenth of April, in Seventy-five;
4 Hardly a man is now alive
5 Who remembers that famous day and year.

6 He said to his friend, "If the British march
7 By land or sea from the town to-night,
8 Hang a lantern aloft in the belfry arch
9 Of the North Church tower as a signal light,—
10 One, if by land, and two, if by sea;
11 And I on the opposite shore will be,
12 Ready to ride and spread the alarm
13 Through every Middlesex village and farm,
14 For the country folk to be up and to arm."

### Greenland Whale Fisheries (1800s)
Traditional Folk song (excerpt)

1 In eighteen hundred sixty-three
2    on June the thirteenth day,
3 Our gallant ship her anchor raised
4    and for Greenland sailed away,

5 The lookout in the crow's nest stood
6    with spyglass in his hand.
7 "There's a whale, there's a whale, there's a whalefish," he cried,
8    "and she blows at ev'ry span."

. . .

29   Oh, Greenland is a dreadful place—
30     it's a land that's never green;
31   Where there's ice and snow and the whalefishes blow
32     and daylight's seldom seen.

## Alushta by Day (1826)
by Adam Mickiewicz, translated by Edna Worthley Underwood (1917)

1   The mighty mountain flings its mist-veil down;
2   With little flowers the gracious fields are bright,
3   And from the forest colors flash to sight
4   Like gems that drop from off a Caliph's crown.
5   Upon the meadows settles shimmering down
6   A band of butterflies in rainbow flight;
7   Cicadas call and call in day's delight,
8   And bees are dreaming in a blossom's crown.
9   The waves beneath the cliff are thunder-pale,
10  Now upward, upward in their rage they rise
11  And tawny are their crests as tigers' eyes.
12  The sun is focused on one white, far sail
13  And on blue, shining deeps as smooth as glass
14  Wherein slim cranes are shadowed as they pass.

## The Star (before 1806)
by Jane Taylor (excerpt)

1   Twinkle, twinkle, little star,
2   How I wonder what you are!
3   Up above the world so high,
4   Like a diamond in the sky.

5   When the blazing sun is gone,
6   When he nothing shines upon,
7   Then you show your little light,
8   Twinkle, twinkle, all the night.

9   Then the trav'ller in the dark,
10  Thanks you for your tiny spark,
11  He could not see which way to go,
12  If you did not twinkle so.

# The Eagle (1842)
### by Alfred, Lord Tennyson

1   He clasps the crag with crooked hands;
2   Close to the sun in lonely lands,
3   Ring'd with the azure world, he stands.

4   The wrinkled sea beneath him crawls;
5   He watches from his mountain walls,
6   And like a thunderbolt he falls.

# The Raven (1844)
### by Edgar Allan Poe (excerpt)

1   Once upon a midnight dreary, while I pondered, weak and weary,
2   Over many a quaint and curious volume of forgotten lore—
3   While I nodded, nearly napping, suddenly there came a tapping,
4   As of some one gently rapping, rapping at my chamber door.
5   " 'Tis some visitor," I muttered, "tapping at my chamber door—
6             Only this and nothing more."

# *Song of Hiawatha* III: Hiawatha's Childhood (1854–1855)
### by Henry Wadsworth Longfellow (excerpt)

1   By the shores of Gitche Gumee,
2   By the shining Big-Sea-Water,
3   Stood the wigwam of Nokomis,

. . .

11   There the wrinkled old Nokomis
12   Nursed the little Hiawatha,
13   Rocked him in his linden cradle,
14   Bedded soft in moss and rushes,
15   Safely bound with reindeer sinews;
16   Stilled his fretful wail by saying,
17   "Hush! the Naked Bear will hear thee!"
18   Lulled him into slumber, singing,
19   "Ewa-yea! my little owlet!
20   Who is this, that lights the wigwam?
21   With his great eyes lights the wigwam?
22   Ewa-yea! my little owlet!"

## Birthday Wishes to a Physician (before 1907)
### by Lizelia Augusta Jenkins Moorer

1 Birthday greetings
2 From a friend,
3 All thy meetings
4 Peace attend.

5 Time extended
6 Be thy store,
7 Bliss appended
8 Evermore.

9 Did the flowers
10 Born of May,
11 From their bowers
12 Choose a day?

13 Music ringing,
14 On the air,
15 Flowers springing
16 Everywhere.

17 Chanting gayly,
18 Five and eight,
19 Make the day we
20 Celebrate.

21 Where's the doctor?
22 Can you tell,
23 How she makes her
24 Patients well?

25 Soul of beauty,
26 Day by day,
27 To her duty
28 Hies away.

29 With the sickest,
30 Day and night,
31 In the thickest
32 Of the fight.

33 Heaven's treasure
34 Be thine end,
35 Is the measure
36 Of a friend.

## Song in a Minor Key (c. 1922)
### by Dorothy Parker (excerpt)

1 There's a place I know where the birds swing low,
2    And wayward vines go roaming,
3 Where the lilacs nod, and a marble god
4    is pale, in scented gloaming.
5 And at sunset there comes a lady fair
6    Whose eyes are deep with yearning.
7 By an old, old gate does the lady wait
8    Her own true love's returning.

## Account of a Visit from St. Nicholas (1822)

### by Clement Moore (excerpt)

1  'Twas the night before Christmas, when all through the house
2  Not a creature was stirring, not even a mouse;
3  The stockings were hung by the chimney with care,
4  In hopes that St. Nicholas soon would be there;
5  The children were nestled all snug in their beds,
6  While visions of sugar-plums danced in their heads;
7  And Mama in her 'kerchief, and I in my cap,
8  Had just settled our brains for a long winter's nap;
9  When out on the lawn there arose such a clatter,
10 I sprang from the bed to see what was the matter.
11 Away to the window I flew like a flash,
12 Tore open the shutters and threw up the sash.
13 The moon on the breast of the new-fallen snow,
14 Gave the lustre of mid-day to objects below,
15 When, what to my wondering sight should appear,
16 But a miniature sleigh, and eight tiny reindeer,
17 With a little old driver, so lively and quick,
18 I knew in a moment it must be St. Nick.
19 More rapid than eagles his coursers they came,
20 And he whistled, and shouted, and called them by name;
21 "Now, Dasher! now, Dancer! now, Prancer and Vixen!
22 On, Comet! on, Cupid! on, Donder and Blitzen!
23 To the top of the porch! to the top of the wall!
24 Now dash away! dash away! dash away all!"

## Comment (1925)

### by Dorothy Parker

1  Oh, life is a glorious cycle of song,
2  A medley of extemporanea;
3  And love is a thing that can never go wrong;
4  And I am Marie of Roumania.

## Charge of the Light Brigade (1854)

by Alfred, Lord Tennyson (excerpt)

I

1   Half a league, half a league,
2       Half a league onward . . .

III

18   Cannon to right of them,
19   Cannon to left of them,
20   Cannon in front of them
21       Volley'd and thunder'd;
22   Storm'd at with shot and shell,
23   Boldly they rode and well,
24   Into the jaws of Death,
25   Into the mouth of Hell
26       Rode the six hundred.

## Rain Music (1918)

by Joseph Seamon Cotter, Jr.

1   On the dusty earth-drum
2       Beats the falling rain;
3   Now a whispered murmur,
4       Now a louder strain.

5   Slender, silvery drumsticks,
6       On an ancient drum,
7   Beat the mellow music
8       Bidding life to come.

9   Chords of earth awakened,
10       Notes of greening spring,
11   Rise and fall triumphant
12       Over every thing.

13   Slender, silvery drumsticks
14       Beat the long tattoo—
15   God, the Great Musician,
16       Calling life anew.

2. Write a poem using some or all the rhyming words on one of the following lists (or choose words of your own). Choose a meter and stanza length appropriate to your topic and audience. You might want to try out a meter you've never used before.

   a. buccaneer, mutineer, persevere, steer, sneer, jeer, career, peer, pier, hemisphere
   b. May, spray, stray, bouquet, decay, dismay, display, repay
   c. guise, disguise, surprise, utilize, devise, recognize, lies, spies
   d. fact, lacked, tact, intact, abstract, impact, react
   e. couch, ouch, crouch, grouch, slouch, vouch

(Continued on page 218.)

f. fence, defense, hence, commence, consequence, difference, negligence, preference, sense, events

(Answers are on page 248.)

## NOTE

Here is the entire text of the George Crabbe poem "A Marriage Ring," which you saw on page 190.

1 The ring, so worn as you behold,
2 So thin, so pale, is yet of gold:
3 The passion such it was to prove—
4 Worn with life's care, love yet was love.

# RHYME AND REASON

Often when people talk about rhyme, they mean two words that differ only in their initial sound, like *growl* and *prowl* or *flipper* and *slipper*. In this narrow sense, some English words do not have an English rhyme word: *orange, silver, month, purple, chimney, breadth, circle, desert, monarch, virtue,* and *wisdom* are some examples. Some words have only one rhyme: *mountain/fountain*. It is a much-lamented fact that the word *love*, while so important to us and so often a subject of poetry, has so few rhymes.

The language we speak determines the vocabulary we have available, and the poet's art partly consists in using the chance characteristics of your language to forge a poem. It is also true, however, that learning the subtleties of rhyming terminology will reveal to you some kinds of rhyme that you may not have been aware of. This may open some new insights into the interpretation of the poetry you read and new possibilities for shaping the poetry you write.

## Rhyme placement

Usually when we speak of rhyme, we mean rhyme at the end of lines. But there are multiple places in poetic lines that rhyme can occur. First, we'll examine these in chart format, for easy reference. In the chart, we will use an X to represent words that are not important except for completing the line.

| Placement of Rhyme | |
|---|---|
| **end rhyme**—also called *tail rhyme, terminal rhyme* | **X X X X X X X X X fill** <br> **X X X X X X X X X spill** <br> Using only one end rhyme for more than three lines consecutively is called **monorhyme**. |
| **initial rhyme**—also called *head rhyme* | **We X X X X X X X X** <br> **Three X X X X X X X X** |
| **medial rhyme** (in the middle) | Rhyme between a word in the *middle* of a line and another word. |
| **internal rhyme** | **X X X thou X X X cow** <br> Rhyme between a medial word (often the word before the caesura) and the end rhyme. |
| **close rhyme** | **Hug X X X lug X X X** <br> Internal rhyme of two words in close proximity, neither at the end of the line. |
| **interlaced rhyme** | **X X X X X door X X X** <br> **X X X floor X X X X** <br> Rhyming words that appear medially in two consecutive lines. |

# Kinds of rhymes

Now, we'll turn our attention to the different sound pairs that are called rhymes in English (the definition of rhyme varies by language). First we'll use a chart to show various types of rhyme. Then we'll talk about the effects that different types of rhymes can achieve and look at examples in published poetry.

The chart uses the abbreviations *S* for syllable, *Z* for initial sound, *V* for vowel, and *C* for consonant. The red letters indicate which parts of the words' sounds are identical. The chart also uses the ictus and breve for stressed and unstressed that we learned in the section on meter ( ´ ˘ ). Again, we will use an X to represent words that are not important except for filling up the line.

| Different Sounds of Rhyme | |
|---|---|
| **Name** | **Representation** |
| **perfect rhyme** —also called *true rhyme, full rhyme* There are six types: | ZS with ZS  *ham/jam* <br><br> ZSS with ZSS  *honey/bunny* <br><br> ZSSS with ZSSS  *higgledy/piggledy* <br> No matter how many syllables rhyme, the initial sounds are different. |
| 1. *strong/ masculine rhyme** | Z̍S with Z̍S  *prize/rise* <br><br> Z̍S with ZS̆Z̍S  *prize/arise* <br> This is perfect rhyme occurring on a single, stressed syllable. Note that the two-syllable word is iambic. |
| 2. *weak/ feminine rhyme** | Z̍S̆S with Z̍S̆S  *darling/starling* <br><br> Z̍S̆S̆S with Z̍S̆S̆S  *reference/preference* <br> This is perfect rhyme beginning on a stressed syllable and ending on the final, unstressed syllable. When three syllables are involved, it is called **triple rhyme**. |

* so called because of masculine and feminine endings in romance languages.

| Name | Representation |
|---|---|
| 3. *apocopated rhyme*—also called *light rhyme* | ZS with ZSZS  *sing/starling* This is a perfect rhyme of a stressed syllable in one word, and an unstressed syllable in the other. Notice that the two-syllable word is trochaic. |
| 4. *unstressed rhyme* | ZSS with ZSS  *prizing/singing* This is perfect rhyme of the unstressed syllables in two trochaic words where there is no rhyme in the stressed syllables—some people question whether this is a type of rhyme. |
| 5. *mosaic rhyme* | ZSS with ZS S  *poet/know it* or ZSSS with ZS SS  *Longfellow/strong fellow* This is perfect rhyme formed by joining some shorter words to rhyme with one multisyllabic word. |
| 6. *broken rhyme* | **X X X X X X X X X ZS** . . . *XX fate* **X X X X X X X X ZS-** . . . *Xawait-* **SX X X X X X X X X X** *ing XX* . . . This is perfect rhyme formed by "breaking" (hyphenating) a word across the end of the line. |
| **identical rhyme**— also called *autorhyme, null rhyme, self-rhyme* | ZS  *bear/bear* ZSS  *hairy/hairy* ZSSS  *element/element* If the rhyme words are homonyms or homophones it is called **rich rhyme**. |

| Name | Representation |
|---|---|
| **near rhyme—** also called *off rhyme, slant rhyme, half rhyme* | Approximate rhymes chosen by the poet for effect. These should not be viewed as failures to attain perfect rhyme (without good reason). There are many kinds. Don't confuse this category with *close rhyme*, which refers to placement. |
| 1. *wrenched rhyme* | *Thermopylæ/properly chum/crem-a-tor-e-um* The pronunciation (and sometimes the spelling) of one or more words is mangled to force a rhyme. This can be done by changing the sound or shifting the stress. It differs from other near rhymes in that it creates a mix of surprise and humor. |
| 2. *eye rhyme—* also called *printer's rhyme* | *move/love* This is the rhyme of two words with homographic ending syllables but different pronunciations. An example in English is the group of words ending in *-ough* and each having a different vowel sound (for example, *bough, cough, dough, through, rough*). |
| 3. *assonance* | ZVC with ZVC    *sad/back* Only the vowel sound in the stressed syllable is repeated. |
| 4. *consonance* | ZSC with ZSC    *shed/pod* Only the final consonant sound is repeated. |
| 5. *alliteration* | CS with CS    *red/rose* Only the initial consonant sound is repeated |

| Name | Representation |
|------|----------------|
| 6. *pararhyme*— also called *frame rhyme* | ZVC with ZVC  *find/fond*<br>The initial and final consonant sounds in the final syllable are repeated, but the vowel sound between them is different. |
| 7. *reverse rhyme* | ZSC with ZSC  *heart/hearth*<br>The consonant sound that begins the final syllable and the vowel sound in it are identical. The final consonant sound differs. |

# The uses of rhyme in poetry

Now that we have some vocabulary to work with, let's look at a chart that shows the poetic effects of various types of rhyme.

### Some Poetic Effects of Rhyme Types

| Rhyme type | Effect(s) |
|------------|-----------|
| **end rhyme** | |
| *strong rhyme/ masculine rhyme* | By emphasizing the last word of the line, it may add to the sense of separateness between consecutive end-stopped lines or suggest conclusive finality at the end of rhymed couplets. Strong rhyme is often used for serious topics |
| *weak rhyme/ feminine rhyme* | Triple rhyme especially is often used for comic effect. Some poets use alternating strong and weak rhymes as end rhymes for variety. |
| *apocopated rhyme* | Used instead of strong rhyme, it can reduce the emphasis and apparent surety of statements. |

| Rhyme type | Effect(s) |
|---|---|
| *unstressed rhyme* | Some people won't read this as rhyme. |
| *mosaic rhyme* | Usually used only for comedy—in mock-epic, satire, and comic songs—mosaic rhyme is surprising and clever. |
| *broken rhyme* | It is often used for comic effect. |
| *monorhyme* (The use of only one rhyme for a whole stanza; see p. 233) | Once the pattern is recognized and the available word bank begins to deplete, it can become predictable—but the poet can then play with the reader's expectations. |
| **medial rhyme** | It adds to the sense of patterning and close relationship within or between lines. |

The key is not to use one particular type of rhyme of another—unless you are completing an assignment or working with a set form. Rather, concentrate on using whatever approach to rhyme works for the poem you are writing. This might include using types of rhyme that aren't even on the charts! To understand this flexible approach to rhyme, let's look at three poems by the same poet.

### Ice (2009)
by Garry Smith

1 Met him on a winter day.
2 Saw him falter
3 and fail to check his fall
4 on the frozen walk.
5 Saw him bleed,
6 ragged tear in his trouser knee.
7 Took his hand,
8 to help him stand,
9 to catch his breath,
10 compose himself and
11 go upon his way.

This poem has some strong rhyme, but it isn't used in a standard way in a regular pattern at the ends of the lines. Strong rhyme appears in lines 2 and 3 (*falter/fall*), lines 7 and 8 (*hand/stand*), and lines 1 and 11 (*day/way*). The strong rhyme in the first and last line helps give the poem a sense of closure.

The poem also incorporates identical rhyme. In lines 2 and 5, *saw him* is repeated. In lines 8 and 9, *to* is repeated, an example of anaphora. Additionally, Smith uses assonance in lines 5 and 6 (*bleed/knee*), and alliteration in lines 2–4 (*falter/fail/fall/frozen*), lines 6–7 (*tear/trouser/took*), and lines 7–8 (*his/hand/help/him*). But again, no pattern is built up.

Both the combination of rhyme techniques and their unpatterned use in the poem are unexpected, like taking a spill on the ice. Perhaps the jagged edges of the unequal line lengths tie into this, with Smith fashioning a poem that reflects its subject in several ways.

### Twilight (2009)
#### by Garry Smith

1   Blame the darkness on sundown
2   and the sunlight on small birds
3   that awaken with songs
4   shivering in their lungs.
5   Blame the silence on darkness
6   flooding the valley
7   from rim to distant rim
8   and sunlit singing on gladness,
9   not unlike sailors, bell-buoys
10   ringing them home and joy
11   quivering on their tongues,
12   as if the night is folded back upon itself,
13   and the day is flung open.

In this poem, Smith uses various types of rhyme to emphasize contrasts and parallels. The identical rhyme in lines 1 and 5 (*Blame the*), another use of anaphora, each introduce a section in which dark and light are contrasted. Identical rhyme also highlights the contrast between **sundown** (line 1), on the one hand, and **sunlight/sunlit** (lines 2 and 8) on the other hand.

Within those two sections formed by reiteration of *Blame the* (lines 1–4 and lines 5–13), the parallels are further pointed to by the weak rhyme of *shivering/quivering* (lines 4 and 11). Meanwhile, unstressed rhyme draws attention to the contrast between *darkness* understood figuratively as well as literally (lines 1 and 5) and *gladness* (line 8).

This poem is not ended by the finality of rhyme. Rather, the bursting forth of day to dispel the darkness provides both a new beginning (in the world) and an ending (for the poem).

### Repose (2009)
#### by Garry Smith

1    The week of all my days feels seven short,
2      dull and dusted with toil and
3      punished with redundancy.
4    The ragged edge of a threadbare day,
5      worn thin but neatly folded at
6      the twelves, hangs from the dim lamplight.
7    A bruised and black-eyed sky begins
8      to groan and lick its wounds and a
9      haggard muscle cramps around the chest.
10    A cup of comfort, a sagging chair and a
11      humble hearth beckon a battered
12      man inside, away from the weather rising.
13    I long for a summer sun to warm my nest,
14      to fold with feathered radiance round
15      the room and shield against the storm,
16    to bundle all the sighs and sorrows
17      with a string and, for the little that I do,
18      bless me with a dreamless sleep.
19    So faithfully I sit, while wind blows round
20      this spinning sphere and another week of
21      endless days becomes another year.

Although this poem shares imagery with "Twilight," Smith uses rhyme differently in creating the sound. First and foremost, the poem includes a great amount of alliteration, whereas in Smith's other two poems, there was not one dominant type of rhyme. In this poem, alliteration is unquestionably the predominant sound effect.

| Line Number(s) | Alliteration |
| --- | --- |
| 1 | *seven/short* |
| 2 | *dull/dusted* |
| 7 | *bruised/black-eyed/begins* |
| 9–10 | *chest/chair; cramps/cup/comfort* |
| 11 | *humble/hearth; beckon/battered* |
| 13 | *summer/sun* |
| 14 | *fold/feathered* |
| 14–15 | *radiance/round/room* |
| 15–17 | *storm/sighs/sorrows/string* |

There is also occasional use of pararhyme (line 16: *sighs/ sorrows*) and consonance (line 2: *dull/toil*).

But besides alliteration, the other key types of rhyme in this poem are strong rhyme and identical rhyme. In both of Smith's first two poems, he used devices to lend finality to the ending. In this poem, he creates finality in two ways. First, he repeats the word *week* from line 1 in line 20 and the word *days* from line 1 in line 21. This makes a strong connection between the end and the beginning. Second, he uses strong rhyme—used only one other place in the poem (lines 13, 15: *warm/storm*)— in lines 20 and 21 (*sphere/year*). Because the last word is a rhyme word, it brings a sense of completion.

# BRAIN TICKLERS
## Set # 42

1. Read the following poems and excerpts. Then using the charts on pages 219–224 for reference, identify the rhymes in each poem. For each selection, draw a conclusion about how the use of rhyme informs meaning.

### There Was an Old Man of Thermopylæ
(1872)
by Edward Lear

1   There was an old man of Thermopylæ,
2   Who never did anything properly;
3   But they said, "If you choose,
     To boil eggs in your shoes,
4   You shall never remain in Thermopylæ."

### Safe Piracy

1   I am a pirate, wondrous bold.
2   I am the bloke who's filched more gold
3   than anyone,
4   purloined more plun-
5   der than the rest.
6   I'm simply best.

7   I hold my spyglass to my eye.
8   Ahoy! A rival ship I spy
9   not far alee!
10   But in my ea-
11   sy chair I'm dreaming,
12   so I easily thwart their wicked scheming.

                   [original]

### Model of a Modern Major-General (1879)
by W. S. Gilbert (excerpt)

1   I am the very model of a modern Major-Gineral,
2   I've information vegetable, animal, and mineral;
3   I know the kings of England, and I quote the fights historical,
4   From Marathon to Waterloo, in order categorical;
5   I'm very well acquainted, too, with matters mathematical,
6   I understand equations, both the simple and quadratical;

7   About binomial theorem I'm teeming with a lot o' news,
8   With many cheerful facts about the square of the hypotenuse.
9   I'm very good at integral and differential calculus,
10  I know the scientific names of beings animalculous.
11  In short, in matters vegetable, animal, and mineral,
12  I am the very model of a modern Major-Gineral.

## A Chant of Mystics (1921)

by Ameen Rihani (excerpt)

1   Whirl, whirl, whirl
2   Till the world is the size of a pearl.

3   Dance, dance, dance
4   Till the world's like the point of a lance.

5   Soar, soar, soar
6   Till the world is no more.

## Auf meines Kindes Tod* (1832)

by Joseph von Eichendorff

1   Von fern die Uhren schlagen,
2   es ist schon tiefe Nacht,
3   die Lampe brennt so düster,
4   dein Bettlein ist gemacht.

5   Die Winde nur noch gehen
6   wehklagend um des Haus,
7   wir sitzen einsam drinnen
8   und lauschen oft hinaus.

9   Es ist, als müßtest leise
10  du klopfen an die Tür,
11  du hätt'st dich nur verirret,
12  und kämst nun mud zurück.

13  Wir armen, armen Toren!
14  Wir irren ja im Graus
15  des Dunkels noch verloren—
16  du fandst dich längst nach Haus.

## On the Death of My Child

translated by Aodhagán O'Broin (2000)

1   The distant clocks are striking,
2   It is already late,
3   The lamp is burning dimly,
4   Your little bed is made.

5   The winds are blowing still
6   They wail around the house,
7   Inside we sit here lonely
8   And often listen out.

9   It seems as if that must be
10  You tapping on the door,
11  You lost your way a little,
12  But now you've made it home.

13  What silly foolish folk we are!
14  It's we who are misled—
15  While we're still lost in darkness
16  You've long since found your bed.

---

* Here you will need to compare the end rhymes of an English translation and the German original. For the German version, just look at the even-numbered lines and go by the spelling to determine the kind of rhyme. You do not have to know German to do this. Did the translator use the same kind of rhymes as the original?

## The Bustle in the House (c. 1866)
### by Emily Dickinson

1 The bustle in a house
2 The morning after death
3 Is solemnest of industries
4 Enacted upon earth.

5 The sweeping up the heart
6 And putting love away
7 We shall not want to use again
8 Until eternity.

## The Whistling Gypsy
### Traditional British Folk Song

1 The Gypsy Rover, came over the hill, down through the valley so shady.
2 He whistled and he sang till the green woods rang, and he won the heart of a lady.

Refrain:

    Ah dee doo ah dee doo da day, ah dee doo ah dee day dee
    He whistled and he sang till the green woods rang
    And he won the heart of a lady

3 She left her father's castle gate, she left her own true lover,
4 She left her servants and her estate, to follow the Gypsy Rover.

5 Her father saddled his swiftest steed, and roamed the valleys all over.
6 He sought his daughter at great speed and the whistling Gypsy Rover.

7 He came at last to a mansion fine, down by the River Clady,
8 And there was music and there was wine, for the gypsy and his lady.

9 "O Father, he's no gypsy free, but lord of these lands all over,
10 And I shall stay till my dying day, with my whistling Gypsy Rover."

## The Fox*
### Traditional Folk Song, originally English, 1700s

1 The fox went out on a chilly night
2 And he prayed for the moon to give him light
3 For he'd many a mile to go that night
4 Before he reached the town-o

---

\* The refrain for "The Fox" changes for every verse, incorporating the last two lines of the verse. Lines 7–9 are the refrain for verse one.

Refrain:

    Town-o, town-o
    He'd many a mile to go that night
    Before he reached the town-o.

5   He ran till he came to a great big pen
6   The ducks and the geese were kept therein
7   He said, "A couple of you are gonna grease my chin
8   Before I leave this town-o"

9   He grabbed the grey goose by the neck
10  Threw the duck across his back
11  He didn't mind the quack-quack-quack
12  And the legs all dangling down-o

13  Then Old Mother Flipper-Flopper jumped out of bed
14  Out of the window she cocked her head,
15  Crying, "John! John, the grey goose is gone,
16  And the fox is on the town-o"

17  Then John, he ran to the top of the hill,
18  Blew his horn both loud and shrill.
19  Fox, he said, "I'd better flee with my kill
20  For they'll soon be on my trail-o"

21  He ran till he came to his cozy den
22  There were his little ones: eight, nine, ten.
23  "Daddy," they said, "you'd better go back again,
24  'Cause it must be a very fine town-o"

25  Then the fox and his wife, without any strife,
26  Cut up the goose with a fork and knife.
27  They never had such a supper in their life,
28  And the little ones chewed on the bones-o.

## Fire and Ice (1920)
### by Robert Frost

1 Some say the world will end in fire,
2 Some say in ice.
3 From what I've tasted of desire
4 I hold with those who favor fire.
5 But if it had to perish twice,
6 I think I know enough of hate
7 To know that for destruction ice
8 Is also great
9 And would suffice.

2. By thinking, using a rhyming dictionary, and/or brainstorming with friends, come up with at least three pairs of triple rhymes. See if you can find a triple set (three words that all rhyme for three syllables).
3. *Challenge:* Can you think of a quadruple rhyme?

(Answers are on page 251.)

## Rhyme schemes

Rhyme schemes are patterns of end rhymes. They are recorded with lowercase letters. Here's how:

1. Check the end rhyme of the first line. If there is at least one other line that rhymes with it, mark all the lines with that rhyme, *a*. If there aren't any others, that's okay. Make sure to check for different types of rhyme, not just strong rhyme.
2. Find the first line in the poem that does not rhyme with *a*. Check for lines that rhyme with it. Mark that line and all lines in the entire poem that rhyme with that line, *b*.
3. Continue with the next unmarked line, following the procedure until all rhyming lines in the poem are marked.
4. You can leave rhymeless lines unmarked, or mark them with an *x*. In quatrains with two unrhymed lines, you will often find the first designated *x* and the second *y*.

To identify the rhyme scheme, list the sequence in order. (In type, you use italic letters.) For example, a poem composed of quatrains (four-line stanzas) might have *abab* in the first stanza.

The chart shows some of the typical rhyme schemes for the shorter stanzas and their names (if they have names).

| Stanza length | Rhyme scheme |
| --- | --- |
| **rhymed couplets—** two-line stanzas | *aa, bb, cc,* etc. |
| **tercets—**three-line stanzas | *axa* or *aaa; bxb* or *bbb,* etc. |
| *terza rima—*a set of tercets with interlocking rhyme | *aba, bcb, cdc,* etc. |
| **quatrains—**four-line stanzas | Six types are listed here. |
| *single-rhyme—*one of the traditional stanzas for ballad meter. (The other is cross-rhyme.) | *xaya, xbyb,* etc. |
| *cross-rhyme—*also called *alternating rhyme* | *abab, cdcd,* etc. |
| *envelope rhyme—*also called *arch-rhyme* or *chiasmic rhyme* | *abba, cddc,* etc. |
| *opposed couplets* | *aabb, ccdd,* etc. |
| *Omar Khayyám stanza* | *aaxa, bbxb,* etc. |
| *monorhyme* | *aaaa, bbbb,* etc. |

Patterns of rhymes set up expectations for the reader. Once a pattern has been established, putting off an expected rhyme creates **delayed rhyme**; moving it up creates **accelerated rhyme**. You can create suspense or surprise the reader with these techniques.

## Writing with rhymes

A rhyme scheme can be planned in prewriting or developed as you draft. A rhyming dictionary may help you identify a pool of possible words, but you still have to judge whether a particular word fits the diction and context in your particular poem. Refrigerator magnets provide an easy way to shift words around and try them in different combinations.

## BRAIN TICKLERS
### Set # 43

1. It's time to apply new learning to familiar poems. Figure out the rhyme scheme and other uses of rhyme in one of the listed poems. Tell how your analysis expands the meaning of the poem for you.
    a. "Stopping by Woods on a Snowy Evening," page 129
    b. "The Raven," pages 214 and 12
    c. "I Wandered Lonely as a Cloud," page 89
    d. "Abraham Lincoln Walks at Midnight," page 177
    e. "The Cremation of Sam McGee," page 23
2. Write about a subject you've never written about, using at least two kinds of rhyme. If you like, use one of these titles to get started:

You Are Cold as Dust
A is for Apple
The Strange Thing in My Basement
Ronald LaRue and Maggie Pew
The Pig and the Polar Bear
Evanescence

(Answers are on page 254.)

# LEFT TO YOUR OWN DEVICES: OTHER USES OF SOUND

## Long and short sounds

When you were learning to read, you were probably taught about long vowels (those that "say their own names") and short vowels (those that appear in CVC—consonant-vowel-consonant—words). But here we are going to discuss the actual length of time it takes to utter certain letter combinations and how poets can use this. This discussion has three parts.

### 1. Vowels in context

Vowels in speech are almost always followed by consonants, if not in the word they're in, then in the following word. The

length of time it takes to say a vowel is partly governed by the type of consonant that follows. There are two types of consonants: voiced and unvoiced. **Voiced consonants** are the kind that set your larynx buzzing as it does when you hum. Try humming and you'll feel it. Put your hand on your throat, and you'll feel it in your fingers, too. When you say **unvoiced consonants** (be careful not to say a vowel sound afterwards) they don't make your larynx buzz.

Look at this chart of voiced and unvoiced consonants. (Notice that it includes some consonant combinations.)

| Voiced | Unvoiced |
|---|---|
| b, d, g as in *goose*, j, l, m, n, ng, r, th as in *then*, v, w, y, z, zh | c, ch, h, f, k, p, s, sh, t, th as in *thigh* <br> *s becomes voiced (pronounced like z) in certain situations |

Now, here's the lowdown: It takes twice as long to say a vowel followed by a voiced consonant as it does to say a vowel followed by an unvoiced consonant. You can prove that voiced consonants take longer to say by pronouncing these sets of words:

> *sap/sad*     *let/leg*     *tick/Tim*     *hush/hug*

Can you hear and feel the difference? (There are more details, but no space to discuss them. If you're interested, look for a book on phonetics or ask a knowledgeable adult.)

## 2. More words take longer to say

It takes longer to say a line of poetry with many monosyllables than one with a few multisyllabic words. This occurs partly because there are short pauses between words.

## 3. Consonant blends

It takes longer to say *strength* than to say *wren* because of those extra consonant sounds that our mouths need to wrap around.

---

# BRAIN TICKLERS
### Set # 44

Read the following poem. Then answer the questions about the poet's use of sound.

### Amoretti LXXV (1592–1594?)
#### by Edmund Spenser

1   One day I wrote her name upon the strand,
2   But came the waves and washèd it away:
3   Again I wrote it with a second hand,
4   But came the tide, and made my pains his prey.
5   "Vain man," said she, "that lost in vain assay,
6   A mortal thing so to immortalize;
7   For I myself shall like to this decay,
8   And eke my name be wipèd out likewise."
9   "Not so," (quod I) "let baser things devise
10  To die in dust, but you shall live by fame:
11  My verse your virtues rare shall eternize,
12  And in the heavens write your glorious name:
13  Where whenas death shall all the world subdue,
14  Our love shall live, and later life renew."

1. What is the connection between the length of word sounds and the theme of the poem?

2. How does Spenser manipulate his vocabulary to reinforce the poem's meaning?

(Answers are on page 255.)

## Onomatopoeia

At one time **onomatopoeia** was only used to refer to words that are imitative of the sounds they name. Onomatopoeia traditionally brings to mind words like *whirr, buzz, zoom, swish, zip, crackle,* and *mew*. But poets can create onomatopoetic effects in other ways as well. Recently its use has been widened to other kinds of imitation. For example, if a poet used long words to describe something large and short words to describe something small (for example, *stupendous, prodigious,* and *tremendous* vs. *wee, puny,* and *tiny*), this could now be called onomatopoeia. Similarly, the sharp, jagged outline of line ends in the poem "Ice" (page 224), which may be imitating the sharp and jagged edges that pieces of ice can have, may be another example of onomatopoeia.

## BRAIN TICKLERS
### Set # 45

Read the following poem. Then explain the effects of the poet's use of alliteration and onomatopoeia.

### Reapers (1922)
#### by Jean Toomer

1  Black reapers with the sound of steel on stones
2  Are sharpening scythes. I see them place the hones
3  In their hip-pockets as a thing that's done,
4  And start their silent swinging, one by one.
5  Black horses drive a mower through the weeds,
6  And there, a field rat, startled, squealing bleeds,
7  His belly close to ground. I see the blade,
8  Blood-stained, continue cutting weeds and shade.

(Answers are on page 256.)

## Cacophony

**Cacophony** is the purposeful use of harsh sounds for effect. It may include the use of alliteration and onomatopoeia, as well as other sound devices. Here's an example in which the harsh sounds and unpleasant subject matter go hand-in-hand, as is often the case with cacophony. Notice how many sounds are /k/, /ch/, /b/, and /t/. In this case these rough sounds are combined with an accentual verse form that has four stresses, and six to nine syllables per line, so that the stresses are erratic and less musical and soothing than they would be in a regular pattern.

### *The Tragedy of Macbeth* (1605)
### Act IV, scene I
by William Shakespeare (excerpt)

FIRST WITCH:
4   Round about the cauldron go:
5   In the poison'd entrails throw.
6   Toad, that under cold stone
7   Days and nights has thirty-one
8   Swelter'd venom sleeping got,
9   Boil thou first i' the charmed pot.

ALL:
10   Double, double, toil and trouble;
11   Fire burn and cauldron bubble.

SECOND WITCH:
12   Fillet of a fenny snake,
13   In the cauldron boil and bake;
14   Eye of newt and toe of frog,
15   Wool of bat and tongue of dog,
16   Adder's fork and blind-worm's sting,
17   Lizard's leg and howlet's wing,
18   For a charm of powerful trouble,
19   Like a hell-broth boil and bubble.

# BRAIN TICKLERS
## Set # 46

Read the following poem. Explain how the poet creates cacophony and what purpose it serves in the poem.

### Beat! Beat! Drums! (1861)
by Walt Whitman

1   Beat! beat! drums!—blow! bugles! blow!
2   Through the windows—through doors—burst like a ruthless force,
3   Into the solemn church, and scatter the congregation,
4   Into the school where the scholar is studying;
5   Leave not the bridegroom quiet—no happiness must he have now with
     his bride,
6   Nor the peaceful farmer any peace, ploughing his field or gathering his
     grain,
7   So fierce you whirr and pound you drums—so shrill you bugles blow.

8   Beat! beat! drums!—blow! bugles! blow!
9   Over the traffic of cities—over the rumble of wheels in the streets;
10   Are beds prepared for sleepers at night in the houses? no sleepers must
     sleep in those beds,
11   No bargainers' bargains by day—no brokers or speculators—would they
     continue?
12   Would the talkers be talking? would the singer attempt to sing?
13   Would the lawyer rise in the court to state his case before the judge?
14   Then rattle quicker, heavier drums—you bugles wilder blow.

15   Beat! beat! drums!—blow! bugles! blow!
16   Make no parley—stop for no expostulation,
17   Mind not the timid—mind not the weeper or prayer,
18   Mind not the old man beseeching the young man,
19   Let not the child's voice be heard, nor the mother's entreaties,
20   Make even the trestles to shake the dead where they lie awaiting the
     hearses,
21   So strong you thump O terrible drums—so loud you bugles blow.

(Answers are on page 256.)

239

## Euphony

In contrast to cacophony, **euphony** is the use of flowing, smooth, harmonious sounds. It makes use of repeated vowel sounds and the so-called liquid consonants, *l* and *r*. Read this excerpt and think about its use of euphony.

### The Lotos-Eaters, Part VIII (1832)
#### by Alfred, Lord Tennyson

145   The Lotos blooms below the barren peak:
146   The Lotos blows by every winding creek:
147   All day the wind breathes low with mellower tone:
148   Thro' every hollow cave and alley lone
149   Round and round the spicy downs the yellow Lotos-dust is blown.

Notice the repetition of and alliteration of *l* and *b* in lines 145 and 146 and the repetition of the long *o* sound (as in the first syllable of *Lotos*) in *below, blow, low, mellower, tone, hollow, lone, yellow,* and *blown,* creating a sense of soothing and lulling. The trochees of "Round and round the spicy downs" rock back and forth.

## BRAIN TICKLERS
### Set # 47

1. Read the following excerpts. Analyze the use of sound in each selection.

### *The Odyssey of Homer,* vol. 1 (c. 700 B.C.E.)
translated by George Chapman (1614–1616) (excerpt)

1    The man, O Muse, inform, that many a way
2    Wound with his wisdom to his wished stay;
3    That wandered wondrous far, when he the town
4    Of sacred Troy had sack'd and shivered down;
5    The cities of a world of nations,
6    With all their manners, minds, and fashions,
7    He saw and knew; at sea felt many woes,
8    Much care sustained, to save from overthrows
9    Himself and friends in their retreat for home;
10   But so their fates he could not overcome,
11   Though much he thirsted it.

### Out of the Cradle Endlessly Rocking (1859)
by Walt Whitman (excerpt)

| | |
|---|---|
| 111 | Hither my love! |
| 112 | Here I am! here! |
| 113 | With this just-sustain'd note I announce myself to you, |
| 114 | This gentle call is for you my love, for you. |
| | |
| 115 | Do not be decoy'd elsewhere, |
| 116 | That is the whistle of the wind, it is not my voice, |
| 117 | That is the fluttering, the fluttering of the spray, |
| 118 | Those are the shadows of leaves. |
| | |
| 119 | O darkness! O in vain! |
| 120 | O I am very sick and sorrowful. |
| | |
| 121 | O brown halo in the sky near the moon, drooping upon the sea! |
| 122 | O troubled reflection in the sea! |
| 123 | O throat! O throbbing heart! |
| 124 | And I singing uselessly, uselessly all the night. |
| | |
| 125 | O past! O happy life! O songs of joy! |
| 126 | In the air, in the woods, over fields, |
| 127 | Loved! loved! loved! loved! loved! |
| 128 | But my mate no more, no more with me! |
| 129 | We two together no more. |

2. Write a poem in which you use various sound devices other than (or in addition to) rhyme to create meaning. Think about the effects your choices will have on your audience.

(Answers are on page 256.)

# BRAIN TICKLERS—THE ANSWERS

Set # 34, page 177

**Possible responses:**

1. Lindsay's simple diction refers to the fundamentally important things in life: *state, town, children, market, man, shawl, sleep, men, kings, world, peasants, terror, weep, sins, heart, free, peace. Peace* is one of the few content words repeated in the poem (lines 28 and 31). This

simplicity makes *portentous* and *dreadnaughts* stand out. I never heard of *Cornlands* before. The *Oxford English Dictionary* says it was first used in 1387 and means "land that is used for or is suitable for cultivating corn."

2. In lines 5–8, there is a series of three prepositional phrases, each starting with *or*—polysyndeton. This emphasizes that Lincoln walks everywhere through the town, not just in one area.

In lines 11 and 12, Lindsay uses the phrases "the prairie-lawyer" and "master of us all" (both epithets) as appositives to expand on "the quaint great figure that men love." These emphasize Lincoln's simple roots, his learning, and his role as president.

In lines 13 and 25 and also in lines 19 and 20 Lindsay uses anaphora. The repetition of "He cannot" expands our understanding of why Lincoln's ghost is walking, recalling us to the central image of the poem. The repetition of "Too many" (lines 19 and 20) emphasizes the breadth of the trouble that has roused Lincoln from his rest.

Lines 19 and 20 also use asyndeton, giving a sense of events breaking forth with no pause.

In lines 20 and 31, "black terror" and "white peace" are metaphors that contrast the situation as it is and as Lincoln. (and the reader) hopes to find it. Here, *black* and *white* are the traditional symbols of evil and good.

Line 28 uses a metonym for Europe, which is composed of *Cornland* (plains/farmland), *Alp* (mountains), and *Sea* (water).

3. The main image in the poem is Lincoln roaming through Springfield (lines 1–18). Lines 19–22 and 25–29 focus on images of war and peace in Europe (but still all seen through Lincoln's eyes). The  final image is of Lincoln again resting in peace. Aside from line 16, where "breathe deep, and start" refers to sound as well as sight, the imagery is all visual.

4. The poem has a title and eight stanzas of four lines each. The second and fourth line in each stanza rhyme. The title is important because it contains the only mention of Lincoln's name, although the description of him in lines 9 and. 10 would be recognizable to most U.S. citizens.

5. The rhythm of the poem makes me think of Lincoln's pacing through the streets.

6. Unlike *Cornland, Alp,* and *Sea,* which are all common nouns (despite being capitalized), *Cornwall* is a proper noun—the old name of the farthest southwest county of England. It would not allow for the metonymy anymore and would make it harder to construe the meaning.

7. "The Great War" (World War I) erupted in the summer of 1914. By September, Austria-Hungary, Germany, and Great Britain had declared war, Luxembourg and Belgium had been invaded, other nations had started fighting without formal declarations of war, and several major battles had been fought.

8. The poem is a reaction to the outbreak of World War I. The speaker says that "peasants fight" (line 19) without knowing why. But he and the readers know that it is because of "the sins of all the war-lords." Lincoln's unrest is a symbol of the unrest so many people and nations in the world felt at the Central Powers' disregard for treaties and promises, their trespasses into neutral territory, and the enormous loss of life and disruption of lives that the war caused.

   This poem is about our connectedness. Lindsay shows a man who is not at peace with his own goal achieved, be it ever so great, and his own country at peace. Lincoln will not find peace until peace is shared everywhere by everyone. The living, the dead, our neighbors, and those across the ocean are all connected, and no one is at peace until all are at peace. This is the interpretation that the two questions suggest.

Set # 35, page 179

1. **Possible responses:**

**The Mahogany Tree**
The words of "The Mahogany Tree" are mostly simple and have only one or two syllables. This is important because the short line length does not allow for many longer words to fit easily. There is still room for variety, however, as can be seen in my chart.

| Line # | Meaning unit | # of words in meaning unit |
|---|---|---|
| 1, 2, 4 | independent clauses | 3 |
| 3 | adjectival phrase | 3 |
| 5–6 | independent clause | 5 |
| 7–8 | independent clause with ellipsis (*we* is understood) | 5 |
| 9–11 | independent clause | 9 |
| rest of 11 | adverbial clause | 3 |
| 12,13 | independent clauses | 3 |
| 14 | adverbial clause | 3 |
| 15–16 | adverbial clause | 9 |

**Casey at the Bat**
"Casey at the Bat" uses the odd combination of baseball jargon ("Mudville nine," "died at first," "get a whack at that") and the high-blown and hyperbolic language of heroic adventure ("so upon that stricken multitude grim melancholy sat," "watching it in haughty grandeur"), along with a lot of clichés ("hope which springs eternal," "muffled roar"). In this, it reminds me of "The Football Match" (page 112). The multisyllabic words coupled with the imagery of sports reporting and epic and the sensory detail work well in the long lines. The poem turns on the use of

paraprosdokian, and the long sentences—several of which are compound-complex and a number of which take up four whole lines—help build the suspense by dragging out the meaning units. For contrast, each of lines 45–48 is a complete sentence, the effect of which is to slow down the action like a stop-action camera in the last moments before the climax.

## Set # 36, page 182

### 1. Possible responses:

**Death of an Old Carriage Horse**
"Death of an Old Carriage Horse" is about a horse pressed into harsh service, or perhaps it is a symbolic poem about slavery (I thought this because "oppressing force" seemed to refer to something larger and more powerful than a harsh master and because I discovered that Horton was born into slavery and liberated at the end of the Civil War.) The use of epistrophe or refrain at the end of every stanza reinforces the constriction of the life the horse lives—the end of every thought is the repeated words that epitomize his servitude: "push along." The last stanza is ironic—even the horse's "sweet and favored friend" uses these words as the horse ended his life. If the poem is symbolic and the slave is being freed from his burden and entering the afterlife, the ending is ironic in a different sense in that the words that epitomized his lack of freedom in this life are the same words that bid him leave slavery behind and enter heaven.

**The New England Boy's Song About Thanksgiving Day**
Child's use of anaphora at the beginning of each five-line stanza shows us that the poem is a light reflection on the journey to a family celebration. The stanzas have lines of different lengths but in a set pattern. This gives the poem a songlike quality.

**When I Set Out for Lyonnesse**
Hardy's six-line stanzas are all based on epanalepsis: Each stanza begins with the same two lines that it ends with and has two lines in between, so we know the end of every stanza as we begin it. The two lines in the middle end the idea of the first two lines and begin the idea of the last two lines. The advance

knowledge of each stanza's ending contrasts sharply with the content of the poem, which is about the mystery and magic of Lyonnesse (a legendary country that has now sunk into the sea, according to Arthurian legend). The second stanza says that what would happen to the speaker in Lyonnesse could not be foretold by either religious prediction (prophet) or magic (wizard), and though we know that something happened there, for the effects are described in the third stanza—we are never told what it is. I think this is a poem about reading Arthurian legend. Each time he reads, the speaker "sojourn[s]" in Lyonnesse and is transformed by the experience.

## Set # 37, page 184

**Possible responses:**

1. The end stops, coupled with alternating questions and answers, signal a dialogue, despite the lack of quotation marks. Each end-stop is the end of what one speaker says.

2. This poem has some elements that I have already seen as symbols. "Stopping by Woods on a Snowy Evening" (page 129) and "On the Death of my Child" (page 229) both referred (directly or indirectly) to journeys, night, sleep, and bed. "Up-Hill" doesn't make sense as a poem about a particular journey. And if it were, who would the speaker be, and how would the inn hold beds "for all who come"? It makes more sense to imagine the questioner as the soul and the answers as coming from God, with the journey being the journey of life, darkness being death, and the bed at the inn being eternal rest.

## Set # 38, page 185

**Possible response:**

The refrain is "And the barber kept on shaving." My understanding of the refrain changed as I read. At first, I thought the barber was just busy. Then I thought the barber was ill-mannered to ignore a man who was trying to help him. Finally, I saw that the barber's silence was a comment on the value of the man's harangue.

## Set # 39, page 186

**Possible responses:**

1. First I thought the poem would reveal a confusing experience that might seem both dreamlike and real. But the first stanza begins "I dreamed" and the events described seem unreal and nightmarish. Within the poem, the dream is not questioned until the second stanza, when the speaker finds evidence to suggest that he or she actually has been in a lake. Without the warning in the title, the poem might have seemed like a trick on the reader.
2. The poem develops Lincoln's action described in the title as a symbol of the unrest caused by World War I. On rereading the poem, I noticed how much enjambment there is: Only the fifth stanza of this eight-stanza poem has every line end-stopped with punctuation. The enjambment gives the poem a sense of always pushing ahead, which mirrors Lincoln's restlessness.

3. (poem difficult to understand without its title)

### Picking Cherry Tomatoes

"Six-feet high and wired for strength"
seems daunting and unnatural in words.

But . . .
no small, burnished, plump, and nearly bursting roundness
ever
leapt into my hand at gentlest touch
—as if it willed connection—
at farmstand, store, or market.

[original]

## Set # 40, page 203

**Possible responses:**

1. He is explaining the need for unity. I agree. It takes more than a couple of great lines to make a poem work—all the parts must form a coherent whole.

2. He is saying that some people evaluate poetry by whether the rhythm matches the meter (does it always have the "right" number of syllables?). Since the rhythm should reflect the sense, and since a perfectly metrical poem would be boring, I agree.

3. He is deploring monotony of meter and rhyme. I agree that variety shouldn't be sought for its own sake, but used to create interest and underline meaning.

4. He's saying that the poem is a unity—you cannot consider the meaning apart from the sound of the poem. I agree. That's one important difference between poetry and prose.

## Set # 41, page 212

1. **Possible responses:**

**Paul Revere's Ride**
"Paul Revere's Ride" is **accentual verse** (8 to 12 syllables per line, but consistently 4 stresses per line).
   The point here seems to be to tell the story fully without omitting details, and so the flexible line of four stresses and however many syllables are necessary works well.

**Greenland Whale Fisheries**
"Greenland Whale Fisheries" is in **ballad meter**.
   This seems to be a work song for sailors. Ballads are often dramatic and sad and this one concludes with a lament about having to go to Greenland, an appropriately bleak end.

## Alushta by Day

"Alushta by Day" is a sonnet in **iambic pentameter**.

I read line 12 as ending with two spondaic feet—these focus the reader's attention on the sail, reinforcing the sense of the line.

## The Star

"The Star" is **trochaic tetrameter with catalexis.**

I knew the first verse as a nursery rhyme, so I was expecting accentual meter, but each line (except line 11 in which there is anacrusis) has seven syllables. I imagine that the trochaic rhythm might reflect the twinkling of the star.

## The Eagle

"The Eagle" is **iambic tetrameter** (with a substituted trochee in foot one of lines 2 and 3).

The alliteration of *c* in the first line reinforces the stress falling on those syllables that begin with a *c*.

## The Raven

"The Raven" is **trochaic octameter** with a refrain.

The trochees mirror the repeated tapping and rapping that the speaker hears.

## Song of Hiawatha

"Song of Hiawatha" is **trochaic tetrameter.**

The spondee substituted in foot 2 of line 21 reinforces the power of Hiawatha's "great eyes."

## Birthday Wishes to a Physician

"Birthday Wishes to a Physician" is **trochaic dimeter** with catalexis in lines 2 and 4 of each stanza.

The rhythm seems quick and cheerful, as does the content of the poem.

## Song in a Minor Key

"Song in a Minor Key" is **ballad meter** (for a literary ballad) with anapests substituted in the first and third foot of the odd-numbered lines.

The substituted anapests give the odd lines a certain bounce and joy, which contradicts the title. I didn't realize until line 6 that the poem is about yearning. This time, Parker is using *meter* ironically.

### Account of a Visit from St. Nicholas

"Account of a Visit from St. Nicholas" is **anapestic tetrameter** with acephalectic lines and substitutions.

I've noticed that people usually develop a rhythm for calling to their pets (for example, "Here kitty, kitty, kitty, kitty!") and the use of anacrustic catalectic dactylic tetrameter in lines 21 and 22 gives a nice rhythm to St. Nicholas's call to his reindeer.

### Comment

"Comment" is **ballad meter** (again, for a literary ballad) but with a regular pattern: dactylic tetrameter with anacrusis in all four lines and catalexis in lines 1 and 3.

The bouncy dactyls underline the frivolous/naïve tone of the first three lines, as well as the irony of the fourth.

### The Charge of the Light Brigade

"The Charge of the Light Brigade" is **dactylic dimeter**.

I have also seen this poem classified as **amphimaceric dimeter**, but some experts say that amphimacers are a classical foot and do not exist in English. Dactyls are certainly more appealing in understanding lines 18 to 21 (with catalexis in line 21), whereas lines 22 to 25 seem to begin with a dactyl and have amphimacers substituted in the second foot. However it's analyzed, the rhythm echoes of the beat of the horses' hooves and the firing of the cannons.

### Rain Music

"Rain Music" is **ballad meter** (in a literary ballad).

Cotter has often thrown two of the stresses to the back of the odd lines (maybe we could call them two tailless trochees in a row), which become imitative of the sound of the earth-drum being pounded.

2. **Possible response:** (Anapestic Dimeter)

On the Hazards of Owning a Cat in UK

OR

(Lost cat, Found Cat) x 2

In the dark of the night,
with the moon at its brightest, my heart was upli-
fted to see that my cat
had returned now to me.

But come morning (the next),
oh! my heart it was vexed,
for my cat had remem-
bered her yen for the Thame-
s she decided to flee.

She went there for the fish.—Oh the fish in that river! She caught them and ate
them and had such a si-
ngular time: now she's sate-
d; she's come back to me.

[original]

## Set # 42, page 228

1. **Possible responses:**
   **There Was an Old Man of Thermopylæ**
   "There Was an Old Man of Thermopylæ" has **wrenched
   end rhyme** between lines 2 and lines 1 and 5—all triple, all
   feminine; **identical end rhyme** between lines 1 and 5; and
   **strong internal rhyme** in line 3. The clever rhyme for
   "Thermopylæ" is the best thing in the poem, in my opinion.

   **Safe Piracy**
   "Safe Piracy" has **perfect rhyme** for all end rhymes:
   **strong rhyme** in lines 1 and 2, 5 and 6, and 7 and 8, **weak
   rhyme** in lines 11 and 12, and **broken rhyme** in lines 4 and
   5 and lines 10 and 11; as well as **internal rhyme** in lines 7
   and 8. The assuredness of the rhymed couplets underscores
   the tone of the pirate who is confident that everything will
   go his way. (There is no name in the chart for the perfect
   rhyming of the first syllable only in a trochaic word with a
   single-syllable word. This occurs in the poem in both the
   internal rhymes and the broken rhymes. For the purposes
   of this exercise, we'll just call it perfect rhyme.)

   **Model of a Modern Major-General**
   The song from *The Pirates of Penzance* has **wrenched end
   rhyme** in lines 1 and 2 (repeated in lines 11 and 12) and
   lines 10 and 11 (the correct—though rare—adjectival form
   of *animalcule* is *animalcular*, says the *Oxford English
   Dictionary*); **mosaic end rhyme** (also wrenched a little) in

lines 7 and 8; **weak triple end rhyme** in lines 3 and 4 and 5 and 6; **identical close rhyme** in lines 1 and 2 (*model/ modern*; *-le/-al/-al*; repeated in line 11); **interlacing rhyme** in lines 4 and 5 (*Waterloo/too*); **reverse close rhyme** in line 5 (*mat-/math-*); and **interlaced rhyme** in lines 5 and 6 (*-quai-/-qua-*). The wrenching and unusual triple rhymes combined with the Major-General's claims of competence in completely unrelated specialties, few of which are relevant to his office, make this very funny. I kept waiting to hear (in the rhyme word) what his next crazy claim was going to be.

### A Chant of Mystics

"A Chant of Mystics" has **strong rhyme** at all the line ends; **identical close rhyme** in lines 1, 3, and 5; and **reverse interlaced rhyme** in lines 1 and 2 (*whirl/world*). I think this is a poem about the Sufi mystics called whirling der- vishes who whirl around in a ritual dance. According to the information I found on a Sufi website, the dance causes "a feeling of soaring," which represents a spiritual journey. The words chosen for repetition, I noticed, have a feeling of speeding up and slowing down because of the blends at the ends of the first two words and the *r*-controlled vowel in the third—like the feeling you get if you try to twirl repeat- edly by pushing off with one foot, gliding around, pushing off, gliding, and so on.

### Auf meines Kindes Tod

"Auf meines Kindes Tod"/"On the Death of My Child," now I can see that they don't always use perfect rhymes in German—stanzas 1, 2, and 4 have end rhyme words that look like **strong rhymes,** but the end rhyme in lines 10 and 12 seems to be **assonance**. The translator has picked up on this and used **assonance** at the ends of lines 2 and 4 and lines 6 and 8. There's a **strong end rhyme** in lines 14 and 16, but I don't know what to call the rhyme (if it is rhyme) in lines 10 and 12. (Both words have *o*'s, but they are not pronounced the same, at least in my dialect of American English—the translator's name is Irish, so it may sound dif- ferent to him.) I noticed that in the translation the speakers are quite certain all through the first three stanzas that they know the correct view of things, but it isn't until their view is completely reversed in the fourth stanza that the perfect rhyme confirms their thoughts with its finality and certitude.

## The Bustle in the House
"The Bustle in the House" has **consonance** at the ends of lines 2 and 4; and **wrenched rhyme** to end lines 6 and 8. Perhaps we cannot have that sense of finality that comes with perfect rhyme in Dickinson's view of this broken life.

## The Whistling Gypsy
"The Whistling Gypsy" has **weak mosaic end rhyme** in the refrain (*day dee/lady*), as well as **weak end rhyme** in lines 1 and 2, 5 and 6, 7 and 8, and 9 and 10; **eye end rhyme** in lines 4 and 5, which is also unstressed rhyme (original pronunciation may have differed); **interlaced strong** rhymes in lines 1 and 2 (*hill/till*), lines 3 and 4 (*gate/estate*), lines 5 and 6 (*steed/speed*), and lines 7 and 8 (*fine/wine*); and **close strong rhyme** in line 12 (*shay/day*), as well as in the nonsense words of the refrain. The rhymes are typical as is the story.

## The Fox
"The Fox" has **monorhyme** at the ends of refrain lines; **identical end rhymes** in lines 1 and 3; **strong end rhymes** in lines 1 and 2, 6 and 7, 10 and 11, 13 and 14, 17 to 19, 21 to 23 (the way I pronounce *again*), and 25 to 27; **consonance** between the last word in line 5 and the **perfect strong end rhyme** in lines 6 and 7 (likewise for line 9 with lines 10 and 11); pararhyme in line 13; **internal rhyme** in lines 15 and 25; and **consonant internal rhyme** in line 15 (*duck/back*). This animal story (especially with the little foxes at the end) seems made for children, and the uncomplicated, repeated rhymes fit the design.

## Fire and Ice
"Fire and Ice" has **strong end rhymes** but only three sounds used as rhymes—*abaabcbcb*; **initial identical rhyme** in lines 1 and 2; and **identical interlaced rhyme** in lines 6 and 7 (*know*). The whole poem is ironic: What difference does it make which of two methods the unavoidable end comes by? If the end is coming, why waste our time arguing about the means? Let's *live*!

2. Set of two triple rhymes: *evermore/nevermore, millionaire/ billionaire*; Set of three triple rhymes: *latitude/attitude/ gratitude*

3. *criticism/witticism*

## Set # 43, page 234

1. **Possible response:** In "Stopping by Woods on a Snowy Evening," Frost has created an interlocking rhyme scheme: *aaba, bbcb, ccdc, dddd*. Each stanza, taken alone, has a single rhyme and introduces the rhyme for the next stanza. The last stanza is monorhyme, with identical rhyme in lines 15 and 16. All the end rhymes are strong, perfect rhymes. The final rhyme (*d*) is hinted at in the early stanzas: The lines are interlaced with long *e* sounds in lines 1, 3, 8, and 12. I think getting that rhyme scheme to work must have required rapt attention, like that the speaker gave to the woods. In both cases, the contemplation of beauty/art is given time, without giving up life for it. It is engaged in freely, with one's whole being for the time allotted; then one moves on to the other demands of life.

2. **Possible response:** topic: laundry; rhyme scheme: rhymed couplets

### Laundry: Dedicated to the Dirty Clothes
#### in *Simple Simon*

The things that can be said about laundry
are various and sundry.

For example, we could explore the fine points of sorting and dividing,
with allusion to the fact that when you want to clean *your* clothes, someone
    *else's* interest in the same activity is sure to be coinciding.
We could also discuss soap and detergent and whether liquid is better than
    powder,
and which company makes the best and quietest washer, and whose machine
    does a worse job and is louder.

Then there's the question of water temperature—cold, warm, or hot;
and the bleach dispenser—whether to use it or not.

How you set the wash cycle is, of course, a matter about which not everyone
  is willing to talk, some people being snooty,
so we may never know the truth about whether people really prefer normal,
  delicate, or heavy duty.

As for me, when I do laundry, the thing that I'm most fearing
is the inevitable phenomenon of socks disappearing.

I put my laundry in, my socks all nicely in pairs, which I attach to each other
  in all kinds of ways,
and no matter what I do, when I open the dryer, I have lonely strays.

So it comes to this: laundry is just a part of life, and with all its peculiarities
  we must somehow, weekly, get through it,
but if you really can't stand it (and are rich enough) you can always take it to
  the cleaners, and let them do it.

[original]

## Set # 44, page 236

1. **Possible response:** Spenser's theme is that his verse will
   make his love's name immortal.

2. **Possible response:** The key lines seem to be lines 10 and
   11. The sounds in line 10 change sharply after the first six
   words, matching the contrast the speaker is stating. When
   he's talking about mortality, he uses short words with few
   voiced consonants ("To die in dust, but you"). Then there is
   a change, with an increase in both word length and voiced
   consonants at the end of each word. In line 11, this continues: Of the seven words, six have voiced consonants
   (mostly *r*'s). This use of voiced consonants draws out the
   line—making it last longer, moving it toward immortality,
   and reinforcing the speaker's claim.

## Set # 45, page 237

**Possible response:**
The regular repetition of *s* sounds (every stressed syllable) in lines 1 and 2 may be imitating the regular hiss of the scythes across the hones. The word *one* is pronounced as if it begins with a *w*, so there is alliteration between lines 4 and 5 as well, covering the transition in topic from the reapers to the mower, but then the sound changes. *Squealing* is onomatopoetic, and the alliteration of *c*'s in the last line is harsh. Though the reapers and the mower are both cutting, the similarity ends there. The poem is contrasting them, and the sound helps show this.

## Set # 46, page 239

**Possible response:**
The single-syllable words with exclamation marks that spit out at the beginning of the poem begin the cacophony, with the word *beat* biting itself off at the end. I notice the emphasis (loudness and intensity) given by the exclamation marks. Dashes, too, break up the flow of the lines and contribute to the effect. Whitman uses onomatopoetic words that name loud, often-unpleasant sounds: *burst, whirr, rumble, rattle,* and *thump.* Lines like 7 interrupt the erratic rhythm preceding it with a strong iambic beat that imitates the drums. The alliteration with /k/ sounds in lines 11 to 13 also breaks up the phrasing. The poem reproduces the sounds of war, just at the time the Civil War was starting.

## Set # 47, page 240

1. **Possible response:**
   "*The Odyssey of Homer*"
   Chapman has alliteration of *m*'s in line 1, shifting to *w*, and carrying into line 3. At the end of line 3, he begins to use *t* (though in a word with a *w*), and through lines 4 he uses both *s* and *t*. In the following lines there are some repetitions of the alliteration with sounds of *s, w, t,* and *f*. There is close reversed rhyme in line 2 and interlacing pararhyme

between lines 2 and 3 *(wound/ first syllable of wondrous)*. The impression I get is of a carefully, thoughtfully wrought story—perhaps this is supposed to be a sign of the Muse's having heard the speaker's prayer.

### "Out of the Cradle Endlessly Rocking"

Like "Beat! Beat! Drum!," this excerpt has apostrophe, but this time to a lover, not to a drum. The stop and start of the phrases here is that of a troubled soul, not the cacophonic roar of battle. There are several onomatopoetic words: the repeated groan of the *O*, along with *whistle* and *futtering*. The repetition of the word *fluttering* creates more fluttering. The widely varying line length emphasizes the speaker's distress, as does the sobbing of the word *loved* repeatedly.

2. alliteration and sound length

### Unwanted Memories

I tape pieces of memories
onto blank pages to make a book.
Then wait,
and look at it again,
and tear each memory's yellowed page in hate,
in four, in eight, in shreds, and then—
I take a new blank page and paste again.

I never fill a book.
I come back to look
at what my life has been,
and see again the memories I've seen.
And with
embarrassment, relief,
despair—
if I could just *not care!*—
I match the corners neatly in a stack:
a pack of cards to deal away.
And almost of their own accord,
the memories and pages fray
beneath my fevered fingers.

I throw them away . . .
and start a new book later in the day.

[original]

# CHAPTER FIVE

# A Goodge Selection of Poetic Forms

As we've discussed before, one of the first things we notice about a poem, even before we start reading, is its shape. Poems come in all kinds of shapes and sizes. Some are "nonce" shapes— made up for writing one particular poem and possibly never used again. At the other end of the spectrum are forms with a long and rich history, specific rhyme schemes, and intricate rules.

In this chapter, we'll explore some of the various forms that poets writing in English have used. We'll look at the classification of forms, and then examine some forms of different lengths. We'll look at syllabic poetry, free verse, and visual or pattern poetry. We'll share some poems that are "useful," and wrap up with some light-hearted parodies.

Poetry is often divided into three categories: narrative, dramatic, and lyric. To get us started, we'll look at a narrative poem by an Australian poet of the nineteenth century.

### A Snake Yarn* (before 1909)
#### by William Thomas Goodge

1  "You talk of snakes," said Jack the Rat,
2  "But, blow me, one hot summer,
3  I seen a thing that knocked me flat
4  Fourteen foot long, or more than that,
5  It was a regular hummer!
6  Lay right along a sort of bog,
7  Just like a log!

8  "The ugly thing was lyin' there
9  And not a sign o' movin',
10  Give any man a nasty scare;
11  Seen nothin' like it anywhere
12  Since I first started drovin'.
13  And yet it didn't scare my dog.
14  Looked like a log!

15  "I had to cross that bog, yer see,
16  And blue I was humpin';
17  But wonderin' what that thing could be
18  A-layin' there in front o' me
19  I didn't feel like jumpin'.
20  Yet, though I shivered like a frog,
21  It seemed a log!

22  "I takes a leap and lands right on
23  The back of that there whopper!" He stopped.
24  We waited. Then Big Mac remarked,
25  "Well, then, what happened, Jack?"
26  "Not much," said Jack, and drained his grog.
27  "It was a log!"

---

\* Here are two notes on the text (courtesy of Dave Campbell, on whose website I found the poem), for items you might have trouble tracking down:

1. *Drovin'* in line 12 is short for *droving*, which means herding sheep or cattle.
2. "And blue I was humpin' " (line 16) means carrying a swag—a bedroll with all one's belongings packed in it.

The speaker is what people in the U.S. call a *hobo* and what Australians call a *swagman*. The practice of traveling like this is sometimes called waltzing matilda—a name you may recognize from the song of that name.

## BRAIN TICKLERS
### Set # 48

Reread "A Snake Yarn." Then answer the questions.
1. Describe the stanzas—length, metrics, use of rhyme, including rhyme scheme.
2. Do you think the poet's use of language is effective? Explain your answer.
3. Is the chosen form effective? Explain your answer.

(Answers are on page 330.)

# THE BIG THREE: NARRATIVE, DRAMATIC, LYRIC

## Narrative

**Narrative verse** recounts a sequence of events with a causal element. It is a story in verse, told by a speaker or narrator (that's where the word *narrative* originates).

The forms most closely associated with narrative poetry include ballads, both folk and literary, and epic. "A Snake Yarn" is a narrative poem. Some other narrative poems you have seen in this book include "The Cremation of Sam McGee," "La Belle Dame Sans Merci," "Dad's Gift," "Casey at the Bat," "Paul Revere's Ride," "Greenland Whale Fisheries," "The Whistling Gypsy," and "The Fox." As different as these poems are and as varied in their treatment of character and setting, for each one, the movement of plot is at the center. Something happens; because of this, something else happens. This is the essence of narrative, in whatever form we find it.

# BRAIN TICKLERS
## Set # 49

If you read this retelling of 2 Kings 19 (Hebrew Scriptures/Old Testament) carefully, you are unlikely to ever forget the vivid simile-induced imagery in the first two stanzas. Tell the plot of the poem in your own words.

### The Destruction of Sennacherib (1815)
#### by George Gordon, Lord Byron

1 The Assyrian came down like the wolf on the fold,
2 And his cohorts were gleaming in purple and gold;
3 And the sheen of their spears was like stars on the sea,
4 When the blue wave rolls nightly on deep Galilee.

5 Like the leaves of the forest when Summer is green,
6 That host with their banners at sunset were seen;
7 Like the leaves of the forest when Autumn hath blown,
8 That host on the morrow lay withered and strown.

9 For the Angel of Death spread his wings on the blast,
10 And breathed in the face of the foe as he passed;
11 And the eyes of the sleepers waxed deadly and chill,
12 And their hearts but once heaved, and for ever grew still!

13 And there lay the steed with his nostril all wide,
14 But through it there rolled not the breath of his pride;
15 And the foam of his gasping lay white on the turf,
16 And cold as the spray of the rock-beating surf.

17 And there lay the rider distorted and pale,
18 With the dew on his brow, and the rust on his mail:
19 And the tents were all silent, the banners alone,
20 The lances unlifted, the trumpet unblown.

21 And the widows of Ashur are loud in their wail,
22 And the idols are broke in the temple of Baal;
23 And the might of the Gentile, unsmote by the sword,
24 Hath melted like snow in the glance of the Lord!

(Answers are on page 330.)

## Dramatic

**Dramatic poetry** is an enactment rather than a narrative. Just as in theatre we see action directly and hear characters speak for themselves, so the characters in dramatic poetry speak to us directly without being filtered through the speaker's voice. Dramatic poetry can appear in the form of a full-blown comedy or tragedy for the stage, on the one hand, or a briefer monologue or dialogue, on the other. Dramatic poetry from which we have read excerpts includes "The Raven," "Ulysses and the Siren," *Romeo and Juliet, Macbeth,* and "The Love Song of J. Alfred Prufrock." "The Death of a Hired Man" has aspects of both narrative and dramatic poetry, and is sometimes called *dramatic narrative.*

There are several different kinds of dramatic poems with a single speaker. **Dramatic monologues** are characterized by the speaker's self-revelation, addressed either to him- or herself (as in a soliloquy in a play), to the reader or listener, or to another character.

# BRAIN TICKLERS
### Set # 50

Read to following excerpts from a dramatic monologue. Then answer each question in a paragraph.

### *Ulysses* (1842)
by Alfred, Lord Tennyson (excerpts)

1  It little profits that an idle king,
2  By this still hearth, among these barren crags,
3  Match'd with an aged wife, I mete and dole
4  Unequal laws unto a savage race,
5  That hoard, and sleep, and feed, and know not me.
6  I cannot rest from travel: I will drink
7  Life to the lees: All times I have enjoy'd
8  Greatly, have suffer'd greatly, both with those
9  That loved me, and alone, on shore, and when
10  Thro' scudding drifts the rainy Hyades
11  Vexed the dim sea: I am become a name;
12  For always roaming with a hungry heart
13  Much have I seen and known; cities of men

14   And manners, climates, councils, governments,
15   Myself not least, but honour'd of them all;
16   And drunk delight of battle with my peers,
17   Far on the ringing plains of windy Troy.
18   I am a part of all that I have met;
19   Yet all experience is an arch wherethro'
20   Gleams that untravell'd world whose margin fades
21   For ever and forever when I move.
22   How dull it is to pause, to make an end,
23   To rust unburnish'd, not to shine in use!
24   As tho' to breathe were life! Life piled on life
25   Were all to little . . .
56                 Come, my friends,
57   'Tis not too late to seek a newer world.
58   Push off, and sitting well in order smite
59   The sounding furrows; for my purpose holds
60   To sail beyond the sunset, and the baths
61   Of all the western stars, until I die.
62   It may be that the gulfs will wash us down:
63   It may be we shall touch the Happy Isles,
64   And see the great Achilles, whom we knew.
65   Tho' much is taken, much abides; and tho'
66   We are not now that strength which in old days
67   Moved earth and heaven, that which we are, we are;
68   One equal temper of heroic hearts,
69   Made weak by time and fate, but strong in will
70   To strive, to seek, to find, and not to yield.

1. Who is the speaker?
2. What does he want?
3. To whom is he speaking?

(Answers are on page 331.)

# Lyric

**Lyric** is the hardest kind of poetry to define because its definition has changed. Originally, it was simple: Lyrics were poems sung to the accompaniment of a lyre. As you may have guessed, the name *lyric* is derived from the word *lyre*. When poetic compositions became literary (written down to be read), the lyre was no longer used and the definition had to be revised. Although many say that the musical quality is still evident in a lyric poem's sound, musicality is a hard quality to define. Some find it easiest to assume that if a poem is neither narrative nor dramatic, it is lyric.

Many lyrics are brief with a high emotional content, revealing the speaker's thoughts and feelings—love poetry and mystic poetry are examples. A list of some of the lyric forms will show you how diverse lyrics can be: carol, cinquain, haiku, hymn, madrigal, nursery rhyme, ode, psalm, Rubáiyát, sea shanty, and sonnet. Lyric poems you have read in this book include "Loveliest of Trees"; "Night"; "To My Dear and Loving Husband"; "Psalm 100"; "I Wandered Lonely as a Cloud"; "Break, Break, Break"; "Sonnet CXXX"; and "A Birthday."

# BRAIN TICKLERS
## Set # 51

Read the following poems. Then answer the questions.

### The Wild Swans at Coole (1917)
by William Butler Yeats

1 The trees are in their autumn beauty,
2 The woodland paths are dry,
3 Under the October twilight the water
4 Mirrors a still sky;
5 Upon the brimming water among the stones
6 Are nine-and-fifty Swans.

7 The nineteenth autumn has come upon me
8 Since I first made my count;
9 I saw, before I had well finished,
10 All suddenly mount
11 And scatter wheeling in great broken rings
12 Upon their clamorous wings.

13 I have looked upon those brilliant creatures,
14 And now my heart is sore.
15 All's changed since I, hearing at twilight,
16 The first time on this shore,
17 The bell-beat of their wings above my head,
18 Trod with a lighter tread.

19  Unwearied still, lover by lover,
20  They paddle in the cold
21  Companionable streams or climb the air;
22  Their hearts have not grown old;
23  Passion or conquest, wander where they will,
24  Attend upon them still.

25  But now they drift on the still water,
26  Mysterious, beautiful;
27  Among what rushes will they build,
28  By what lake's edge or pool
29  Delight men's eyes when I awake some day
30  To find they have flown away?

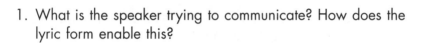

1. What is the speaker trying to communicate? How does the lyric form enable this?

### The Pasture (1914)
#### by Robert Frost

1  I'm going out to clean the pasture spring;
2  I'll only stop to rake the leaves away
3  (And wait to watch the water clear, I may):
4  I shan't be gone long.—You come too.
5  I'm going out to fetch the little calf
6  That's standing by the mother. It's so young,
7  It totters when she licks it with her tongue.
8  I shan't be gone long.—You come too.

2. By Frost's direction, the preceding poem is placed at the front of every collection of his works. Is it a lyric, a dramatic address to the audience, or both? Explain your answer.

3  Write either a lyric, a dramatic, or a narrative poem. Make it as artful as you can, choosing devices appropriate to your subject, tone, purpose, and audience.

(Answers are on page 331.)

# MAKE MINE MEDIUM: MID-SIZED POEMS

In this section we will focus on one of the most popular mid-length poems, the sonnet (fourteen lines). But you should know that medium-sized poems can also be created by building up sets of couplets, quatrains, other shorter stanzas, or any structure that works for the particular poems.

## Sonnets

Some sonnets are called Italian and English after the countries in which the forms originated, but they are written in many countries outside of Italy and England. Whether you know it or not, you have already read (in entirety or in excerpt) twelve sonnets in this book.

There are three main sonnet forms with which you should be familiar to start: Italian (or Petrarchan); English (or Shakespearian); and Spenserian. The Italian sonnet has two parts: An eight-line stanza called an **octave** and a six-line stanza called a **sestet**. The other two sonnets each have four parts: Three quatrains and a rhyming couplet, but with different rhyme schemes. Here is a chart to help you distinguish them:

| Name | Stanzas | Rhyme scheme |
|---|---|---|
| Petrarchan/ Italian | 1 octave 1 sestet | *abbaabba cdecde* or *cdcdcd* or any combination except one that ends with a rhyming couplet |
| Shakespearian/ English | 3 quatrains 1 rhyming couplet | *abab cdcd efef gg* |
| Spenserian | 3 quatrains with interlocking rhyme 1 rhyming couplet | *abab bcbc cdcd ee* |

The variations in the forms are mirrored in the different ways ideas are presented in each of the three kinds of sonnets. The Italian sonnet develops a thought in the octave. Then there is a change (the technical word is *turn, volta* in Italian), and the sestet varies the idea of the octave and completes the thought in a (somewhat or completely) unexpected way. The other two forms express a different idea in each quatrain, each extending, playing off of, or arguing with the preceding one, the turn often coming after the completion of twelve lines, and the whole being concluded with finality in the rhyming couplet.

## BRAIN TICKLERS
### Set # 52

1. Here is an example of each type of sonnet. Read each one and answer the questions.
   • What kind of sonnet is it? How do you know?
   • How does the thought develop in the octet/sestet or quatrains/couplet? Explain this turn of thought.

   a. This is a sonnet from one of the first sonnet sequences written in English. A sonnet sequence is a cycle of sonnets on a particular theme and/or to a particular individual.

## Delia XVII (1592)
### by Samuel Daniel

1 Why should I sing in verse, why should I frame
2 These sad neglected notes for her dear sake?
3 Why should I offer up unto her name
4 The sweetest sacrifice my youth can make?
5 Why should I strive to make her live forever,
6 That never deigns to give me joy to live?
7 Why should m'afflicted muse so much endeavor
8 Such honor unto cruelty to give?
9 If her defects have purchased her this fame,
10 What should her virtues do, her smiles, her love?
11 If this her worst, how should her best inflame?
12 What passions would her milder favors move?
13 Favors, I think, would sense quite overcome,
14 And that makes happy lovers ever dumb.

b. This is one of the earliest sonnets written. The famous
   Italian poet Dante Alighieri called its author the "father of
   Italian love poetry."

## Of Moderation and Tolerance (late 1200s)
### by Guido Guinicelli, translated by Dante Rossetti (1861)

1 He that has grown to wisdom hurries not,
2 But thinks and weighs what Reason bids him do
3 And after thinking he retains his thought
4 Until as he conceived the fact ensue.
5 Let no man to o'erweening pride be wrought,
6 But count his state as Fortune's gift and due.
7 He is a fool who deems that none has sought
8 The truth, save he alone, or knows it true.
9 Many strange birds are on the air abroad,
10 Nor all are of one flight or of one force,
11 But each after his kind dissimilar:
12 To each was portioned of the breath of God,
13 Who gave them divers instincts from one source.
14 Then judge not thou thy fellows what they are.

c. This sonnet (you've read it already) is from a sonnet sequence written about the same time as Daniel wrote the Delia sonnets.

### Amoretti LXXV (1592–1594?)
by Edmund Spenser

1   One day I wrote her name upon the strand,
2   But came the waves and washèd it away:
3   Again I wrote it with a second hand,
4   But came the tide, and made my pains his prey.
5   "Vain man," said she, "that dost in vain assay,
6   A mortal thing so to immortalize;
7   For I myself shall like to this decay,
8   And eke my name be wipèd out likewise."
9   "Not so," (quod I) "let baser things devise
10  To die in dust, but you shall live by fame:
11  My verse your virtues rare shall eternize,
12  And in the heavens write your glorious name:
13  Where whenas death shall all the world subdue,
14  Our love shall live, and later life renew."

2. Read the following poems, here and on page 272. Then answer the questions.

### Soneto de repente,* from *La niña de plata* (c. 1600)
by Lope de Vega

1   Un soneto me manda hacer Violante,
2   que en mi vida me he visto en tanto aprieto;
3   catorce versos dicen que es soneto,
4   burla burlando van los tres delante.

5   Yo pensé que no hallara consonante
6   y estoy a la mitad de otro cuarteto,
7   mas si me veo en el primer terceto,
8   no hay cosa en los cuartetos que me espante.

9   Por el primer terceto voy entrando,
10  y parece que entré con pie derecho
11  pues fin con este verso le voy dando.

12  Ya estoy en el segundo y aun sospecho
13  que voy los trece versos acabando:
14  contad si son catorce y está hecho.

___

* Yes, the following poem is in Spanish. And yes, you will be able to work with it, just as you worked with the German poem earlier. You're just going to compare the spellings of the words that end the lines to find out which ones rhyme.

## Instant Sonnet
### translated by Alix Ingber (1995)

1   A sonnet Violante bids me write,
2   such grief I hope never again to see;
3   they say a sonnet's made of fourteen lines:
4   lo and behold, before this line go three.

5   I thought that I could never get this far,
6   and now I'm halfway into quatrain two;
7   but if at the first tercet I arrive,
8   I'll have no fear: there's nothing I can't do!

9   The tercets I have just begun to pen;
10  I know I must be headed the right way,
11  for with this line I finish number one.

12  Now I am in the second, and suspect
13  that I have written nearly thirteen lines:
14  count them, that makes fourteen, and look—it's done.

## Improvised Sonnet
### translated by Aodhagán O'Broin (1999)

1   "Make me a sonnet?" Violante's plea
2   performance-fear and promises combines:
3   they say a sonnet must have fourteen lines,
4   and stealthily before this one go three.

5   I thought that finding words would be a chore,
6   and here I've half another quatrain done!
7   If I achieve the first tercet, I've won;
8   those quatrains just don't scare me anymore.

9   The first tercet is just beginning here,
10  so far, so good, the bearing still seems right,
11  since I can see that this line's end is near.

12  And now I'm on the second, and suspect
13  that thirteen finished lines will expedite
14  the count to fourteen, and the end perfect.

a. Note the structure, including rhyme scheme for each of the three previous sonnets. How are they similar? How do they differ?

b. What is there to recommend each translation as a sonnet in its own right?

c. Find all the complete sonnets that appear in the first four chapters of this book. List them, separating them by type.

(Answers are on page 332.)

# BRAIN TICKLERS
## *Set # 53*

1. Read the following poems, that use definite forms neither of which is a sonnet. Then describe each poetic form and how it fits the poet's purpose.

### Sorrow (1914)
by Edna St. Vincent Millay

1   Sorrow like a ceaseless rain
2       Beats upon my heart.
3   People twist and scream in pain, —
4   Dawn will find them still again;
5   This has neither wax nor wane,
6       Neither stop nor start.

7   People dress and go to town;
8       I sit in my chair.
9   All my thoughts are slow and brown;
10   Standing up or sitting down
11   Little matters, or what gown
12       Or what shoes I wear.

### Transience (1912)
by Sarojini Naidu

1   Nay, do not grieve tho' life be full of sadness,
2   Dawn will not veil her splendor for your grief,
3   Nor spring deny their bright appointed beauty
4   To lotus blossom and ashoka leaf.

5   Nay, do not pine, tho' life be dark with trouble,
6   Time will not pause or tarry on his way;
7   To-day that seems so long, so strange, so bitter,
8   Will soon be some forgotten yesterday.

9   Nay, do not weep; new hopes, new dreams, new faces,
10   The unspent joy of all the unborn years,
11   Will prove your heart a traitor to its sorrow,
12   And make your eyes unfaithful to their tears.

2. Write a mid-sized poem, either a sonnet or another form. Subject idea: Use the poem to comment on or respond to an issue, opinion, or attitude presented in one of the poems in this chapter.

(Answers are on page 335.)

# SHORT GUYS AND LONGFELLOWS: FORMS AT THE EXTREMES

In this section, we will explore very brief and very long poetic forms. Brief poetry is often humorous, satiric, or witty—and lends itself to lyric poetry. Long poetry tends to be dramatic or narrative.

## Short forms

### Couplet

We're going to start with two lines—the shortest poem that includes both meter and end rhyme. A two-line poem is a **couplet**. This term is also used to refer to two consecutive rhymed lines that form the building blocks of a larger stanza. Stand-alone couplets have been used through history for epigrams—pithy, satiric statements or maxims. Here is an example of a couplet epigram.

**To Fool or Knave** (1616)
by Ben Jonson

1  Thy praise or dispraise is to me alike:
2  One doth not stroke me, nor the other strike.

### Tercet

Next in length is the **tercet**. It is still short, but it allows for more development of thought. Here is another epigram, but this time, the three lines of the tercet are used to develop an extended metaphor which is "thrown away" with the final elliptical sentence fragment.

### On Spies (1616)
by Ben Jonson

1  Spies, you are lights in state, but of base stuff,
2  Who, when you've burnt yourselves down to the snuff,
3  Stink and are thrown away. End fair enough.

## Quatrain

The four-line **quatrain** is long enough to include idea development, contrast, or opposition (see page 233 for quatrain rhyme schemes). This single-rhyme quatrain reflects on the relationship of faith and knowledge.

### "Faith" is a fine invention (c. 1860)
by Emily Dickinson

1  "Faith" is a fine invention
2  For gentlemen who *see*.
3  But *Microscopes* are prudent
4  In an emergency!

## Limerick

Take five lines (chiefly anapestic) of accentual verse with (usually) an *aabba* rhyme pattern, throw in some unusual thoughts, and you have a **limerick**. Lines 1, 2, and 5 are trimeter, whereas lines 3 and 4 are dimeter. It's easier to hear the meter than to figure it out from the verbal description. Here are two anonymous examples.

1  A flea and a fly in a flue
2  Were imprisoned, so what could they do?
3    Said the fly: "Let us flee"
4    Said the flea: "Let us fly!"
5  So they flew through a flaw in the flue.

1  There was a young man from Darjeeling,
2  Who got on a bus bound for Ealing;
3    It said at the door:
4    "Don't spit on the floor."
5  So he carefully spat on the ceiling.

# Long forms

## Ballads

Long forms lend themselves to deep thoughts, to episodic adventures, and to major investments of time and artistry. But that doesn't mean that they are never humorous. **Ballads,** partly because they partake of both folk origins and literary heritage, treat a variety of subjects from the tragic ("Greenland Whale Fisheries," page 212) to love interest ("The Whistling Gypsy," page 230) to the comic, which you are about to read.

This sample ballad is a humorously ironic folk song written in octaves.

### Father Grumble (pre-1825, originally Scottish)

1 There was an old man who lived in the woods,
2 as you can plainly see,
3 who said he could do more work in a day
4 than his wife could do in three.
5 "If that be so," the old woman said,
6 "why this you must allow:
7 That you shall do my work for a day
8 while I go drive the plough.

9 "Now you must milk the tiny cow
10 for fear she should go dry,
11 and you must feed the little pigs
12 that are within the sty,
13 and you must watch the speckled hen
14 for fear she'll lay astray,
15 and you must wind the reel of yarn
16 that I spun yesterday."

17 The old woman took the staff in her hand
18 and went to drive the plough;
19 the old man took the pail in his hand,
20 and went to milk the cow.
21 But Tiny hinched, and Tiny flinched,
22 and Tiny cocked her nose.
23 And Tiny hit the old man such a kick
24 that the blood ran down to his toes.

25 'Twas, "Hey, my good cow!" and "Ho, my good cow!"
26 and "Now, my good cow, stand still!
27 If I ever milk this cow again,
28 'twill be against my will."
29 And when he'd milk'd the tiny cow
30 for fear she should go dry,
31 why then he fed the little pigs
32 that were within the sty.

33 And then he watched the speckled hen,
34 lest she should lay astray.
35 But he forgot the reel of yarn
36 his wife spun yesterday.
37 He swore by all the leaves on the trees,
38 and all the stars in heaven,
39 that his wife could do more work in a day,
40 than he could do in seven.

Did you notice that the ballad started off with masculine rhymes and ended with a feminine rhyme? Pretty clever work!

## Epic

The grandest of poetic forms in scale and scope, **epics** treat the origins of civilizations, early mythologies, heroic adventures, and memorable deeds . . . usually at great length. To give you an idea of the length, the first twelve books of the *Odyssey* (there are twenty-four in all) have 6,213 lines of dactylic hexameter.

Here is the opening of the Roman epic, the *Aeneid*.

### Aeneid of Virgil (19 B.C.E.)
translated by John Dryden (1697) (excerpt)

1 Arms, and the man I sing, who, forc'd by fate,
2 And haughty Juno's unrelenting hate,
3 Expell'd and exil'd, left the Trojan shore.
4 Long labors, both by sea and land, he bore,
5 And in the doubtful war, before he won
6 The Latian realm, and built the destin'd town;
7 His banish'd gods restor'd to rites divine,
8 And settled sure succession in his line,
9 From whence the race of Alban fathers come,
10 And the long glories of majestic Rome.
11 O Muse! the causes and the crimes relate;
12 What goddess was provok'd, and whence her hate;
13 For what offense the Queen of Heav'n began
14 To persecute so brave, so just a man;
15 Involv'd his anxious life in endless cares,
16 Expos'd to wants, and hurried into wars!

## Blank verse

**Blank verse** is the term for unrhymed iambic pentameter. It is used in verse dramas (like the plays of Shakespeare) and lengthy narrative poetry—it was the meter Frost chose for "The Death of the Hired Man" (page 31). Here is the beginning section of a poem in blank verse based on Arthurian legend.

### Morte D'Arthur (1835)
by Alfred, Lord Tennyson (excerpt)

1     So all day long the noise of battle roll'd
2     Among the mountains by the winter sea;
3     Until King Arthur's table, man by man,
4     Had fallen in Lyonnesse about their Lord,
5     King Arthur: then, because his wound was deep,
6     The bold Sir Bedivere uplifted him,
7     Sir Bedivere, the last of all his knights,
8     And bore him to a chapel nigh the field,
9     A broken chancel with a broken cross,
10    That stood on a dark strait of barren land.
11    On one side lay the ocean, and on one
12    Lay a great water, and the moon was full.

13      Then spake King Arthur to Sir Bedivere:
14    "The sequel of to-day unsolders all
15    The goodliest fellowship of famous knights
16    Whereof this world holds record. Such a sleep
17    They sleep—the men I loved. I think that we
18    Shall never more, at any future time,
19    Delight our souls with talk of knightly deeds,
20    Walking about the gardens and the halls
21    Of Camelot, as in the days that were.
22    I perish by this people which I made,—
23    Tho' Merlin sware that I should come again
24    To rule once more—but let what will be, be,
25    I am so deeply smitten thro' the helm
26    That without help I cannot last till morn.

Of course, other meters and forms can be adapted for long poems. Remember Henry Wadsworth Longfellow's "The Song of Hiawatha" (page 214), written in trochaic tetrameter?

## BRAIN TICKLERS
### Set # 54

Write a short poem or a long poem, different from anything you've ever done before. Don't choose a short poem because you think it will take less time: Getting an epigram "right" can require hours of thought! Consider your audience as you write.

If you want to write an epigram, consider using a politician or a recent political event or speech as your topic. You might find material on C-SPAN's coverage of the House or Senate, or in a news article.

(Answers are on page 337.)

# YOU CAN COUNT ON THIS: SYLLABIC AND WORD COUNT POETRY

In order to understand this section, keep in mind that:

- Accentual-syllabic verse (metered verse) is composed with attention to both stress and syllables;
- Accentual verse counts stresses and allows great variation in the syllable count;
- Syllabic poetry counts syllables (with great variations possible in the number and placement of stresses); and
- Didactic verse is composed by counting words.

## Syllabic poetry

Syllabic poetry is developed around a specified number of syllables in each line. The use of counted syllables can result in a rough conformity to a visual pattern, but since syllables can be different lengths, the shape changes with the words.

### Haiku

One of the most popular forms of syllabic poetry is **haiku**, a Japanese form that sounds very simple: one line of five syllables, one line of seven syllables, and a final line of five syllables. But there are some underlying rules that characterize haiku:

- It is made of fragments.
- It speaks of everyday things using concrete language.
- It makes (usually indirect) reference to nature or to a season.
- Much is left unsaid.
- It presents material in the present tense.

In English, we are used to explaining everything in detail in most of our writing. In haiku, as the saying goes, "less is more." A Native American poet captured this idea in the first stanza of a poem.

### More Than a Moment Ago (1998)
by John-Crow Bigler (excerpt)

> Love is like Haiku
> Its depth in what's
> not said, its quality
> hidden between words
> where silence dwells
> and the heart blossoms
> like a spring flower.

Here are some translations from two of the most famous haiku poets, Basho and Issa. Mitsuko Yamamoto, a native of Japan, explained each one to me at length, and I tried to translate them into English poetry. But it seemed impossible both to preserve the haiku 5-7-5 form using English as native speakers customarily use English in poetic contexts and also to structure the poem with the brevity and inference that Mitsuko says is characteristic in Japanese. So once for Basho and once for Issa, I did two translations: one that keeps the 5-7-5 pattern and is characteristic of writing in English and the other to convey the Japanese style.

## Basho (1686)

### Frog haiku English style

1  Soft, summer twilight,
2  suddenly a sound: Frog leaps
3  in the old pond—Splash!

### Frog haiku Japanese style

1  Old pond,
2  Frog leaps—
3  Splash!

### Cicada haiku

1  In summer stillness,
2  cicada's clamoring cry
3  pierces even rocks.

## Issa (c. 1800)

### Frog haiku English style

1  Two frogs wrestling.
2  Issa cheers the under-frog:
3  "Don't lose—I'm with you!"

### Frog haiku Japanese Style

1  "Thin Frog,
2  don't lose the match!
3  I'm cheering for you.

### Sparrow haiku

1  Little sparrow child
2  plays in the road. "Oh, watch out!
3  Watch out! Horse tramps by!"

Exploring the issues and choices that arise when translating forms such as haiku is a good way to learn about the different cultural expectations in Japanese and English poetry. Online, you can compare a number of different translations of one particular Japanese poem (a tanka—like a haiku with two

---

* To get the count on Issa's frog poem in English style, pronounce *wrestling* with three syllables.

additional lines of seven syllables each) to gain some insights into the translator's art.

http://etext.lib.virginia.edu/japanese/hyakunin/english.html

Here, for comparison, is a poem on the same topic as Issa's frog haiku by a contemporary Vermont poet. Notice the differences in treatment not only in terms of length, but also with regard to development, the role of the speaker, and what you take away as a reader.

### Debate (1989)
by Geof Hewitt

1  On the stack of cherry firewood
2  cut in a sweat last August
3  2 squirrels alternate and squabble
4  for dominion. The off-squirrel
5  soothes his feelings foraging
6  under the hanging feeder.

7  He urges the chickadees
8  to nudge the feeder, chucks at them
9  to spill their seed
10  while the lordly squirrel preens at the top
11  of my wood, and with piggish eye
12  regards his peer.

13  Tails up, they also engage
14  in races over the crusted snow
15  in and out of brush piles and up the giant dead pine
16  for a stand-off on the second lowest limb.

17  Last spring 2 downy male woodpeckers
18  in a mating altercation
19  tumbled repeatedly to the ground
20  until I pounced on them and captured one.
21  He blinked, repentant,
22  as I cupped and admonished him

23  in the ways of peace,
24  then released him to the sky where
25  without missing a beat his wings unfolded
26  and carried him back to the fight.

## BRAIN TICKLERS
### Set # 55

1. Compare and contrast the frog haiku by Issa and "Debate" by Geof Hewitt.
2. There's nothing to prevent you from borrowing stanza forms from other languages besides Japanese.

For example, one Spanish stanza, the **lira**, is composed of five lines with the following syllable counts:

| Line number | Number of syllables | Rhyme scheme |
|:-----------:|:-------------------:|:------------:|
| 1 | 7 | *a* |
| 2 | 11 | *b* |
| 3 | 7 | *a* |
| 4 | 7 | *b* |
| 5 | 11 | *b* |

Try writing a stanza in English using this form. If you're feeling brave, use the rhyme scheme, too. Or, if you're studying a foreign language other than Spanish or Japanese, you can try a syllabic form from that language.

(Answers are on page 337)

## Cinquain

One report says that the **cinquain** was invented by Adelaide Crapsey, inspired to syllabic verse after translating haiku and tanka into English from French in 1909. Another report says that her system was at first accentual-syllabic (written in sets of iambs) and evolved, afterward into a syllabic form. Whichever is true, the cinquain is a twentieth-century American invention and is now undoubtedly syllabic. It is a five-line poem with the following numbers of syllables per line:

| Line number | Number of syllables |
|:---:|:---:|
| 1 | 2 |
| 2 | 4 |
| 3 | 6 |
| 4 | 8 |
| 5 | 2 |

Here are two examples from the few that Crapsey wrote before her early death from tuberculosis.

### November Night (1911–1913)
#### by Adelaide Crapsey

1 Listen . . .
2 With faint dry sound,
3 Like steps of passing ghosts,
4 The leaves, frost-crisp'd, break from the trees
5 And fall.

### The Grand Canyon (1911–1913)
#### by Adelaide Crapsey

1 By Zeus!
2 Shout word of this
3 To the eldest dead! Titans,
4 Gods, Heroes, come who have once more
5 A home!

## BRAIN TICKLERS
### Set # 56

Write either a set of at least three haiku or two cinquains. Here are some possible topics:

| | | |
|---|---|---|
| newborns | toothpicks | staplers |
| moonrise | tiddlywinks | saffron |
| emeralds | rhinoceros | car racing |
| architecture | Sri Lanka | swordfish |
| movies | pudding | injustice |
| newts | integrity | crayons |
| Atlantis | the phoenix | |

(Answers are on page 338.)

## Didactic or word count poetry

Didactic poetry is a growing and changing set of poetic forms that were created or adapted for use in school classrooms. In general, their aim is to make poetry easy and accessible for students. Because it's easier to count words than it is to count syllables or figure out stresses, didactic poetry is often based on a number of words per line. The arrangement of words tends to create a pattern.

### Didactic cinquain

The didactic cinquain is a variation on the cinquain that we've already covered. Instead of depending on syllable count, like the other type of cinquain, the didactic cinquain is a five-line poem with the following number of words per line:

## Didactic Cinquain

| Line Number | Number of Words |
|:-----------:|:---------------:|
| 1 | 1 |
| 2 | 2 |
| 3 | 3 |
| 4 | 4 |
| 5 | 1 |

Here are two sample didactic cinquains by middle school student Ivan Krizanac. Notice how he has arranged them on the page.

Water
Transparent, tasteless
      Filling, running, streaming
           A human's only hope
                Life

Books
An adventure
Unravels in yourself
Just like in dreams
Enjoy

### Lunes, lanterns, and diamantes

Lunes, lanterns, and diamantes are didactic poetry that is also pattern poetry. This means that the poetry is meant to be displayed in a certain way on the page. In each case, the name of the poem refers to the shape it is intended to make.

## Lune

| Line Number | Number of Words |
|:-----------:|:---------------:|
| 1 | 3 |
| 2 | 5 |
| 3 | 5 |

*Lune* is French for "moon," and the poem is meant to look like a new moon when turned on its side.

## Lantern

| Line Number | Number of Words |
|:-----------:|:---------------:|
| 1 | 1 |
| 2 | 3 |
| 3 | 5 |
| 4 | 3 |
| 5 | 1 |

The lantern form is meant to look like a lantern.

Here are a sample lune and lantern by Michael Podhaizer.

Grow up now.
Actually, unemployment is too high.
Keep being young.

love
the urban life
while you are young and
can take the
muggings.

**Diamantes,** invented by Iris Tiedt, take their name from their diamond shape. The rules don't control the number of syllables; they control the parts of speech used. But poets have to attend to word length or the size in which they print the words on the page, if they want to get a real diamond shape.

Here is the pattern:

| Line number | Description |
|---|---|
| 1 and 7 | a pair of antonyms (usually nouns) that will appear at the top and bottom of the poem, framing the rest of the content. |
| 2 | 2 adjectives that describe the word in line 1 |
| 3 | 3 participles that describe the word in line 1 |
| 4 | 2 nouns related to line 1 followed by 2 nouns related to line 7 |
| 5 | 3 participles that describe the word in line 7 |
| 6 | 2 adjectives that describe the word in line 7 |

And here's an example:

1    Music
2    Tender, Evocative
3    Consoling, Beautifying, Enchanting
4    Counterpoint, Orchestration, Wail, Cry
5    Scraping, Scrunching, Screeching
6    Harsh, Grating
7    Noise

[original]

## BRAIN TICKLERS
### Set # 57

Write a lune, a lantern, or a diamante.

(Answers are on page 338.)

# FREE VERSE AND PATTERN POETRY

## Free verse

Since **free verse**—verse not measured by the count of accents or syllables—often relies on visual patterning, it makes a good grouping with **pattern poetry**—poetry with an intended visual as well as an aural component. In the absence of meter and usually of end rhyme, free verse demands special attention to line length, to other sounds within and between lines, to arrangement on the page, and to rhythmic patterns that are not metrical. These are all poetic elements, not characteristic of prose, that allow us to make meaning of free verse not only in ways related to what we've been learning but also with new methods. Here is a free verse poem.

### A Man Said to the Universe (1894)
#### by Stephen Crane

1  A man said to the universe:
2  "Sir, I exist!"
3  "However," replied the universe,
4  "The fact has not created in me
5  A sense of obligation."

After reading this poem, we can apply many of the same analytical techniques that we have been using. We can point out the two characters with differing points of view, discuss the speaker's role in transmitting the scene, compare the humility and briefness of the man's statement with the coldness and length of the universe's reply. But once we give reign to our free-verse thought-processes, we may realize that we can also see that the small, relatively insignificant "I" is sandwiched between large weighty layers.

## BRAIN TICKLERS
### Set # 58

1. Read the following poem. Then tell how the shape of the poem interacts with its content.

### Languages (1916)
by Carl Sandburg

1  There are no handles upon a language
2  Whereby men take hold of it
3  And mark it with signs for its remembrance.
4  It is a river, this language,
5  Once in a thousand years
6  Breaking a new course
7  Changing its way to the ocean.
8  It is mountain effluvia
9  Moving to valleys
10  And from nation to nation
11  Crossing borders and mixing.
12  Languages die like rivers.
13  Words wrapped round your tongue today
14  And broken to shape of thought
15  Between your teeth and lips speaking
16  Now and today
17  Shall be faded hieroglyphics
18  Ten thousand years from now.
19  Sing—and singing—remember
20  Your song dies and changes
21  And is not here to-morrow
22  Any more than the wind
23  Blowing ten thousand years ago.

2. Write a poem in free verse. Choose a topic that you think is particularly suited for free verse—perhaps love, or reflection, or exploration of some important idea or insight. Plan your form carefully.

(Answers are on page 338.)

## Pattern poetry

Pattern poetry can take many different forms. As mentioned in the discussion of syllable and word count poetry, patterns can reflect the number of syllables (e.g., cinquain) or words (e.g., didactic cinquain), or both count and arrangement (e.g., lune). In other words, all of the poetry discussed so far in this section is pattern poetry. Some patterns form an arrangement on the page to create a particular profile or image. A pattern that is invented for a particular situation is sometimes referred to as a *nonce pattern*.

Here is a comic pattern poem from *Alice in Wonderland* that is onomatopoetic. ("Mine is a long and a sad tale," says the mouse who recites the poem; "it *is* a long tail certainly," replies Alice.)

## Fury said to a mouse . . . (1866)

by Lewis Carroll

1 Fury said to
2 a mouse, That
3 he met
4 in the
5 house,
6 'Let us
7 both go
8 to law:
9 *I* will
10 prosecute
11 *you.*—
12 Come, I'll
13 take no
14 denial;
15 We must
16 have a
17 trial:
18 For
19 really
20 this
21 morning
22 I've
23 nothing
24 to do.'
25 Said the
26 mouse to
27 the cur
28 'Such a
29 trial,
30 dear sir,
31 With no
32 jury or
33 judge,
34 would be
35 wasting
36 our breath.'
37 'I'll be
38 judge,
39 I'll be
40 jury,'
41 Said
42 cunning
43 old Fury:
44 'I'll try
45 the whole
46 cause,
47 and
48 condemn
49 you
50 to
51 death.'"

## BRAIN TICKLERS
### Set # 59

Read the following poem. Tell how you relate its shape to its meaning.

### Poetry (1919)
by Marianne Moore

1  I too, dislike it: there are things that are important beyond all this fiddle.

2    Reading it, however, with a perfect contempt for it, one discovers that there is in

3    it after all, a place for the genuine.

4      Hands that can grasp, eyes

5      that can dilate, hair that can rise

6        if it must, these things are important not because a

7  high sounding interpretation can be put upon them but because they are

8    useful; when they become so derivative as to become unintelligible,

9    the same thing may be said for all of us, that we

10      do not admire what

11      we cannot understand: the bat,

12        holding on upside down or in quest of something to

13  eat, elephants pushing, a wild horse taking a roll, a tireless wolf under

14    a tree, the immovable critic twitching his skin like a horse that feels a flea, the base-

15    ball fan, the statistician—

16      nor is it valid

17      to discriminate against "business documents and

18  school-books": all these phenomena are important. One must make a distinction
19      however: when dragged into prominence by half poets, the result is not poetry,
20      nor till the poets among us can be
21          "literalists of
22          the imagination"—above
23              insolence and triviality and can present

24  for inspection, imaginary gardens with real toads in them, shall we have
25      it. In the meantime, if you demand on one hand,
26      the raw material of poetry in
27          all its rawness and
28          that which is on the other hand
29              genuine, then you are interested in poetry.

(Answers are on page 339.)

## Working with poetic forms

Sometimes poems seem made for a particular form. But sometimes it's harder to get to the point at which it feels "right." When you have an idea for a poem and it's not working as you hoped, one of the approaches you may find valuable is working out the idea in a different form. It's an interesting exercise to do this even when you're satisfied with the poem as you wrote it: a new form may open up new possibilities. Here is an example of playing with the same poem in two different forms, courtesy of Wendy Zuckerman.

Read this lune:

> Beneath clouds, contrails
> I swim with fish, cool
> under lily umbrellas.

Because of the word lengths, this is not an ideal poem for the lune form: it doesn't form a moon shape. But move one word up a line, and it fits the haiku form:

> Beneath clouds, contrails,
> I swim with fish, cool under
> lily umbrellas.

Not all transformations are so simple. Sometimes poems must be partly or completely rewritten to fit into another form. This can give you an opportunity to see your subject in a new light. You may also realize that what you wanted to communicate can succeed in fewer words, requires more words, works better with a set rhyme scheme, works better without a set rhyme scheme, etc.

Poets develop the ability to choose a form that fits what they want to communicate. They also feel free to invent a new form whenever it fits their purposes. The only measure of its quality is whether the form fits the subject, tone, purpose, and audience. Think about the usefulness of each form you encounter. How is it used most effectively?

# BRAIN TICKLERS
## Set # 60

Each of the three pairs of poems that follow share a subject. Read the pairs. Then tell which you prefer and why.

1. Lune and haiku by Wendy Zuckerman

> The old maple
> catches my hair, whispers secrets
> in my ear.

> An old maple tree
> catches up my hair, whispers
> secrets in my ear.

2. Lune and lantern by Wendy Zuckerman

> Leaving the reef,
> I wring the Coral Sea
> from my hair.

> Fresh
> from saltwater sojourns
> I wring the Coral Sea
> from my hair,
> enchanted.

3. Haiku and double dactyl* [original] (Nikolai Rimsky-Korsakov was a Russian composer. *The Five* is an allusion to a group of composers of which he was a member.)

Rimsky-Korsakov
musically conveyed Russia's
winter, summer, spring.
                    [original]

Higgeldy, piggedly,
N. Rimsky-Korsakov
nationalistic, and
one of The Five;

Keen orchestrator, who
extraordinarily
wrote fifteen fairytale
operas: What drive!
                    [original]

(Answers are on page 340.)

# POETRY PLUS: VARIOUS USES OF POETRY

Others, besides Moore, have found poetry "useful." This section provides a brief survey of poems that, besides being, *do* something. There aren't Brain Ticklers to direct your reading, yet each one is worthy of a full study to apprehend its value. You know what to do.

---

* A double dactyl is an eight-line verse form that American poets Anthony Hecht and John Hollander invented in 1966. The poem has rules, which different people state differently. Here is one version:
- The poem is one sentence long.
- It has two stanzas.
- The first three lines of each stanza are dactylic dimeter. The last line of each stanza has a dactyl followed by one stressed syllable.
- The first line is rhyming nonsense.
- The second line is a person's name.
- The sixth line is a six-syllable word that makes a double dactyl (strong weak weak strong weak weak).

## Poetry as song

This poem provided the lyrics for one of the earliest songs I remember, a lullaby. Notice how Tennyson achieves euphony in this lyric in which some lines sway like a cradle, and some flow like the "rolling waters."

### From *The Princess* (1850)
by Alfred, Lord Tennyson

1  Sweet and low, sweet and low,
2    Wind of the western sea,
3  Low, low, breathe and blow,
4    Wind of the western sea!
5  Over the rolling waters go,
6  Come from the dying moon, and blow,
7    Blow him again to me;
8  While my little one, while my pretty one, sleeps.

9  Sleep and rest, sleep and rest,
10    Father will come to thee soon;
11  Rest, rest, on mother's breast,
12    Father will come to thee soon;
13  Father will come to his babe in the nest,
14  Silver sails all out of the west
15    Under the silver moon:
16  Sleep, my little one, sleep, my pretty one, sleep.

## Poetry as description

This sonnet-length section, the final lines in the poem from which it was taken, uses a simile and an allusion to create a striking final image. But notice how, early in the section, the poet uses interlacing rhymes to interlock the lines for both eye and ear: *down/powdery* (42–43); *blown/meadows* (43–44); and the half anagrams that create links for the eye within lines: *dust/sun* (45); *settled/rest* (46); *stole/slope* (48); *beauty/peace* (49).

### The Winter Scene (1929)
by Bliss Carman (excerpt)

IV

42  When the day changed and the mad wind died down,
43  The powdery drifts that all day long had blown
44  Across the meadows and the open fields,
45  Or whirled like diamond dust in the bright sun,
46  Settled to rest, and for a tranquil hour
47  The lengthening bluish shadows on the snow
48  Stole down the orchard slope, and a rose light
49  Flooded the earth with beauty and with peace.
50  Then in the west behind the cedars black
51  The sinking sun stained red the winter dusk
52  With sullen flare upon the snowy ridge,—
53  As in a masterpiece by Hokusai,
54  Where on a background gray, with flaming breath
55  A scarlet dragon dies in dusky gold.

## Poetry as prayer

Poetry has been used in religious rituals for thousands of years, but it can also be the form of individual prayers. That this poem is a prayer is not clear until the ninth line (you know from the outset only because I've told you). Note the personification in line 6 and the metaphor of lines 7 and 8.

### Where the Mind Is Without Fear (1918)
by Rabindrath Tagore

1  Where the mind is without fear and the head is held high
2  Where knowledge is free
3  Where the world has not been broken up into fragments
4  By narrow domestic walls
5  Where words come out from the depth of truth
6  Where tireless striving stretches its arms towards perfection
7  Where the clear stream of reason has not lost its way
8  Into the dreary desert sand of dead habit
9  Where the mind is led forward by thee
10  Into ever-widening thought and action
11  Into that heaven of Freedom, my Father, let my country awake.

## Poetry to educate

This excerpt is from a book on husbandry by a farmer who wanted to share his knowledge of agriculture. To this end, he wrote a whole volume of poems called *Five Hundreth Points of Good Husbandry*. And his book was a best seller in Elizabethan and Jacobean England!

### A Description of the Properties of Winds All the Times of the Year (1580)
by Thomas Tusser (excerpt)

1 North winds send hail, south winds bring rain,
2 East winds we bewail, west winds blow amain;
3 Northeast is too cold, southeast not too warm,
4 Northwest is too bold, southwest doth no harm.

## Poetry as philosophy

This poem shares a heritage with "Ulysses" but makes its point in a very different way, suggesting a very different course of action. Try comparing them. What do you find?

### On Living, Part I
by Nazim Hikmet (1948),
translated by Randy Blasing and Mutlu Konuk (1994)

1 Living is no laughing matter:
2     you must live with great seriousness
3         like a squirrel, for example—
4   I mean without looking for something beyond and above living,
5         I mean living must be your whole occupation.
6 Living is no laughing matter:
7     you must take it seriously,
8     so much so and to such a degree

9    that, for example, your hands tied behind your back,

10                        your back to the wall,

11    or else in a laboratory

12        in your white coat and safety glasses,

13        you can die for people—

14    even for people whose faces you've never seen,

15    even though you know living

16        is the most real, the most beautiful thing.

17  I mean, you must take living so seriously

18    that even at seventy, for example, you'll plant olive trees—

19    and not for your children, either,

20    but because although you fear death you don't believe it,

21    because living, I mean, weighs heavier.

## Love poetry

Love poetry dates back thousands of years. In this example, notice how the poet uses metaphor in the first line of each stanza, direct description in the second, and personification in the third to move toward the simple yet powerful conclusions in the last line of each stanza.

### To-night (1917)
by Sara Teasdale

1  The moon is a curving flower of gold,

2    The sky is still and blue;

3  The moon was made for the sky to hold,

4    And I for you;

5  The moon is a flower without a stem,

6    The sky is luminous;

7  Eternity was made for them,

8    To-night for us.

## Poetry as retelling/comment

Retelling a well-known story gives the poet and reader a common ground to start on. But watch out for the poet who chooses to give the story a twist! Each of the following two poems retells a well-known story, one from the Hebrew Scriptures/Old Testament, and the other from Greek mythology. How does each use the original? What new insights does each give us?

# The Mad Fisherman (1998)

### by Patrick Hodgkin

1   They call me crazy!

2   Baalak the mad fisherman; and snicker

3   As I go along the brick jetty

4   To my boat. For I carry no net

5   (What net would hold him?)

6   And for fishing line, well—rope

7   Not twine; and for bait, a goat.

8   Perhaps they are right.

9   But what would you? Had you been there

10   And seen him too, might you not deem

11   Such a catch worth fishing for?

12   I am a simple man, but not without ambition.

13   It was a year or more ago he came on shore

14   —Maybe four or five.

15   Sometimes the mind clouds.

16   I was scrounging in the rocks to find

17   Crabs or octopus for my bait box,

18   When I heard a roar of water—not the waves.

19   I turned then, and saw him breaking surface,

20   A fish, yes, but such a fish!

21   Bigger than my brother's barn, foam pouring

22   Down his scaled flanks (like the flash floods

23   That fill our stream to its banks) as he

24   Neared the land, working his way

25   Into the shallows, where the sand

26   Shelves to the bay. There he lay exhausted,

27   Then as I ran—

28   As who would not for such a prize!

29   He opened wide his mouth,

30   Barnacled, whiskered with seaweed,

31   And discharged, yes, large as life, a man!

32   He seemed drowned. (The man, I mean.)

33   But as I approached, I saw him stir.

34   Slowly he crawled, hauling himself forward

35   From the sea, until I reached him, caught him

36   By the armpits as he retched and choked,

37   And brought him to land.

38   There he sat awhile,

39   Dazed in the sand dunes, muttered, seemed not

40   To understand where he was or why—

41   Hardly surprising!—

42   Sucked a cut on his knuckle. Then suddenly:

43 "Which way to Nineveh?" he cried,
44 And rose, as though ready to go.
45 I pointed dumbly. I could find no word.
46 "Thank you, friend, for your courtesy," he said.
47 "They call me Jonah,
48 And now I know my road."

49 He turned and strode off as if
50 Nothing was amiss. And when I looked,
51 My fish was gone, and I was left alone.

Did you figure out which story Hodgkin is retelling? It's from the Book of Jonah in the Hebrew Scriptures/Old Testament. Read the original. How does the shift in point of view from the original to Hodgkin's poem change the emphasis of the story? Notice the elaborate play with rhyme, as tangled as a fishing line. Hodgkin not only interlaces internal rhyme within lines and skipping lines and unexpectedly reintroduces end sounds to make rhymes after you thought they were gone, but also uses identical rhyme, assonance, close rhyme, and eye rhyme.

In the next poem, the poet uses an Italian sonnet to give Arachne a chance to answer the charges against her by giving her the speaker's role. Pull out a mythology book and read or reread the story before you look at the poem.

### Arachne (1993)
#### by Richard Foerster

1 I worked with all aurora at my loom—
2 the merchants at my father's house, my thralls,
3 brought me gold and silken threads from Bengal,
4 Tyrian dyes and flax and peacock plumes.
5 Evenings when I danced in my rich costumes,
6 I watched the women's eyes beneath their shawls
7 and heard a whispered curse at each footfall.
8 I learned how blazing envy can consume.

(Continued on page 304.)

> 9   When father died, the house no longer filled,
> 10  age and solitude like friends settled in.
> 11  Yet my weaving shuttle has not been stilled;
> 12  I weave new curses; my pride was no sin;
> 13  before the waiting wooden frame I thrill
> 14  to quicken space where nothingness has been.

Now that you've read the poem, think about these questions: How does the poem create atmosphere? Were you expecting the word *silver* where Foerster used *silken*? Which is a better choice and why? What do you make of the repetition of *curse*? Why would it be appropriate to call Arachne a *spinster* (look up the word to find out its original meaning)? How is the weaver like the poet? How does this poem compare to the other two spider poems in the book, "Arachne" (page 198) and "A Noiseless Patient Spider" (page 148)?

## Poking fun—parodies

**Parody** mocks one or more aspects of an existing piece of literature or body of work or uses a well-known piece of literature for social commentary. Parody is like caricature: It contains elements of similarity and elements of distortion. Balancing these can be tricky. If parody is too similar, it loses its ironic edge. If it's too distorted, it may be unrecognizable.

Parody is one of the most sophisticated art forms because in order to write parody well (or understand it as a reader), you have to analyze well. Style, tone, subject matter, diction, literary techniques, and ideas are all open to parody, and the better the analysis, the better the parody. Parody can be done to make a point, but sometimes it's written just for fun.

To enjoy a parody of a particular poem, you first need to recognize which poem is being parodied: Only then can you really understand it . . . and enjoy it. But sometimes parodists will use a particular poem, not to disparage it, but as a vehicle for social or cultural commentary. Poetic social commentary may also make its point without being based on a particular poem.

# BRAIN TICKLERS
### *Set # 61*

1. Read the following poems. Then tell what each poet is parodying. How does the chosen form work?

### I Feel (Verse Libre) (before 1942)
by Lucy Maud Montgomery

1 I feel
2 Very much
3 Like taking
4 Its unholy perpetrators
5 By the hair
6 Of their heads
7 (If they have any hair)
8 And dragging them around
9 A few times,
10 And then cutting them
11 Into small, irregular pieces

12 And burying them
13 In the depths of the blue sea.
14 They are without form
15 And void,/ Or at least
16 The stuff they/ produce
17 Is./ They are too lazy
18 To hunt up rhymes;
19 And that
20 Is all
21 That is the matter with them.

### There was a young bard ... Anonymous

1 There was a young bard of Japan
2 Whose limericks never would scan;
3    When they said it was so,
4    He replied: "Yes, I know,
5 But I make a rule of always trying to get just as many words into the last line as I possibly can."

# Poeta Fit, Non Nascitur* (1883)

## by Lewis Carroll

1 "How shall I be a poet?
2 How shall I write in rhyme?
3 You told me once 'the very wish
4 Partook of the sublime.'
5 Then tell me how! Don't put me off
6 With your 'another time'!"

7 The old man smiled to see him,
8 To hear his sudden sally;
9 He liked the lad to speak his mind
10 Enthusiastically;
11 And thought "There's no hum-drum in him,
12 Nor any shilly-shally.

13 "And would you be a poet
14 Before you've been to school?
15 Ah, well! I hardly thought you
16 So absolute a fool.
17 First learn to be spasmodic—
18 A very simple rule.

19 "For first you write a sentence,
20 And then you chop it small;
21 Then mix the bits, and sort them out
22 Just as they chance to fall:
23 The order of the phrases makes
24 No difference at all.

25 "Then, if you'd be impressive,
26 Remember what I say,
27 That abstract qualities begin
28 With capitals alway:
29 The True, the Good, the Beautiful—
30 Those are the things that pay!

31 "Next, when we are describing
32 A shape, or sound, or tint;
33 Don't state the matter plainly,
34 But put it in a hint;
35 And learn to look at all things
36 With a sort of mental squint."

37 "For instance, if I wished, Sir,
38 Of mutton-pies to tell,
39 Should I say 'dreams of fleecy flocks
40 Pent in a wheaten cell'?"
41 "Why, yes," the old man said: that phrase
42 Would answer very well.

43 "Then fourthly, there are epithets
44 That suit with any word—
45 As well as Harvey's Reading Sauce
46 With fish, or flesh, or bird—
47 Of these, 'wild,' 'lonely,' 'weary,' 'strange,'
48 Are much to be preferred."

49 "And will it do, O will it do
50 To take them in a lump—
51 As 'the wild man went his weary way
52 To a strange and lonely pump'?"
53 "Nay, nay! You must not hastily
54 To such conclusions jump.

55 "Such epithets, like pepper,
56 Give zest to what you write;
57 And, if you strew them sparely,
58 They whet the appetite:
59 But if you lay them on too thick,
60 You spoil the matter quite!

61 "Last, as to the arrangement:
62 Your reader, you should show him,
63 Must take what information he
64 Can get, and look for no im-
65 mature disclosure of the drift
66 And purpose of your poem.

67 "Therefore to test his patience—
68 How much he can endure—
69 Mention no places, names, or dates,
70 And evermore be sure
71 Throughout the poem to be found
72 Consistently obscure.

---

*Poets are made, not born

73  "First fix upon the limit
74  To which it shall extend:
75  Then fill it up with 'Padding'
76  (Beg some of any friend)
77  Your great SENSATION-STANZA
78  You place towards the end."

79  "And what is a Sensation,
80  Grandfather, tell me, pray?
81  I think I never heard the word
82  So used before to-day:
83  Be kind enough to mention one
84  'Exempli gratiâ.' "

85  And the old man, looking sadly
86  Across the garden-lawn,
87  Where here and there a dew-drop
88  Yet glittered in the dawn,
89  Said "Go to the Adelphi,
90  And see the 'Colleen Bawn.'

91  "The word is due to Boucicault—
92  The theory is his,
93  Where Life becomes a Spasm,
94  And History a Whiz:
95  If that is not Sensation,
96  I don't know what it is.

97  "Now try your hand, ere Fancy
98  Have lost its present glow—"
99  "And then," his grandson added,
100  "We'll publish it, you know:
101  Green cloth—gold-lettered at the
      back—
102  In duodecimo!"

103  Then proudly smiled that old man
104  To see the eager lad
105  Rush madly for his pen and ink
106  And for his blotting-pad—
107  But, when he thought of publishing,
108  His face grew stern and sad.

2. In *Alice in Wonderland* and *Through the Looking Glass, and What Alice Found There,* Lewis Carroll parodies a number of poems. Which poem is being parodied here? How can you tell?

### Twinkle, Twinkle, Little Bat (1866)
by Lewis Carroll

1  Twinkle, twinkle, little bat!
2  How I wonder what you're at!
3  Up above the world you fly,
4  Like a tea-tray in the sky.

3. Do you know this poem (and have you ever seen such a long title)?

### The Purple Cow's Projected Feast:
### Reflections on a Mythic Beast
### Who's Quite Remarkable, at Least
(before 1895)
by Gelett Burgess

1  I never saw a Purple Cow,
2  I never hope to see one;
3  But I can tell you anyhow,
4  I'd rather see than be one.

Carolyn Wells, in 1918, published a group of parodies of this famous quatrain under the title *Diversions of the Re-Echo Club*.

For each parody, identify the "author" and the poem that is being parodied.

1  All that I know
2    Of a certain Cow
3  Is it can throw,
4    Somewhere, somehow,
5  Now a dart of red,
6    Now a dart of blue
7  (That makes purple, 'tis said).
8    I would fain see, too.
9  The Cow that dartles the red and the blue!

1    Open then I flung a shutter,
2    And, with many a flirt and flutter,
3  In there stepped a Purple Cow which gayly tripped around my floor.
4    Not the least obeisance made she,
5    Not a moment stopped or stayed she,
6  But with mien of chorus lady perched herself above my door.
7  On a dusty bust of Dante perched and sat above my door.

8    And that Purple Cow unflitting

9    Still is sitting—still is sitting

10  On that dusty bust of Dante just above my chamber door,

11    And her horns have all the seeming

12    Of a demon's that is screaming

13    And the arc-light o'er her streaming

14  Cast her shadow on the floor.

15  And my soul from out that pool of Purple shadow on the floor,

16  Shall be lifted Nevermore!

4. a. Write a poem that fulfills one of the functions mentioned in the beginning of this section: A song, a description, a prayer, a statement of philosophy, a declaration of love, or a comment/retelling. Choose a form that works for your purpose, topic, audience, and tone.

   b. Write a parody of a particular poet and poem (for this assignment, chose a published poet) or use whatever poetic means seem appropriate to parody an attitude, behavior, practice, or idea in society. If you parody a particular poem and are doing this as a classroom assignment, supply a copy of the original when you turn yours in.

(Answers are on page 340.)

# POETRY AS PERFORMANCE

## What is poetry performance?

There are a variety of ways in which poetry can go from the page to sound. By yourself, you can sit silently in a chair letting the words reverberate within your mind and heart or saying them aloud as you read; you can stand on a hilltop and shout the words of a poem you know by heart into the fury of a storm; or you can rehearse a comforting poem to share with a child who is in the hospital. Reading, reciting, and rehearsal are all ways of bringing the text of a poem to life by oneself.

But poetry can also be performed. *Performance* implies an audience, someone besides yourself whose response you care about. It could be a single person or a huge crowd listening to you, and your performance could be live or recorded or transmitted by telephone or video chat or sound recording. Because there is an audience, performing poetry has elements of art combined with elements of communication. Even though our reading, reciting, and rehearsal of poetry may be done aloud, it is different when other people are involved as well.

## Types of poetry performance

There are a number of different ways to perform poetry, each with its own characteristics and variables. Generally, the most elaborate are theatrical productions of dramatic works written in verse, like Shakespeare's plays. Theatrical productions differ from the other types of poetry presentation in that they often include the use of makeup, costumes, lights, sets, props, blocking, singing, music, etc.—that is, many elements besides the voice. Some poems are turned into lyrics and set to music. Again, a great deal is added to the original poem in its performance. Additionally, there are a number of common ways to perform poetry that concentrate on the flexibility and expressiveness of the human voice.

## Poetry Readings, Poetry Recitals, and Oral Interpretation

Three of the most common types of performance poetry in school are poetry readings, poetry recitals, and oral interpretation, the last of which may be conducted as an exercise or as a contest.

## Poetry Reading

A **poetry reading** is different than simply reading poetry. It is a planned event at which one or more people read poems to an audience. Professional poets often give readings of their own poetry. Poetry readings given by poets are unified by the fact that the poet is reading his or her own work. Poetry readings are also used to give students experience in interpreting poetry in front of an audience of their classmates, the whole school, or their parents. Having the text of a poem means that the reader doesn't have to worry about forgetting the lines. The presence of a text to read can help reduce stage fright. This, in turn, can allow the reader to focus on using his or her voice to convey the poem. Conveying a poem in a poetry reading involves close attention to elements of poetic form, such as rhythm, rhyme, meter, stanza, and lines, as well as punctuation and the emotional impact of the poem's content.

Gestures and movement are usually very limited in poetry readings, and dress is street clothes or slightly formal "presentation" outfits (i.e., not costumes). Usually, poems are introduced simply with title (and author, if the author is not the reader). If the author *is* the reader, he or she may provide information about the poem's origins, or other background of interest that nobody else would know.

## Poetry Recital

A **poetry recital** differs from a poetry reading in that there is no text: all the presentations are memorized or learned by heart. Provided that the reciters are confident, having the poem inside them frees them from the piece of paper or the book. They can focus on making eye contact with the audience and communicating the poem. Without the paper, recitals may have more gestures, facial expression, and movement than poetry readings.

Sometimes poetry recitals are set as a task for students who are practicing memorization. In this case, students may be graded more on accuracy in rendering the words of the poem than on interpretation, and more on the proficiency and fluency than on the audience response.

## Oral Interpretation

**Oral interpretation** is also called *interpretive reading* or *dramatic reading*. In school settings, it is distinguished from both reading, on the one hand, and drama or theatre, on the other hand. In general, the interpreter's interaction with the text is expected to be limited. Instead, the interpreter is expected to primarily focus on the audience, which differentiates oral interpretation from reading. Also, props, costumes, and stage movements are usually not allowed, separating it from a dramatic performance. Gestures may be limited by the requirement to hold a folder with the script of the performance. In some places, interpreters may be required to memorize their pieces, in which case, gestures and a little movement may be allowed.

### Actor vs. Interpreter

| Actor | Interpreter |
|---|---|
| Brings work to life in action | Communicates work to audience directly through speech |
| Accessories: costumes, make-up, props, lighting, stage, set, sound, etc. | No accessories |
| One person per role | One communicator of whole |
| Director creates coherent vision | Interpreter creates coherent vision |
| Actors relate to each other in view of the audience | Interpreters relate to the audience |

Oral interpretation is done in speech competitions and tournaments, and the focus—as the name suggests—is on using the voice (and sometimes gestures or movement) to convey meaning, emotion, and story. In this context, oral interpretation often features an introduction written by the presenter that provides background for the audience, both about the work's origins (the author, title, and date of origin, for example), as well as anything the audience might need to know, particularly if the piece to be interpreted is an excerpt. The introduction is often delivered from memory, with the folder closed. The folder is opened when the interpretation begins. Descriptions of oral interpretation differ in describing the presenter as impersonating the speaker of the poem and in presenting the material as him- or herself or, alternatively, representing the poet discovering the poem.

There are some other, less common but very interesting, ways of performing poetry. These include choral readings and reader's theatre. The first requires a group of people to speak in unison. This requires careful training and can be impressive when done well. The second often has the performers seated in a row, facing the audience, and doing theatre just with their voices and faces—no costumes, make-up, set, stage, etc.

## Competitions and tournaments

Many middle schools and high schools have Speech Clubs or Forensic Teams or Speech and Debate Clubs. These organizations give students training and an opportunity to present poetry—along with other types of material—in competition with other students their age. Students gain valuable feedback from both coaches and judges, a chance to see other students perform, and an opportunity to hone their performance skills. In contest situations, a number of elements other than the actual performance of the poetry are at stake. Timing requirements are strict, and various penalties are enacted for failing to meet them. Performances may be judged from the first moment the performer is on stage to the last, and attention is paid to dress and demeanor, not just the communication of the poem. Oral interpretation is often one of the categories of competition.

## Poetry Slams

Both inside and outside of school, a newer type of poetry competition has been taking hold. It is called the **poetry slam**. Like oral interpretation, it has a set time period (often three minutes) and judges (often five). But slams are usually—unless otherwise indicated—situations in which the poet performs his or her own work, unlike oral interpretation, which is often required to be published poetry. And slam judges are different from speech competition judges, who are often teachers. Slam judges are most often chosen from the audience and are expected to *not* have any special qualifications for the job, except a willingness not to show favoritism. A poetry slam is emceed by a *slam master*, the master of ceremonies for the event. Additionally, the slam is more open to variations in the rules. There are one-minute slams: team slams; music slams (in which musical accompaniment is used as backing for the performance of the poem); and freestyling slams, in which the poets make up poetry on the spot and perform it. One of the newest variations on poetry slamming may be podslamming, in which the poetry slammer records a reading of a poem and posts it on a website for audience comments. A link to an example appears on my *Painless Poetry* website.

Thaddeus Rutkowski slamming.

Despite all these possible variations, the key difference between a poetry slam and an oral interpretation contest is the role of the audience. Visibly involving the audience in the performance is an important part of poetry slamming, but not an important part of oral interpretation. Slammed poetry is meant to move the audience, who are allowed to respond with cheers, groans, applause, and whistles—unlike oral interpretation contests in which the audience is usually expected to be silent.

Poetry slams are not just for young people. Adults slam too, and poetry slams by and for adults may have different standards for the language that is allowed than poetry slams held specifically for students.

## Preparing to perform poetry

Any time that a poem is going to be performed, whether for a recital, a speech contest, or a slam, there are some tasks that often go into the preparation, which include selecting a suitable poem and developing a performance of it. Here are some tips for each stage of preparation. More detailed information and tips about preparing to perform a text can be found in *Painless Speaking* (1$^{st}$ edition, Barron's, 2003), which I also wrote.

### Finding a Poem

Sometimes your teacher, coach, or advisor may provide you with one or more texts that—based on his or her experience and knowledge of both the poem and you—seem to be good choices. Other times, you may need or want to seek out your own material, and this book and other print anthologies may prove useful. In the case of a poetry slam, you may be required to perform a poem of your own, in which case you will be constructing your own text. In any case, the selection is important.

Factors to consider in seeking appropriate poems include:

- Type of performance and the expectations, including any rules (for example, a length limit)
- Text requirements—some contests require poems that are published in print (not on the Internet) and prohibit anonymous or original poems; others require poems written by the performer
- Language—It's wise to consider any explicit or implicit language limitations, especially with regard to any words that might seem out of place or offensive.
- Quality—It's useful to have and to be able to apply a set of standards; it's also useful to recognize when poetry moves you and to be able to predict which poems might translate well into performance
- Appropriateness for you as speaker, given your interests and abilities
- Appropriateness for and appeal to audience

If you find a poem that is appropriate but too long, consider whether there are ways you can adapt it if doing so is allowed by the rules. In most cases, it is best to avoid texts that you have heard performed by others because your performance might be influenced by what you've seen and heard. If you can, choose several poems to work with, so that if one doesn't stand up to the rest of the process, you have something on which to fall back.

## Testing for Time Limit

Doing a rough test for a time limit right away is important. It helps avoid the frustration of investing a lot of time in a poem, only to find that it can't comfortably fit within the given time. When doing your estimate, don't cut it too close. Performing a poem takes longer than reading it. If adapting the text is allowable, your test will give you a preliminary idea of how much needs to be adapted or cut.

## Analyzing the Poem

As you prepare your presentation, having a deep understanding of the poem will be crucial. In some performances, a premium is set on the quality of interpretation. Here are some steps that often help with that task:

- Identify the type of poetry (narrative, lyric, dramatic, etc.).
- Identify the speaker and the speaker's audience, as well as other characters, figuring out their personalities and goals.
- Identify the mood of the poem.
- Identify the setting (time/season/place).
- Identify the subject/topic of the poem.
- Identify the poet's attitude toward speaker/subject (tone).
- Identify themes in the poem.
- Identify conflict if any.
- Identify transitions within the poem.
- Find the high point of poem, if it has one.

Some venues specifically forbid changing genders set by the poet, but allow males to speak female parts and females to speak male parts. Also, depending on the performance rules, adapting in any manner other than cutting may be prohibited, so make sure you know what is allowed. If you are adapting or cutting, make sure that a coherent whole is left (no unexplained references, for example). It is often best to keep some of each of the beginning, middle, and end. Read the results of your alterations several times to make sure everything makes sense.

Besides understanding the poem's meaning, you also need to understand the language and sound of the poem. This includes looking at all the elements of poetic language that have been discussed in this book: rhetorical devices, dialect and diction, sensory detail, rhythm and meter, rhyme, and other uses of sound, such as onomatopoeia, cacophony, and euphony. Of course, this whole process may go much more quickly if you wrote the poem, because you know so much about it already. But running through the list is a good idea in any case, to bring all the elements of poetry to the forefront of your thought. If you've made any alterations or cuts, it's particularly important to review the language and sound of your adapted version.

## The Tools of the Trade

After you thoroughly understand the poem, the next step is to apply the tools of the performer's trade to rendering it into a performance. These tools include the technical elements of the voice: articulation/clarity, emphasis, inflection/intonation, intensity, pacing, pauses, phrasing, pitch, projection, quality, rate/tempo, rhythm, subordination, tension and resolution, vocal variety, and volume. Voice is used to distinguish multiple characters, and the performer works to accurately render dialect and convey the different characters, who may also be distinguished by different facial expressions, gestures, energy levels, posture, and stance. If allowed by the rules, you can use all these elements to bring the poem to life.

## Preparing the Text for Rehearsal and Performance

Once you deeply understand your poem, you need to prepare it for rehearsal and performance. This may require one preparation or two. There are at least two possible key differences between rehearsal and performance. One occurs if you have to perform without a text. In this case, your text for rehearsal is used only for rehearsal. The second case is when your rehearsal involves video recording yourself with your computer, in which case you may want to have an onscreen rehearsal text to work with.

In any case, for the time during which you are working with a text in preparing or performing, you want it to have several attributes:

- It should be easy to read. For many people, this is accomplished by using a clear serif font (serifs on letters—those extra little lines—are considered by many to make the letters more easily distinguishable though some prefer the clean look of sans serif type) and 14-point type, double-spaced.
- You may want to write in or otherwise mark directions for speed, dynamics, emphasis, pitch, pauses, facial expressions, eye contact with audience, and the pronunciations of difficult words, etc. (*Painless Speaking* provides examples of marked texts.)
- Make sure your page turns work. Ending a page at a point where you intend to pause is a useful approach.
- Some competitions may require that the performance matches the prepared script, which must be submitted. In this case, make sure to enter any changes you intend to make.
- Put page numbers on the pages, particularly if you are working without a folder. If you drop your papers, it will be easier to find your place.
- If there are requirements, such as a certain color folder of a certain size, etc., make sure you know them. You may want to begin your rehearsals with whatever format works best for you, even if it's different from what you'll use in performance, but if you do take this approach, be sure to allow yourself time to become comfortable working within the requirements.
- If possible, do your final rehearsals on-site, or at a reasonable facsimile of the performance venue.

In your rehearsal sessions, you may want to use vocal warm-ups, feedback from trusted people, and audio or video recording to help you prepare for and improve your performance. If you are practicing at a time when other people and equipment are not available, try using a mirror. As you review your own work, aim to avoid a singsong presentation. It's a good idea to use punctuation and meaning, rather than line breaks and rhymes, to forge phrases.

Rehearsal is the best place for overcoming the fear that can accompany performing in front of an audience. Whether it is called *speech anxiety, stage fright,* or *communication apprehension,* being nervous is no fun. Sometimes, this can come from not having a choice about what you're performing or the fact that you're performing, if the performance is part of an assignment, or that you have to memorize. But even professionals who choose to spend their lives in the theatre, on live television, etc., and students who volunteer for speech contests or poetry slams can feel anxious. This leads to the tentative conclusion that some amount of nerves may just be in the nature of performance.

The best approach is to figure out exactly what is causing the discomfort, and what you can do to make yourself feel better. For some people, it is the time constraint, while for others, it is fear of forgetting the poem. Still other people don't like speaking to strangers. The first two fears might be somewhat lessened by extra preparation. It may take you longer, but you can spend the time practicing until you feel more comfortable with the time limit and your knowledge of the material. Arriving early and practicing in the actual performance area may also help. If speaking to strangers is an issue, try spending a few minutes studying the audience and picking out some friendly-looking faces to focus on as you present.

Memorizing is required for some performances and forbidden for others. The simple act of repeated rehearsal, combined with your detailed analysis of the poem, will probably put you a good way toward memorization, if that is your goal. In any case, it's usually a good idea to have the first few words after any page turns memorized.

For your final rehearsal, even though you may not be doing theatre, you may want to do a dress rehearsal, wearing whatever you're planning to wear to the performance. The dress standards are different for, say, a poetry slam and for the National Forensic League, and having your attire selected and ready will give you one less thing to worry about. Whatever level of formality or informality your presentation clothes are, they should be neither distracting, wrinkled, nor dirty. Rehearsing in your performance outfit will help you make sure that it won't get in the way.

## Writing an Introduction

The job of the introduction, which often has its own time limit, is to engage the audience and judges, creating interest and preparing them for what is to follow. This always involves providing them with the name of the poet and the title of the poem. What else the introduction contains and how long it is depends on the circumstances, including the rules. Your introduction and your interpretation of the poem both contribute to the full experience of your performance.

Introductions may include factual, contextual, and interpretive information. They may also explain allusions or references that might elude the audience either because the references are not well known or because the aural medium doesn't provide enough time for listeners to fully appreciate and process all the details. But be sure you don't spoil the poem by telling too much. No matter what persona you use for performing the poem, the introduction is characteristically given in your own person and should be primarily or entirely your own words.

Often, the introduction is the beginning of the performer's relationship with the audience and judges. But in some performances, the introduction is not the first part of the presentation. Sometimes a *teaser*—a bit of the performance text—is spoken first, followed by the introduction. Because of the interdependence of the stanzas of poetry, this type of interruption might not work very well unless the performance features several short works of poetry and the intro came after the first one. Whether this technique can be effective will depend very much on the material to be presented: don't use it unless it works well.

The delivery of an introduction is generally memorized, so it should be written with that fact in mind. In addition, it should directly address the audience and be written for you to speak directly to them. When you've decided how to introduce the work, you may need to research the poet, the poet's other works, allusions and references in the poem, literary criticism of the poem, and unknown word definitions and pronunciations. Intro sets up expectations that will be fulfilled.

## Blocking, Gestures, and Expression Planning

Some competitions may restrict gestures and prohibit movement, so make sure to find out the rules. And though blocking and gestures may or may not be part of your performance, facial expression should certainly be. It is best to seek movements, gestures, and expressions that are purposeful, appropriate, meaningful, and varied, but coherent.

Creating characterization can be done with a variety of performance elements including voice, gesture, appearance, attitude, posture, stance, and focus. If you are representing more than one character, it is possible to position the characters in slightly different places around center (see the illustration for "White and Wong" on page 326 for an example).

Varied advice is given for making eye contact with the audience. Most agree that you shouldn't focus only on a single point or person, on the one hand, or try to look at every single person, at the other extreme. Looking toward individuals at the front, back, and sides of the audience can help everyone feel included.

## Poems on the page and in performance

Here are six poems—five very recent, and one from the 1980s. There are links to performed versions of them on my *Painless Poetry* web page. Two of the performances are at poetry slams. One is a podslam. Two are audio recordings made by the poets themselves. One is a professional video of a poet. You will likely notice that some of the poems might appear at first glance to be prose. In each case, you have the opportunity to look at the poem as it exists as a text and to examine how the poet—or, in one case, a performer given permission by the poet—performs the poem.

In this poem, the poet draws a parallel between two near-disasters.

### The Sandman (2000)
#### by Geof Hewitt

So I was coming around the corner and the car ahead of me has stopped and I'm on sheer ice and my car starts to skid and there's this guy on the sidewalk with a shovel and just before my car crunches into the car ahead of me he throws a shovelful of sand under my rear tires and my car comes to a stop ten feet from disaster.

Half an hour later I'm at the Xerox machine with a job I've gotta have copied in time for the mail, which leaves in ten minutes, and the machine jams and I'm trying to get the paper out and something throws a spark and ignites the paper so smoke is starting to curl from the ink drum and I'm trying to figure whether I should run to the men's room for a handful of water when this guy appears with a shovel and throws a shovelful of sand into the machine's underbelly and the smoking stops.

Geof Hewitt slamming "The Sandman."

The first poem by this poet provides some context for the second poem.

## What's in the Name (1999)
### by Thad Rutkowski

The name is Thaddeus, but the choice of the name was ill-advised, I think. No doubt my parents wanted something classical, or something radical. Oedipus and Orpheus would not do, and Theodore and Thelonius would not, either. So my father decided. My mother, it seems, did not have much say in the matter. She picked Xiao Lin, which means Little Forest and sounds something like *her* first name, Chia In, which means Good Tidings. But I don't go by Xiao Lin. What I go by is a little stranger.

To many people, I am Thad, which is easy to spell and fairly easy to say, unless you think it's Fab, as in "Oh Fab, I'm glad, they put real Borax in you!" My first and middle initials, J.T., are even easier, so I use them when I make reservations, arrange for deliveries, or sign my name on lists. One of my old friends calls me J.T., except for the times he calls me Stud. Other people I know call me T-Bone. Some of my friends think T-Bone is too casual, but I like it better than Fazool, which is the nickname of another guy I know. I have not been called Tadpole for a long while, but an old girlfriend used to call me A. Tad, which was short for A. Tad Weird. Some of my close relatives still call me Tad, but so far no one else has adopted the shortest form.

When I meet people and tell them my name is Thaddeus, they say, "That sounds like a Biblical name," or "That sounds like a nineteenth-century name," or "That sounds like a plumber's name." Sometimes my new friends take an initiative and shrink my name to Chaddy, Teddy or Patty, or Chad, Ted or Pat. For a while, people in my office confused me with another Asian guy who looked like me and called him Thad and me Henry.

My last name is no less problematic. Rutkowski just does not fit my face. At times, however, to my great surprise I pass for Eastern European. Someday, I might change my last name to my mother's maiden name, which is simpler and more descriptive, and become Mr. Wong.

**325**

In the next poem, the poet makes wordplay using the facts of his naming and his Caucasian and Asian heritage.

## WHITE AND WONG (1998)
### by Thaddeus Rutkowski

Hi. I'm Mr. **White**.

*That's **White**, and I'm **Wong**.*

We're here to discuss the difference between us, the difference between **White** and **Wong**.

*That's **White**. We're going to get lots of attention for no reason.*

That's **Wong**. We're going to make some interesting points.

*Pure **White**. We're going to ask pointed questions, then ridicule the answers.*

Utterly **Wong**. There is no answer, and that's the answer.

*Almost **White**, but not quite. If you lean on the edge, on your chin and your elbows, you will see the answer where it lies, which is within.*

**Wong**, **Wong**, **Wong**. If you see the answer, why ask pointed questions?

*I'm losing track of the difference between **White** and **Wong**.*

**Wong** again. The difference is as plain as day or night, or dusk and dawn.

*All **White**. All **White**. I've been **Wong**-headed.*

On the contrary, I've been **Wonged**.

*Let's put things to **Whites**.*

I know I'm **White**, and I think you're **Wong**. But remember: Two **Wongs** don't make a **White**.

*Might makes **White**, or at least it might, if you don't go **Wong**.*

Some **Wongs** will never be **Whites**.

*The **White** side of my brain says, "**White**," but the **Wong** side tells me, "**Wong**."*

**Wong** you are. There is no absolute **White** or **Wong**.

*If you're **White**, can we both be **Wong**?*

Thaddeus Rutkowki performs "White and Wong," shifting position to show the two characters.

This next poet reflects on the immortality that poetry can bestow on the poet.

## Remember Me (2008)
### by Bridget Iverson

I'm good at hiding pain.
I don't even flinch.
I'm good at arguments.
I don't give an inch.
I can fade away
until I'm not there.
I'm good at pretending
I don't even care.
I don't care.
Yes, I care.

REFRAIN.
I will write a thousand words
in ink upon my hand
and I will read a thousand books
to try to understand
and I will post a thousand poems
in the hope that one
will be read and remembered
when my life is done.

I'm trying to figure out
my reality
so that there'll be something left
to remember me.
I try to find what might be there
deep inside my mind
So in the end, when I die
I'll leave something behind.

REFRAIN.
I don't know if I'll succeed
but I have to try
because the only thing I know
is I don't want to die.
I don't want to die.

BRIDGE.
I'm fifteen years old.
Fifteen years
worth of thoughts, worth of tears.
Fifteen years old
and already
I'm afraid you won't remember me.

REFRAIN.
I don't know if I'll succeed
but I have to try
because the only thing I know
is I don't want to die.
I don't want to die.
Please don't let me die.

327

The following poet acknowledges that her attitude towards poetry changed because of a new insight.

### Write. Writer. Writing. (2009)
by Anna Rutenbeck

I write
Some would call me
A writer
I guess you could say
I'm good at it.
It hasn't always
Been this way.
I used to
Hate writing
Despise it with a passion.
Until someone
Showed me
My writing
Could be
MINE
It could mirror
Me.
It could be
short
It could be
Long
I could
Crumple my words
Up into a paper ball
And throw them across the room
Have a war
Of poetry
With my neighbor.
I could throw them off
The edge of a cliff

Watch them break
And bind
At the bottom.
Then
Throw them on a page
And call
It
Art.
I could lace them
With brittle fingers
And brittle thread
Make them
Delicate
And breakable
Make sure they realize
How much they
Mean to me.
How much they should mean
To everyone
Who reads
Them.
They're not perfect.
Nothing is ever
Perfect.
But they're
Me
(The best of me anyway)
And I
Love them.

This poet reflects on people, language, and labels.

## We are (2009)
by Sossina Gutema

Nouns
People, places, things
We are not
We mean actions, movements
What we are is verbs
In an
Unspoken tense.
I am
You are
He is
She is
They are
We are
We are
Nouns,
No, that makes no sense
I am not somewhere you can go
Something you can pick up
Hold.
We are
Written, we are spoken, thought
I am
You are
We are defined by the things we do.
It is physically impossible,
    a contradiction of
Terms, for us to be anything
But who we are.
There's no pretending.
We are simple, basic
We can be conjugated
Untangled

Found.
So don't call me a
Wannabe; I'm not faking
Don't tell me to stop trying
To be somebody else.
It's impossible.
I am me
We are
Hoping, tasting,
Trying. We are coasting.
I am crying, chasing, fighting
You are, raining, running, waiting.
I am tossing; turning,
You are trying
We are dancing.
Nouns.
We are not
Things, we do not fit
We do not have subjects;
Articles
(Definite or indefinite).
We are scribbling, frantically.
We are leaping, bounds, taking
    chances,
We exist in moments, movements,
    noises.
I am changing
You are falling
We are
Living.
We are not
Nouns.

The performance of this poem, linked on my *Painless Poetry* web page, is a pod slam by Grady Farnham-Rendino, done with permission of the poet. If you are going to slam someone else's poem, get some guidance from a teacher or slam coordinator about whether permission is needed.

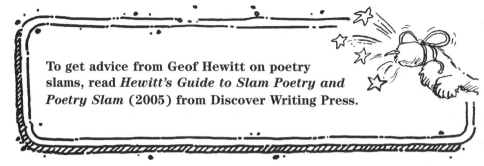

To get advice from Geof Hewitt on poetry slams, read *Hewitt's Guide to Slam Poetry and Poetry Slam* (2005) from Discover Writing Press.

# BRAIN TICKLERS—THE ANSWERS

## Set # 48, page 262

**Possible responses:**

1. The poem is three stanzas of seven lines and a final stanza of six lines. The first three stanzas are *abaabcc*, whereas the last is *wxyzaa*. The syllable count for the first three stanzas is 8-7-8-8-7-8-4 (except that line 16 is one syllable short), but for the final stanza, it is 8-9-8-6-8-4. The first three stanzas appear to be modified ballad meter with a refrain.

2. The slang and the accent that drops the *g* on the *-ing* endings help with the characterization, as does the simple diction. The slight variations in the refrain help to continue the reader's interest. It tricked me, so I guess it worked!

3. The changes and pauses in the last stanza added to the suspense. I had come to expect the rhythm and rhyme of the first three stanzas. If I'd been more on my toes, I might have taken this as an indication that something unexpected was happening.

## Set # 49, page 263

**Possible response:**

The Assyrian army attacked the Hebrew camp with full strength at sunset; but during the night, the Angel of Death passed by and killed the host and their horses, so that they were defeated, not by the sword but by "the Lord."

## Set # 50, page 264

**1–3. Possible responses:**

The speaker is Ulysses (Odysseus), who is home ("by this still hearth"), having finally returned from the Trojan War. He is dissatisfied with his stay-at-home life ("Life piled on life/were all too little . . . ") and the companionship of those who "know not me." These are contrasted to "those that loved me," the friends to whom he is speaking and proposing a new journey (" 'Tis not too late to seek a newer world"). He would rather risk his life in adventure than rest on his laurels (be "a name").

## Set # 51, page 266

**Possible responses:**

1. The speaker is reflecting as he watches some swans swim, not for the first time. Lines 1 and 7 quickly call our attention to the passage of time. "All's changed" since the first time he saw the swans, says the speaker in stanza 3, introducing his reflections and then contrasting himself with the unchanging swans in stanza 4. By his description of them, we may gain some insight into the changes that afflict him: They are unwearied, they are paired, "their hearts have not grown old," and they still feel passion and the desire to conquer. We may gather that these are all the things that the speaker feels the loss of in the last nineteen years. Now, he is only the observer, and someday, he reflects, the swans will have flown away, and he will no longer be even that (lines 28–30).

   What may appear at first to be just a careful description suddenly becomes the spilling of spontaneous thoughts and observations about beauty, love, and the passage of time— a lovely lament about the inevitable losses experienced in life.

2. I think it is both a lyric and a dramatic address: Frost, the poet, is the speaker, inviting his reader to "come" join him in an excursion into the land of lyric poetry. That it is placed at the beginning of every collection reinforces its interpretation as the poet's invitation to the reader.

3. (narrative poem)

*The History of a Confrontation of Great Moment,*
*Reduced Through the Great Dexterity of the Poet*
*to Ten Brief Lines of Monorhymed Iambic Monometer*

A rat,
quite fat,
once sat
on a mat.
"Oh, drat!
A cat!"—
whereat
the rat
did scat.
That's that.

[original]

## Set # 52, page 269

**Possible responses:**

1. a.
   - It's an English sonnet. I can tell because of the rhyme scheme: There's a couplet at the end, and it doesn't have the interlocking rhyme of a Spenserian sonnet.
   - The first twelve lines ask questions about the speaker-poet's occupation of immortalizing his beloved in verse, with reference to many inducements to quit. In the first four lines, it becomes clear that she ignores his poems and he feels that he is using up his youth. In the second quatrain, he explains that she ignores him and asks why he should repay cruelty with kindness. There is a shift of emphasis with line 9; now he imagines what her favors would be like based on the evidence of her defects. In the couplet, he answers his own questions. He must sing because he is unhappy and his love is unrequited; if she loved him, it would be overwhelming, and he would find it impossible to speak.

   b.
   - It's a Petrarchan sonnet. The rhyme scheme shows a sestet and no couplet.

- The octave describes the man of wisdom—what he does and does not do. He does not rush into action but behaves in accord with reason, checking to see if his deliberations are accurate. He is not such a fool as to take credit for his own state in the world or think himself the only wise person in the world. The direction of the tercet is not immediately obvious because it is so different from the octave. The octave points out the attitudes and actions common to all the wise, but the tercet reminds us that each person is unique, and that we should not judge by differences.

c.
- This sonnet is Spenserian—it's by Spenser, it's the only type left, and it has the interlocked rhyme scheme.
- In the first quatrain, the speaker attempts to immortalize his beloved by writing her name in sand, but twice the waves wash it away. In the second quatrain she tells him that it is a vain activity, and that mortal things cannot be immortalized. In the third quatrain, he refutes her claim, telling her that in his verse her name will become immortal, not only on earth, but in heaven. The couplet predicts that their love will be remembered even after their deaths. It is a self-fulfilling prophecy, for here we are, 400 years later, reading this poem and remembering their love.

2. a.

| Poet | Rhyme scheme | |
| --- | --- | --- |
| Lope de Vega | *abbaabba* | *cdcdcd* |
| Ingber (*x* is unrhymed lines) | *xaxaxbxb* | *xxcxxc*\* |
| O'Broin | *abbacddc* | *efegfg* |

---

\*I had to think before I did this. There is assonance at the ends of lines 1 and 3; an apocopated rhyme in lines 5 and 7; and consonance in lines 9 and 11. Should I include this? Looking at lines 10, 12, and 13, 1 decided that they were not intended as part of the scheme, and this fits my overall interpretation.

Lope de Vega wrote a standard Petrarchan sonnet. Ingber includes a simpler rhyme scheme than the standard Petrarchan forms. O'Broin uses an unusual rhyme scheme for a Petrarchan sonnet but keeps every line end a rhyme.

b. Ingber's translation—The sonnet is about someone writing a sonnet for the first time in response to a lover's request. Most of the content of the sonnet is spent discussing the sonnet form and the speaker's quavering attempts to get through it. The simplified rhyme scheme (which in another case one might put down to the difficulties of translation) in this case works excellently with the content; we are shown here a beginner-level sonnet. The diction reinforces this simplicity; the speaker has the names of the sonnet parts correct, but, other than that, the diction is very basic. Whether or not I recognize the assonance, consonance, and apocopated rhyme as intentional (if I do, it underlines the lack of control the beginning poet would exercise over his medium), the poem is a brilliant rendition of a beginner's attempt at a sonnet.

O'Broin's translation—This translation casts the speaker in a different light. The diction is more sophisticated (*performance-fear, expedite, perfect* as a verb) and every line has end rhyme. This creates irony because, even though the form of the sonnet is good (although not exactly a Petrarchan rhyme scheme), the content is not at all what I imagine Violante would have wished (praise of her beauty, graciousness, and the like). Violante asked for a sonnet to create a situation in which her suitor would reconsider her charms. Instead, the speaker devoted his attention solely to the poetry.

Now I wish I could read de Vega's original with the perfect rhyme scheme—I wonder what the tone is.

c.

| Type of Sonnet | Examples |
|---|---|
| Petrarchan | "Sonnets from the Portuguese"<br>"The New Colossus" |
| Elizabethan | "Samarkand: for Seamus Daly"<br>"Sonnet CXXX" |
| Spenserian | "Amoretti LXXXV" |
| Other | "Ozymandias"<br>"Success"<br>"Sonnet: On the Sonnet"<br>"Alushta by Day" |

## Set # 53, page 273

1. **Possible response:**
   **Sorrow**
   "Sorrow" is set in trochaic tetrameter in sextains with the
   rhyme scheme *abaaab*. The trochees beat through the
   poem like the sorrow beating on the speaker's heart.
   Because of the long wait for the second line in each stanza
   to be rhymed, there is a sense of unease, which mirrors
   the unease of the speaker, who cannot understand how the
   world just moves on despite the pain. The first stanza is the
   speaker's personal disclosure; the second sets the speaker
   in the context of society and contrasts her responses to
   those of others.

   **Transience**
   Even before I started reading "Transience," the anaphora in
   lines 1, 5, and 9 caught my eye. The poem consists of three
   single-rhyme quatrains of iambic pentameter. The poem
   develops step by step. In the first stanza, the speaker tells
   the listener (who is grieving) that nature will not succumb
   to the listener's grief. In the second stanza, the speaker
   continues: Time will not tarry either, and today's grief will
   be forgotten at some point. In the third stanza, the speaker
   concludes, suggesting implicitly that nature and time are

not to be blamed, for the listener him- or herself will move on and betray what now seems of greatest importance. The three-part structure works well with the three-part development of the thought. The strong rhymes lend assurance to the speaker's statements. The poem's title makes it seem philosophical, rather than harsh.

2. **Possible response:** an impatient and harried person's response to the stoicism of "Transience" (notice stanza 1: single-rhyme; stanza 2: cross-rhyme; stanza 3: monorhyme; stanza 4: opposed couplets)

### Ode to an Autobus

Phooey! and Confustication!
Bother! And Annoyment!
Must this city transit always
Ruin my enjoyment?

Late to get to work this morning!
Late to go to lunch!
Then it's early without warning!
I have got a hunch

That quite soon it will start pouring,
That my seatmate will be snoring
Loudly, with the muffler roaring,
When the bus gets here, to Warring-

ton, and I get on it, seething,
turning red from too-deep breathing.
Don't think this day is unique—
I do this five days every week!

[original]

## Set # 54, page 279

**Possible response:** (Couplets—Epigram)

### Poetic Diction: In Summary

I shun any poetic entity
that harbors the too-oft used *threnody*.

*Spindrift* is another clear presage
to shun the poetical message.

Finding *limn* used barefaced in a poem
makes me drop the book and run home.

And may anyone using *quotidian*,
get what Gideon delivered to Midian.*

[original]

## Set # 55, page 283

1. **Possible response:** The haiku does a fine job of capturing a brief glimpse of an interaction. Its brevity works well for its subject. The longer length of "Debate" allows Hewitt space to compare two occasions of animal squabbles, as well as show us a (fruitless) attempt at intervention. Each works well for the poet's treatment of the subject.

2. **Possible response:** (Unrhymed lira)

I sometimes ski cross country:
I head down to the pond, watching the snow fall
under the leafless birch trees,
over the barren oak trees,
and covering up the woods in winter stillness.

[original]

---

* The story of Gideon's conquest of Midian is in the Hebrew Scriptures/Old Testament, Book of Judges 6–7.

## Set # 56, page 285

**Possible response:** (haiku)
Note: Pronounce *flowers* as having two syllables.

### The Garden in Various Moods

Key times are marked now:
dawn's morning glories; then four
o'clocks; moon flowers last.

Birds fight the Earth. "Give
up your worms to me!" In most
cases, Earth loses.

Japanese beetles
mate on my rose's blossoms,
but not for long. Squish.

Crabgrass, I hate you!
I shall eradicate you!
Now . . . dissipate, You!

[original]

## Set # 57, page 290

**Possible response:** (diamante)

### The Predator and the Prey (2000)
by Michael Podhaizer

Cats
Sleek, Strong
Hissing, Stalking, Pouncing
Hunters, Mammals, Rodents, Prey
Squeaking, Running, Hiding
Small, Agile
Mice

## Set # 58, page 291

**Possible responses:**

1. Sandburg's speaker contends that uses of language with
   which we are comfortable ("broken to shape of thought")
   are passing but, at the same time urges the readers with an
   imperative to "Sing." This may, in fact, be a poem about the

innovation of free verse replacing metrical verse. But whether it is or not, the margins on the right side of the poem run in and out "like rivers," and make the poem's shape appropriate for the message.

2. Notice the use of repeated and related end words in the lines of each stanza.

### Remember (2000)
by Katie Turner

I sit at my window and look
out into the night.
I put my arms around me
as if to hold tight and feel
the memories and never forget

anything. I'm scared to forget.
I'm scared that I feel
the night
will take me
away and I can't look.

To look
back at the feelings
of him and me
makes me sometimes want to forget.
I get chills but the night

comforts me. The night
surrounds my
inner thoughts and looking
back I will never forget
the feelings

I get when I feel
those memories. The dark night,
the stars bright, the look
in his eyes. I almost forget
because of my

unwillingness to let myself
peer deep inside the thick night.
The cold air, the feel
of his breath on my neck, the look
I gave. *Never forget*

*and hold tight*, I tell myself.
Feelings and nights and looks
are never to be forgotten.

## Set # 59, page 294

**Possible response:**

This is a hard question. The sound "shape" of the poem is punctuated with rhyme, but irregularly. The rhyme occurs most often in the fourth and fifth lines of the six-line stanzas, focusing attention on the narrow "neck" of each one. I can imagine the shape in several different ways, but here's my favorite. They are five wheelbarrows, big solid ones, much larger than Williams's little ones, sitting in the garden (the bottom two lines of each stanza) waiting for the toads to come. The solid, practical, simple, useful object that the poem makes reinforces the poem's statement.

## Set # 60, page 296

**Possible responses:**

1. I prefer the lune because of the way the words fall into lines.

2. I prefer the lune because it seems to work well as is, and not need the added words in the lantern.

3. I prefer the double dactyl because the haiku doesn't seem to be the best use of the form, whereas the double dactyl is clever and uses the form well.

## Set # 61, page 305

1. **Possible responses:**
   **I feel (Verse Libre)**
   Montgomery is parodying free verse attitudes and techniques in a free verse form.

   **There was a young bard . . .** This limerick is a parody of unskilled limerick writers who can't get even the limerick's simple and flexible rhythm scheme right (and maybe cultural miscommunication, too).

   **Poeta Fit, Non Nascitur** Carroll uses a poem to parody those who want to "be poets" because they think it's a romantic calling but don't necessarily have something to say that can be communicated well in poetic form. The particular techniques he sends up are free verse, overuse of emphasis, obscurity, bombastic phrasing, so-called "poetic" vocabulary, and not knowing when to quit. At the end, he mocks the lure of publishing before anything at all (let alone something of value) has been penned. I noticed Carroll's use of wrenched rhyme (lines 8 and. 10), wild changes in diction (lines 4 and 11–12), and broken rhyme (lines 62 and 64), all of which make mockery of the supposedly serious conversation being recounted.

2. Carroll is parodying the sincere and reverent tone of Jane Taylor's "The Star," recognizable by the meter and the *twinkles*.

3. The first example is parodying "My Star" by Robert Browning. The second is parodying "The Raven" by Edgar Allan Poe.

4. a. [Retelling/comment; blank verse with interludes]

### Penelope's Tale (excerpt)

Practiced I was in weaving and in knots,
in picking out the tangled, snarled skeins
and in untangling all the mazy threads;
in tracing misdirected strands to source,
and in devising complicated schemes
for looms, resourceful in devising plans,
marrying harmonious shades together.

To and fro and to my shuttle sang,
a small rhythm of hope within the house,
producing pleated piles of purple cloth,
with glinting gold embellishment and trim,
fair cloth that clothed my husband and myself,
loomwork for labor, comfort, and delight.

But then he left for Troy,
and my life came undone
the threads all lolling loose,
as if the warp had snapped,
leaving the weft hanging weak and useless . . .

And since, my life is spent not only weaving
but unweaving in efforts to avoid
besetting suitors in my husband's home,
encamped, to weave their way into my heart.

My husband went to war to rescue Helen,
from an unsuited suitor—she, a wife;
to help lay siege to Troy and take her back.
But his unwitting absence brewed a war
within his own four walls, a siege against
my heart, battles I cannot win alone.
For my life's pattern has become enmeshed
and tangled in the suitor's strong desires,
and my son's too, for all he does not wish
his inheritance used up by their rich feasts,
his only sign of unknown father's love.

Their coming wrecked the pattern of my life.
I thought, "What can I do? I'll make a plan:
I'll only wed when I've finished the shroud
of proud Laertes." Then I wove by day;
by night I raveled threads, my work undid.
Oh, what an awful pattern for a life:
to do, undo, do, stop, undo again.
Then, I became entrapped in my own web—
they caught me in my un-weaving. And now,
I don't know how to fend them off again.

My husband's all my thought,
but is he living still?
What is it I preserve,
by turning from their suits?
Is anything gained by this putting off?
. . . .

[original]

b.

## The Power of Words (1837)

by L. E. L. (Letitia Elizabeth Landon)

'Tis a strange mystery, the power of words!
Life is in them, and death. A word can send
The crimson colour hurrying to the cheek,
Hurrying with many meanings; or can turn
The current cold and deadly to the heart.
Anger and fear are in them; grief and joy
Are on their sound; yet slight, impalpable:—
A word is but a breath of passing air.

## The Power of Germs

| | |
|---|---|
| 'Tis a strange mystery, the power of germs! | A |
| Life is in them, and death. A germ can send | B |
| the crimson color hurrying to the cheek, | C |
| as fever rises; or bring coughs and sneezes | D |
| with a cold. Deadly to the heart are some diseases | D |
| that people get: the outlook, bleak. | C |
| And yet, our guts, for instance, on bacteria depend. | B |
| Ironic that the same thing can strengthen or make infirm. | A |

[original]

# INDEX

Asterisks indicate excerpts of poems.
Pages in boldface indicate where terms are defined.
More grammar and reference resources are available at
*www.edreinvented.com/products/painless-poetry/*.